Strategies for
Sustainable Development

Strategies for Sustainable Development

LOCAL AGENDAS FOR THE SOUTHERN HEMISPHERE

Edited by

MICHAEL REDCLIFT

and

COLIN SAGE

Wye College, University of London, UK

JOHN WILEY & SONS
Chichester · New York · Brisbane · Toronto · Singapore

Other Wiley Editorial Offices

John Wiley & Sons, Inc., 605 Third Avenue,
New York, NY 10158-0012, USA

Jacaranda Wiley Ltd, 33 Park Road, Milton,
Queensland 4064, Australia

John Wiley & Sons (Canada) Ltd, 22 Worcester Road,
Rexdale, Ontario M9W 1L1, Canada

John Wiley & Sons (SEA) Pte Ltd, 37 Jalan Pemimpin #05-04,
Block B, Union Industrial Building, Singapore 2057

Library of Congress Cataloging-in-Publication Data

Strategies for sustainable development: local agendas for the
  Southern Hemisphere / edited by Michael Redclift and Colin Sage.
      p. cm.
  Includes bibliographical references and index.
  ISBN 0-471-94278-2
  1. Sustainable development.   I. Redclift, M. R.   II. Sage,
  Colin.
  HC79.E5S768   1994
  338.973—dc20   93-3272
                                                        CIP

British Library Cataloguing in Publication Data

A catalogue record for this book is available from the British Library

ISBN 0-471-94278-2

Typeset in 10/12pt Times by Acorn Bookwork, Salisbury, Wiltshire
Printed and bound in Great Britain by Biddles Ltd, Guildford, Surrey

Contents

About the Contributors

Michael Redclift is Professor of Rural Sociology at Wye College, University of London. He is also the Research Coordinator of the ESRC's Global Environmental Change Programme.
Department of Agriculture and Environment, Wye College, University of London, Wye, Nr Ashford, Kent TN25 5AH, UK

Colin Sage is Lecturer in International Environmental Policy at Wye College. His PhD thesis was concerned with small farmers in highland Bolivia. He is currently working in Indonesia and China.
Department of Agriculture and Environment, Wye College, University of London, Wye, Nr Ashford, Kent TN25 5AH, UK

Graham Woodgate is Lecturer in Environmental Sociology at Wye College. His doctoral research was undertaken in Mexico.
Department of Agriculture and Environment, Wye College, University of London, Wye, Nr Ashford, Kent TN25 5AH, UK

Kwasi Nsiah-Gyabaah works with the Bureau for Integrated Rural Development (BIRD), University of Science and Technology in Kumasi, Ghana.
Bureau for Integrated Rural Development (BIRD), University of Science and Technology, Kumasi, Ghana

Amador Remigio is an environmental consultant working in the Philippines.
Townhouse 2, Diamond Corner Pearl Sts, Carmel 5, Banlat, Near Tandang Sora, Quezon City, Metro Manila, Philippines

Preface

This book is the result of collaborative research, much of it at the local level, in developing countries. The authors were, or are, all members of the Environment Section at Wye College. If sustainable development is to mean anything it must be capable of translating into *local* action: in the United Kingdom as much as in the Philippines, Ghana, Mexico or Bolivia. The strength of our approach, we believe, is that each of us undertook research with the idea of matching the "big" global idea with local sensitivities and cultural understanding. There is abundant evidence here that Agenda Twenty One can and *should* be everybody's agenda.

The Editors
10 August 1993

1 Introduction

MICHAEL REDCLIFT AND COLIN SAGE
Wye College, University of London, UK

This book examines the potential of "sustainable development": as an idea, as a focus for planning and as a source of moral and political regeneration. It also points to problems in each of these areas. In the early chapters the philosophical and epistemological dimensions of sustainability are explored, and the sources of confusion exposed to view. Later chapters concentrate on the possibility of combining "sustainability" with "development" from the standpoint of policy and management in a number of developing countries. The countries chosen, Bolivia, the Philippines, Ghana and Mexico, each illustrate dimensions of the problem. They suggest that our understanding of sustainable development will be advanced by both conceptual clarification *and* much more attention to "real world" situations. Three issues emerge clearly from the discussion.

First, the way that people value nature in other cultures materially affects our own ability to "manage" the environment in sustainable ways. Second, environmental management represents a tension between structural changes in the economic and political system, often at an international level, and the potential of human agency in responding to these structural changes. Third, environmental policy interventions have tended to ignore the potential release of human energy currently devoted to handling unsustainable development processes. To what extent does successful environmental management depend on local empowerment?

This book expresses the trade-off between economic goals and mechanisms, and their effects on the ecological systems which underpin human existence. Development is about the creation of economic (often market) "value" as natural resources are transformed into "goods", into commodities. The process of economic development involves the substitution of resources by human-made capital. From one standpoint, then, we need to enlarge our view of "capital", to include nature, if we are to preserve life-forms on the planet (Ekins 1992, Ekins and Max-Neef 1992).

Second, at the same time, our enlarged view of what constitutes "natural capital" poses a problem for us in a number of ways, which are not always obvious. By valuing the environment predominantly in monetary terms, we

Strategies for Sustainable Development: Local Agendas for the Southern Hemisphere
Edited by Michael Redclift and Colin Sage. © 1994 John Wiley & Sons Ltd

may be *de*valuing its importance. We may end up, as Oscar Wilde put it, ". . . knowing the price of everything and the value of nothing". One of the goals of this book is to open up the question of natural values to more critical scrutiny.

Whether it takes place under the rubric of "sustainability" or merely in the name of "development", economic growth clearly poses problems for the biological and climatic systems which are indispensable to our survival. The "laws" which govern the workings of nature, like the First and Second Laws of Thermodynamics, involve the conversion of one form of energy into another. The natural capital of the globe is transformed, through economic growth, in ways which modify such processes, but our environmental accounting procedures still fail to reflect this. The real costs to the environment, and the households which depend on it, are not counted, since they frequently involve imbalances in bio-physical systems. Sustainable environmental management can make use of economic policy mechanisms, but in the final analysis needs to be cognizant of the fundamental laws of nature, as much as those of economics.

The third aspect of natural capital that cannot be ignored is that of culture. The ways in which the environment is conceptualized within other cultural systems, and the implications this holds for policy, have been the subject of some useful discussion recently (McNeely and Pitt 1985, Ghai and Vivian 1992, Parkin and Croll 1992). It is increasingly recognized that development cannot be "sustainable" unless it works with, rather than against, other cultural traditions. This challenge, to recognize that environmental "management" should draw on distinctive epistemologies and perspectives on resource management, very different from those of Northern institutions, is perhaps the most difficult one to grasp. It involves looking at how people value nature in other cultures, as well as the view they take of the interests of future generations. Frequently the accumulation of human-made capital in the South is inversely related to the preservation of natural capital there. The virtual disappearance of some cultural groups, such as dryland pastoralists in Africa, threatens not only the physical environment but the capital stock of knowledge on which such groups have traditionally drawn. At the same time, features of sustainability, such as the preservation of biodiversity, cannot be strengthened without preserving the cultural diversity on which they depend. Culture not only represents the prism through which we view nature, it also represents an essential part of our natural capital stock.

SUSTAINABLE DEVELOPMENT: CONSIDERING THE FUTURE TODAY

It is easy to forget that, although the concern of global environmental problems clearly did not commence with the Brundtland Report in 1987, the

Report represented a watershed in thinking about the environment and development. The environmental debates of the early 1970s focused on the threat posed by continued economic growth to the dwindling natural resource base (Meadows *et al* 1972, Eckholm 1976). The Man and the Biosphere Programme, launched by Unesco in 1971, attempted to chart human impacts on natural ecosystems, and issued warnings about the neglect of these impacts. The United Nations Conference on the Human Environment (Stockholm, 1972) concentrated minds on the dangers of ignoring environmental problems, but its cautions about the negative effects of economic growth were better received by some ideological camps in the developed countries than in developing countries, where growth was seen as a prerequisite for conserving resources. Even a pioneering treatment of the connections between ecology and economic development argued that ". . . much economic development may take place without having an obvious, direct effect upon the environment of its natural resources . . . Development of natural resources contributes to providing an increasing share of the necessities of life, and material luxuries of civilisation, to the people of a country . . ." (Dasmann *et al* 1973).

By 1980, when the World Conservation Strategy was published, together two years later with the Global 2000 Report, the relationship between the preservation of ecosystems and the course of economic development was becoming clearer. However, the environmental problem, on the global scale, was still depicted as essentially a scarcity problem: too many consumers placed an unacceptable burden on a declining resource base. It is important to recognize, for example, that the Brandt Commission, which paved the way for a serious treatment of the environment within the development problematic, took the view that absolute limits in the supply of fossil fuels (rather than their profligate use) constituted the main threat to the planet: "In the crucial field of fuel energy mankind still behaves as if all these resources—up to now so abundantly wasted—were renewable. The oil stock of our planet has been built up in a long process over millions of years. . . . Exhaustion of these resources is foreseeable but their replacement by alternative fuels is not . . . (Brandt Commission 1980).

During the 1980s a number of new concerns were added to those which had stimulated discussion a decade earlier. The links between economic and social development and environmental degradation received much more attention, and this began to be reflected in the discussion and documentation of several international bodies. The *World Conservation Strategy* (IUCN 1980) which effectively coined the term "sustainable development", confined the discussion of economic development to the last section of the report. In this section the emphasis was placed on raising finance for conservation objectives, rather than considering economic development and the environment together. The approach adopted in the second document, a decade later, *Caring for the Earth* (IUCN 1991) is to pose economic development, initially, as a potential problem for achieving environmental objectives. (Other influential reports in this period include Global 2000, *Report to the President* (Penguin, 1982), and F di Castri and M Hadley, *Ecology in Practice* (Unesco, Paris, 1984).) At the same time, the urgency of environmental problems in the South received much more attention from social scientists. In 1987 the World Commission on Environment and Development (Brundtland Commission) gave expression to an agenda of issues specifically designed to counteract the sectoral bias and compartmentalism which had dogged so much work on the environment. It also raised other issues of concern, notably the belief that considerations of intergenerational equity needed to be addressed from a global perspective (Markandya and Pearce 1988).

By the end of the decade, however, a parallel discussion was under way, which carried implications for sustainable development but cast the argument in rather different terms. It also re-awakened an older debate about changes in climate associated with the absorptive capacities of nature (Wilson 1858). The discovery of an "ozone hole" over the Antarctic, followed by increasing evidence that climate was changing under the influence of increased carbon emissions, and other gases, led to a new sense of urgency within the industrialized countries. It could be argued, then, that global warming placed heavy responsibilities on the developed world to use energy more efficiently, and to pay more attention to renewable sources of energy. As Buttel and co-workers observe, attention to climate change, unlike the environmental concerns of the 1970s, was prompted not by considerations of scarcity but by apparently profligate energy consumption (Buttel *et al* 1990). This echoed a theme of the Brundtland Commission— that the North's development was every bit as unsustainable as that of the South. But it also brought more urgency to the discussion of policy alternatives. If one accepted that global warming was already occurring, then more "sustainable pathways", in the language of the European Commission, were not only desirable—they were imperative (Draft EEC Research Programme on Environmental Socio-Economics, Commission of the European Communities 1990).

FROM BRUNDTLAND TO RIO: GLOBAL PRIORITIES

By 1989 the decision had been taken, by the UN General Assembly, to call an Earth Summit in Rio de Janeiro in 1992. The stage was set for the discussion of environmental issues at a global level. However, the basis for international agreements to protect the environment did not exist, for several reasons.

First, the environmental concerns of the North were only partially shared by the developing countries. The preoccupations of the North—carbon dioxide emissions, stratospheric ozone depletion, the loss of rare species, the disposal of toxic wastes—although important to the countries of the South, were not their own priorities.¶Developing countries were more concerned about poor water supply, bad sanitation, soil erosion, the depletion of wood supplies and environmental health generally. In their view resources needed to be channelled towards these pressing concerns, rather than towards more "global modelling" or expensive preventative measures designed to help the North, such as seawall defences.

Second, many of the developing countries were burdened by onerous debt loads, to Northern banks and governments. International financial institutions, such as the World Bank and the International Monetary Fund, sought to persuade indebted governments to remove the obstacles to economic growth and to take a more "realistic" view of the market. In the view of many people in the South, environmental problems could only be addressed by paying more attention to the protection and enhancement of poor people's livelihoods, and the policies of leading Northern institutions undermined these livelihoods (Hewitt 1992). Even august bodies like the Latin American and Caribbean Commission on Development and Environment, commented:

> The worsened economic situation of countries in the region makes it very difficult to adopt measures for environmental conservation and sustainable use of natural resources and has a particularly sharp effect on cutbacks in budgetary allocations for investment in environmental programs. (*Our Own Agenda* 1990, p. 83)

Any expectations of success, from the standpoint of the developing countries, was predicated on measures to reduce the burden of debt, to reverse the flows of capital from South to North or, at the very least, to convert these funds into mechanisms to enhance the natural capital of the South.

Third, in the view of the developing countries, the environmental problems of the North, the sources of their anxiety about the future, were seriously misconceived. A succession of reports from the South had made it clear that the implications of global warming, for example, were more severe for poor countries than for rich ones *Nairobi Declaration on Climate Change* (Institute for African Alternatives 1990); *Our Own Agenda* (Latin American and Caribbean Communism on Development and Environment 1990; Global Warming in an Unequal World (Agarwal and Narain 1991).

Moreover, the view from the South was a dissenting view in a number of ways. First, there was criticism that institutions like the World Resources Institute in Washington, had produced misleading accounts of the shared responsibility of North and South. The WRI had calculated the proportion of the world's greenhouse gases produced by India, and had then used this proportion to calculate India's share of global responsibility for global warming. Agarwal and Narain argued that this ignored the role developing countries played, especially through their forest "sinks", in absorbing emissions. In addition, countries in the North contributed much more to carbon emissions on a *per capita* basis, since their populations consumed more than their "share" of resources (Agarwal and Narain 1991). Finally, of course, it was the North which bore historical responsibility for the problem, and which continued to equate "luxury" emissions with the "survival" emissions of paddy rice producers in the South

The developed countries of the North viewed population as a global responsibility which most governments in the South were unwilling to shoulder. The view that the debate about global warming had little to do with the more urgent environmental issues was put by *The Economist* in advance of the Rio meeting:

> In fact, the main certainty about global warming is that its consequences are uncertain and far off, whereas the measures needed to prevent it are immediate and (in some cases) costly. But much of the damage that could result from climate change in the next century is occurring right now, and it has nothing to do with carbon dioxide. Deserts are advancing, forests are vanishing, crops are failing, species are becoming extinct. The root cause of this damage is a continuation of population growth and poverty in the third world. These are the gravest threats to environment and development, the twin themes of the Earth Summit. Tackling them matters far more for man's future than preventing global warming . . . (*The Economist*, 30 May 1992, p. 11)

The Earth Summit in 1992 was preceded by a number of preparatory meetings and negotiations. It was proposed that the governments attending the Rio meeting would already be asked to sign a number of specific legal measures, on biodiversity and climate, before the conference convened. In addition, an *Agenda 21* was actively negotiated during early June 1992, which set out a work programme into the next century, together with targets, costs and a division of responsibilities (IIED 1991).

It would clearly prove impossible to secure meaningful agreements without the financial means to carry them out. The Secretariat preparing for UNCED (United Nations Conference on Environment and Development) estimated these costs at 125 billion US dollars through the establishment of a new "Green Fund", the Global Environmental Facility. In addition measures would need to be taken to ensure that the transfer of technology, especially energy technologies, from North to South, paid more attention to the environmental effects of the technology. The Northern countries were accused of exporting "dirty" technology, often at a discount, and leaving it to the poorer countries to clean up the cost of their use and live with the environmental consequences. These costs should be incorporated within the costing of energy options, not ignored, in the interests of economic growth. As the *World Development Report* (World Bank 1992) expressed it:

> . . . many (environmental) problems are exacerbated by the *growth* of economic activity. Industrial and energy-related pollution (local and global), deforestation caused by commercial logging, and overuse of water are the result of economic expansion that fails to take account of the value of the environment. Here the challenge is to build the recognition of environmental scarcity into decision making. (World Bank 1992, p. 7)

Even before the ink had dried on the agreements to establish the Global Environmental Facility, critics were adamant that it was little more than window-dressing. The criticisms were that "costing environmental problems in the language of development diverts attention from the policies, values and knowledge systems that led to the crisis, and the interest groups that have promoted them" (*The Ecologist* 1992). The governments of the South were only represented within the GEF after the decisions had been taken about its role and organization. The governments of the South had called for a new agency or for the new funds to be managed by an existing UN agency which was more democratically accountable. Voting rights in the World Bank, and as a consequence in the GEF, were determined according to a country's contribution to the budget, not on a one country–one vote basis.

In addition, the GEF will concentrate its attention, in the view of its critics, on "helping" developing countries to contribute towards solving global environmental problems, when the real challenge is to change the habits and practices of the North. Its terms of reference are restricted to financing "environmental" projects which are global in conception, rather than national or local ones, which "would benefit the world at large". The four main priorities for the GEF—the protection of biodiversity, the mitigation of global warming, the control of pollution in international waters, and the management of stratospheric ozone depletion—are all areas of *global* concern, but ones usually removed from ordinary people's lives, especially in the South. The more pressing problems of ordinary people, such as the questions surrounding land ownership, the provision of basic health facilities, the provision of clean drinking water and the erosion of soils, are not subject to the "benefits" of the GEF. In the event, early reports suggest that the expected finance, without which the post-UNCED agenda is unlikely to advance, will not materialize. The "brave new world" consequent upon the deliberations at Rio looks uncomfortably like the cowardly old one (Grubb *et al* 1993).

The following chapters discuss the more immediate threats—and challenges—affecting poor people in the South. However, the context of this discussion, like the Rio Summit itself, carries implications for the North. In the first part of this book we consider the legacy of thinking surrounding sustainable development and the discussion of population and the environment. These chapters are concerned to establish the assumptions and values behind the current uncritical clamour for "sustainable development". The second part of the book uses case material to explore the strategies under which more sustainable development might be achieved, concentrating on the livelihoods and values of poor people in the south. The chapters on the Philippines, Ghana, Mexico and Bolivia each focus on different "levels" of organization, and policy implementation. They examine the driving forces behind environmental problems, and the obstacles to more sustainable management. They also examine the role of people themselves in future environmental management strategies. They seek to do this not so much as "participants" in the policy goals of others, but more as empowered individuals seeking to achieve greater security for themselves and future generations of their families.

SUSTAINABLE DEVELOPMENT AND ENVIRONMENTAL MANAGEMENT

The case studies discussed in this book provide evidence of the central role which local people, in the South, can play in implementing sustainable development. In the next chapter the concept of "sustainable development" is explored in more detail. However, it is important to provide some discussion of the term before proceeding.

'Sustainable development", although a useful overarching term to describe normative *objectives*, has little explanatory power. In this sense it is hardly a *concept* at all. After the global restructuring that followed the debt crisis of 1982, the environment emerged from the shadows of the "development" debate.

The impetus behind sustainable development came from the biological sciences, as we shall argue in the next chapter. The literature on the concept reflects this debt (Caldwell 1984, Dasmann 1985, Rees 1990). At the same time economists found in "sustainable economic development" a juxtaposition with which they could tackle head-on some of the limitations that had become endemic to their discipline (Barbier 1987, Pearce *et al* 1989, Jacobs 1991). What emerged from this discussion was a debate *within* economics, as well as between economists and others (Ekins and Max-Neef 1992, Dietz *et al* 1992, Anderson 1991; Young 1992). Green economists, more critical of policy than of the idea of "sustainability", sought to argue that the neo-classical tradition, could not accommodate radical, Green ideas (Sachs 1991, a view echoed by political science (Dobson 1990).

At the same time the discussion of sustainable development from a Southern perspective has come to occupy an important place in the literature, concerned as it is with the realities of unsustainable development in the South. The intention of this volume of essays is to focus upon the resources, human and natural, which exist in developing countries, and which provide historical and cultural continuity. Our concern is with the context in which environmental management is pursued. The chapter by Sage, for example, makes the point that the "war on drugs" can be viewed, differently, from Northern and Southern perspectives. From the North the conflict is often viewed as a "crusade" where beneficiaries are the unwilling economies of the North. From the South the dependence on drugs is viewed as a facet of the consumer society, and the production of narcotics as a market opportunity. Where does development meet "sustainability" in this discourse? Clearly, the answer lies in the role of economic necessity and the existence of policy alternatives.

MARKET MECHANISMS AND ENVIRONMENTAL OUTCOMES

Using market mechanisms to ensure better environmental outcomes, rather than regulatory interventions, has much to recommend it. The case for this approach was put most persuasively in Pearce *et al* (1989). However, in addressing the problems of developing countries, in particular, we need to be aware of the role played by wider livelihood considerations in the behaviour of rural people, especially the rural poor. To many of them external policy constraints are established within an institutional domain that they have no control over, and little knowledge of. The strategies of the rural poor in managing their environments are designed to secure their livelihood—including subsistence agriculture and "basic needs" goods such as fuelwood and water supplies—as well as negotiation with the market. Their sphere of activity is that of the so-called "informal sector", in rural areas as well as urban ones, which exists in the interstices of law and regulation. The establishment of environmental "value" within informal livelihood-based economies may have more to do with cultural codes, and traditional community practices, than the apparatus of centralized policymaking.

If we acknowledge that much environmental decision-making occurs outside the battery of formal policy, then it follows that environmental concerns need to be fed into agricultural policies from the "demand side" as well as the "supply side". (This concern with "supply side" policy is also widely illustrated in the chapter by Sage in this volume on cocaine production.) If we take an exclusively supply side approach, valuable as this is, we may be surprised to find that responses to policy change are not those we expected. Important moves to improve natural resource accounting, for example, and to remove disincentives to better environmental management, will have unpredictable effects if we do not also consider the perspective of most environmental "managers" within the rural sector. What may be termed "demand side" issues have only been touched upon in the past: they have inevitably been confined to the margin of the analysis. From the perspective of the resource-poor household, public preferences, often communal preferences, are important as well as private ones. Enlisting people in more sustainable practices, within the agricultural sector, means embracing their social goals and aspirations, which frequently govern the way in which they manage their immediate environment. It should not be confined to adjusting the fiscal and other constraints which originate from central governments, or the international economic system. It may be the case, for example in a country such as Brazil, that the removal of subsidies which a small minority of rich agricultural producers receive from the state can serve as a vehicle for making structural reforms, under which small farmers secure better property rights, linked to sustainable agricultural practices (Guaniziroli 1990). The point is that agricultural policies have environmental impacts that are mediated by human agents. Effective environmental policies, along the lines of the precautionary principle, can only succeed if we have a fairly clear view of the responses of these agents, in the face of new supply side policy innovations. At the heart of this issue lie fundamental questions about the integrity of local knowledge systems, and the ability of rural people to communicate effectively their strategies and goals through the plethora of existing development institutions. As I shall argue below, we may risk losing the potential for more integrated agricultural and environmental policy initiatives, by enlisting local people in policy objectives which they have had no real opportunity to influence.

THE REFORM OF POLICY INCENTIVES

It has been suggested that sustainable production requires the reform of economic *dis*incentives to better resource management, through the removal of subsidies and the more accurate pricing of environmental costs and benefits. The management of the environment for sustainable production also requires attention to *incentives*. Together, incentives and disincentives provide the carrot and the stick for motivating behaviour that will bring about more sustainable development (McNeely 1988). Direct incentives, in the form of cash or in kind, can be applied to specific objectives, such as the management of a protected area. Indirect incentives are likely to be much more important outside protected areas like Biosphere Reserves: they assist local people in conserving their resources, and serve to reward human effort in developing sustainable systems.

Incentives can smooth the uneven distribution of costs and benefits in conserving resources, mitigate the negative impact on local people of regulations controlling exploitation, and reward local people for assuming externalities through which the wider public benefits. To function effectively, incentives require a certain amount of regulation, enforcement and monitoring, but it needs to be emphasized that they cannot function at all without local goodwill and support—a preliminary to the establishment of local people, and their systems of knowledge, in environmental decision-making. Biological resources are often under threat because the responsibility for their management has been taken away from local people and transferred to distant, government agencies. The rural people who live closest to valuable environmental resources, such as tropical forests or wetlands, are often those who are most economically disadvantaged, and have least stake in their exploitation. Excluded from management of their local environment local people cease to act like stewards, and become poachers. The objective of designing workable incentive schemes is that they should become stewards again and, in the case of particularly valuable environments, gamekeepers.

Among the most appropriate measures for effecting this change is the assignment of management responsibilities to local institutions, strengthening community-based resource management systems, and introducing a variety of property rights and land tenure arrangements, which can reinforce the positive effect of more sustainable pricing and fiscal policies. These approaches can serve to rekindle traditional resource management practices, and focus the attention of the local community on the value of indigenous knowledge and experience. This case is strengthened where natural environments are particularly rich—for example in biodiversity. People living in and around the forests, wetlands and coastal zones often exercise more power than governments in the use that is made of biological resources; but the conservation of these resources is rarely linked with more sustainable livelihoods.

Support for better incentives need not be confined to the national level. Because the international community as a whole benefits from better conservation, it should contribute to the costs of conserving biological resources. Governments in the South seldom have sufficient capital or labour to manage their nation's biological resources in an optimum way, even though investments in conservation can be very cost-effective. Programmes of environmental protection are usually implemented through resource management agencies which lack reliable budgets and trained personnel. Some incentives require little more than an administrative decision or regulations, while others involve bilateral agreements or cooperation with international agencies, such as food for work programmes.

One of the most effective ways of introducing environmental management incentives is as part of externally supported project development. According to IUCN, additional mechanisms for supporting incentives include:

- tax deductibility for donations of cash, land or services
- charging entry fees to protected areas

- returning profits from exploiting biological resources to the people living in the area
- implementing water-use charges for the water produced by an area
- building conditionality into extractive concession agreements
- seeking support from international conservation organizations for initiatives such as "debt-for-nature" swaps
- considering conservation "concessions" rather like extractive concessions for forestry and mining (McNeeley 1988, p. 12)

Paradoxically, granting user-rights may prove a more effective incentive to control the use that is made of natural resources than attempting to police protected areas. Such products as firewood, medicinal plants, and meat can often be made available to local communities more effectively through direct harvesting than through middle-men, and effective user-rights can often provide economically disadvantaged communities with highly valued resources.

Among the elements that need to be borne in mind when designing and implementing incentive packages through which the rural poor might play a larger part in environmental management include:

(1) The incentives should serve to catalyse initiative. They should be considered fair compensation for work done, and lead to greater accountability within local populations.
(2) The incentives should emphasize local management of resources, rather than cash in hand. Women should play a large role in these management plans, since it is they who usually shoulder the major burdens of resource management.
(3) The technology and pricing incentives surrounding an incentive package need periodic review, and constant monitoring.
(4) The incentives should seek to correct market failure and market distortions before introducing policies specifically aimed at conservation objectives.
(5) The incentives should be designed with a view to intergenerational equity and, in view of the importance of local feeling, interregional equity. To be effective they should provide short-term benefits, and a stake in longer-term outcomes.
(6) Incentives should be culturally sensitive, and sufficiently flexible to meet community compliance. For example, it is usually the case that farmers treat their own fields first, making it difficult to move from a water-catchment approach to a farm/village emphasis. Where labour is limiting, as in most of Africa, much of South and Central America and parts of Asia, community involvement in catchment conservation and cooperative efforts is extremely difficult to achieve, and unlikely to occur spontaneously (Belshaw et al 1990). The approach to land-use planning

in Lesotho targets the village and uses locally accepted land division and soil names. In seeking to reduce runoff from farmed land, it makes sense technically to address whole catchments, but practically such divisions have little meaning to land users. Clearly the design of effective incentives requires a balance to be struck between what can be achieved locally, through the participation of local communities, and the removal of structural policies, at the intersectoral, national and international level, that impact on the rural poor, regardless of their individual commitment to better environmental management.

LOCAL INVOLVEMENT IN ENVIRONMENTAL MANAGEMENT

The rethinking of environmental economics, and the incorporation of sustainable criteria within the management framework of development projects, in rural areas has enormous potential for policy intervention, but cannot work successfully unless it is matched by much greater local involvement in environmental management decisions. Any serious discussion of participation and local empowerment in managing the environment, in turn, needs to consider the framework of demands which are formulated by the rural poor themselves. Ultimately, sustainable development is only practicable when it is endorsed by local communities and groups, whose own experiences of managing the environment are forged through contact with outside development agencies, government departments and local policy institutions.

The articulation of demands by local groups, governing the use they make of natural resources, inevitably means the exercise of power, and resistance to it. It should come as no surprise, then, to discover that environmental demands affect the content of social relationships, as well as their form. Conflicts over the management of environmental resources, which policy interventions seek to mediate in various ways, help to bring new social relationships into being—most notably, between government institutions, non-governmental organizations (NGOs) and groups of local people. In some cases a radical break is achieved, through which existing relations are democratized, or opened up, but there is no guarantee that the new relations of power will be more stable than those they replaced. As Foucault argued, every strategy of confrontation dreams of becoming a relationship of power, of finding a stable mechanism to replace the free play of antagonistic forces. The clear implication of this kind of reasoning is that a concern with local environmental policy interventions should also address the ways in which the rural poor seek, through their own struggles, to effect more control over the resources they command. It is the relationship between agency (as represented by local people) and structure (as represented by outside institutions and policies) which determines the outcome of social conflicts in rural areas, and the way the environment is ultimately managed. Among the critical issues that need to be addressed in this context are the following:

(1) Do the rural poor, who are most vulnerable to the effects of environmental degradation, understand the full implications of using technology provided by outside institutions? How can policy interventions highlight the environmental costs (and benefits)—many of which are passed on to poor, rural households—of using technologies that did not originate with the rural poor themselves?

(2) Correcting market failures and distortions, implies reassessing the value of environmental goods and services. How are these new valuations incorporated in policy interventions? Have the calculations of the rural poor, in seeking to improve or maintain their livelihood, been incorporated into the system of incentives (and the removal of disincentives) which guides local resource management?

(3) Where does the balance of responsibility (and power) lie in managing the local environment? If new, and more sustainable, policy interventions require the local population to expose themselves to greater risk or uncertainty, or to trade present benefits forgone against future expected benefits, are these factors adequately reflected in the measures which have been taken to gain the support of poor, rural households? In particular, have women's responsibilities for meeting basic household needs from environmental resources (water, energy, fuelwood etc) been translated into policy terms: for example, by ensuring that more sustainable management practices do not lead to greater demands on their time, or income?

(4) What interests does the local population have in intergenerational equity? Is the system of land tenure, and land use, conducive to longer-term security for the rural poor? What measures can be taken to ensure that better environmental policy interventions increase the security of the rural poor?

The implications of designing policy interventions that encourage sustainable development are not confined to the rural poor, of course, and consideration also needs to be given to ways in which institutions coordinate policies, and remove bottlenecks to the implementation of sustainable rural development programmes. In many areas of development policy, sectoralism is entrenched in procedures and planning mechanisms. Coordinating mechanisms, to replace sectoral responsibilities, will fail if the sectoral mandates of different government agencies remain unchanged. The answer is not to try and abolish sectoralism by inventing new, overarching, institutions, but to change the mandate of, and procedures for, each sector, so that institutions behave cross-sectorally. In particular, the rewards for staff within sectoral institutions should reflect their commitment to these coordination functions, as well as their own, narrow sectoral responsibilities. At the national level, sustainable development objectives should be incorporated in the terms of reference of those cabinet and legislative committees dealing with national economic policy and planning, as well as those dealing with key sectoral and international policies. There is an urgent need to take decision-making at the individual household level as seriously as decision-making at the level of government agencies and institutions. A failure to recognize the ways in which they are linked is a hallmark of the kind of unsustainable development which has characterized much of the rural sector in developing countries, often aided and assisted by governments (and international organizations) more interested in short-term economic gain than in long-term environmental and economic security. The case studies undertaken for this book illustrate the centrality of local people's experience in achieving more sustainable development. However, before examining these cases in detail, we need to explore the idea of sustainable development in more depth.

REFERENCES

Agarwal, A. and Narain, S. (1991) *Global Warming in an Unequal World.* Centre for Science and Environment, New Delhi.

Anderson, V. (1991) *Alternative Economic Indicators.* Routledge, London.

Barbier, E.B. (1987) "The concept of sustainable economic development". *Environmental Conservation*, 14, 101–109.

Belshaw, D., Blaikie, P. and Stocking, M. (1990) *Key Land Degradation Issues and Applied Research Priorities.* Overseas Development Natural Resources Institute, Chatham.

Brandt Commission (1980) *North–South: A Programme for Survival.* Pan Books, London.

Brundtland Commission (1987) *Our Common Future.* Oxford University Press, Oxford.

Buttel, F.H., Hawkins, A.P. and Power, A.G. (1990) "From limits to growth to global change: constraints and contradictions in the evolution of environmental science and ideology". *Global Environmental Change*, 1, 57–66.

Caldwell, K.L. (1984) "Political aspects of ecologically sustainable development". *Environmental Conservation*, 11, 299–307.

Castri, E. di and Hadley, M. (1984) *Ecology in Practice.* Unesco, Paris.

Dasmann, R.F. (1985) "Achieving the sustainable use of species and ecosystems". *Landscape Planning*, 12, 211–219.

Dasmann, R.F., Milton, J.P. and Freeman, P.H. (1973) *Ecological Principles for Economic Development.* John Wiley, Chichester.

Dietz, F.J., Simonis, V.E. and Van der Straaten, J. (1992) *Sustainability and Environmental Policy.* Edition Sigma, Berlin.

Dobson, A. (1990) *Green Political Thought: An Introduction.* HarperCollins, London.

Eckholm, E.P. (1976) *Losing Ground: Environmental Stress and World Food Prospects.* Pergamon, Oxford.

The Ecologist (1992) 22 (3) May/June, 82–83.

The Economist (1992) "The Question Rio Forgets". 30 May, 263–294.

Ekins, P. (1992) *Wealth Beyond Measure*. Gaia Books London.

Ekins, P. and Max-Neef, M. (eds) (1992) *Real Life Economics: The Emergence of a Living Economics School of Thought*. Routledge, London.

Ghai, D. and Vivian, J. (eds.) (1992) *Grassroots Environmental Action*. Routledge, London.

Global 2000 (1982) *Report to the President*. Penguin, Harmondsworth.

Grubb, M., Koch, M., Munson, A., Sullivan, E. and Thomson, K. (1993) *The Earth Summit Agreements: A Guide and Assessment*. Royal Institute of International Affairs, London.

Guaniziroli, C.E. (1990) "*Agrarian reform in the context of modernised agriculture: the case of Brazil*". PhD thesis, University College London.

Hewitt, C. (1992) "Economic adjustment and the maize producer in Mexico". United Nations Research Institute for Social Development, Geneva.

IIED (1992) "Rio: the lessons learned". *Perspectives*, No. 9, International Institute for Environment and Development, London.

Institute for African Alternatives (1990), *Nairobi Declaration on Climate Change*, London.

IUCN (International Union for the Conservation of Nature) (1980) *World Conservation Strategy* IUCN/WWF/UNEP, Gland, Switzerland.

IUCN (International Union for the Conservation of Nature) (1991) (World Conservation Strategy II) *Caring for the Earth*. Gland, Switzerland.

Jacobs, M. (1991) *The Green Economy*. Pluto Press, London.

Latin American and Caribbean Commission on Development and Environment (1990) *Our Own Agenda*, Washington DC.

Markandya, A. and Pearce, D. (1988) *Environmental Considerations and the Choice of the Discount Rate in Developing Countries*. Environment Department, The World Bank, Washington DC.

Meadows, D.C., Meadows, D.L., Randers, D.H. and Behrens, W.W. (1972) *The Limits to Growth*. Pan Books, London.

McNeely, J. (1988) *Economic and Biological Diversity*. International Union for Conservation of Nature and Natural Resources, Gland, Switzerland.

McNeely, J. and Pitt, D. (1985) (eds.) *Culture and Conservation*. Croom Helm, London.

Parkin, D. and Croll, L. (1992) (eds.) *Bush Base: Forest Fallow*. Routledge, London.

Pearce, D., Markandya, A. and Barbier, E. (1989) *Blueprint for a Green Economy*. Earthscan, London.

Rees, W.E. (1990) "The ecology of sustainable development". *The Ecologist*, **20**, 18–23.

Sachs, W. (1991) "The story of a dangerous liaison". *The Ecologist*, **21**, 252–257.

Wilson, J.S. (1858) "On the general and gradual desiccation of the earth and atmosphere". *Transactions of the British Association*, pp. 155–156.

World Bank, (1992) *World Development Report*, Washington DC.

Young, M.D. (1992) *Sustainable Investment and Resource Use*. Unesco/Parthenon, Paris.

2 Sustainable Development: Economics and the Environment

MICHAEL REDCLIFT
Wye College, University of London, UK

Sustainable development remains a confused topic. Like motherhood, and God, it is difficult not to approve of it. At the same time, sustainable development is fraught with contradictions (Redclift 1987). This has not prevented "sustainability" from being invoked in support of numerous political and social agendas. This chapter argues that sustainable development has gained currency precisely because of the way it can be used to support these varying agendas.

The idea of sustainability is derived from science, but at the same time highlights the limitations of science. It is used to carry moral, human, imperatives, but at the same time acquires legitimacy from identifying biospheric "imperatives" beyond human societies. Married to the idea of "development", sustainability represents the high-water mark of the Modernist tradition. At the same time, the emphasis on cultural diversity, which some writers view as the underpinning of sustainability, is a clear expression of Postmodernism. The strength of sustainable development lies in its ambiguity, and its range. In wresting control of the idea of sustainable development we are faced with an apparent choice between acknowledging that all such ideas are socially constructed, and a realist position, which engages with urgent environmental problems, and seeks to fashion better environmental policies, and better-informed human agents.

ANTECEDENTS: THE ETYMOLOGY OF "SUSTAINABLE"

The word "sustainable" is derived from the Latin *sus-tenere*, meaning to uphold. It has been used in English since 1290, but the etymology of "sustainable" carries interesting, and important, implications for the way the word is used. As de Vries (1989) reminds us, "sustainable" can mean supporting a desired state of some kind or, conversely, enduring an undesired

Strategies for Sustainable Development: Local Agendas for the Southern Hemisphere
Edited by Michael Redclift and Colin Sage. © 1994 John Wiley & Sons Ltd

state. If we believe that enhanced personal welfare is important, for example, we are encouraged by the fact that it is "sustainable". Similarly, the absence of personal welfare is frequently attributed to a lack of "sustainability". The verb "to sustain" carries a passive connotation; while the adjective "sustainable" is used in the active sense. Sustainable refers to an act or process which is capable of being upheld or defended. On the other hand "sustainable" in the active voice suggests a disposition towards something, it carries a clear prescriptive message that something should, and can, be done. As we shall argue below, the juxtaposition of both normative/active, and positive/passive meanings, has enabled the idea of sustainability to be employed in a variety of contradictory ways.

One route into the problem is to formulate propositions about sustainable development, which can serve to illustrate some of these competing, but powerful, interpretations.

(1) The first proposition is that sustainable development *has proved useful as a concept, precisely because it combines the idea of prescriptive action, with that of enduring, defendable properties, located in scientific principles.* As we shall see, the reference to scientific principles, which may be undermined by human actions, is central to the environmental message. At the same time, of course, Green thinking takes issue with much reductionist science, regarding it as part of the problem.

(2) The second proposition is that sustainable development *is born of intellectual necessity, as much as political necessity. It emerges, in fact, from problems generated by Modernism itself, including our faith in science.* As David Cooper argues, ". . . the shift in the idea of environment is symptomatic not only of a predilection for a scientific perspective, but of the situation of today's intellectuals" (Cooper and Palmer 1992, p. 171). It follows from this proposition that the idea of sustainability reflects unease about the human condition; we use nature and the environment to mirror the discontents of human societies.

We will return to these propositions later. For the present, it is worth considering the historical legacy from which the idea of sustainable development has grown. Although we increasingly refer to other cultures, and other epochs, in defence of the idea of sustainability, it should properly be seen as the outcome of a quite specific set of events, beginning with the idea of progress, and associated with the Enlightenment in Western Europe. Again, our willingness to authenticate sustainability by reference to societies which possess no such concept, is both historically and intellectually revealing. As we shall see, it carries serious implications for "global" strategies of development, which ensure the continued economic hegemony of the northern, industrialized countries.

SUSTAINABILITY AND DEVELOPMENT: THE DISCOURSE
SURROUNDING NEEDS

In his classic study of the environmental idea, Clarence Glacken argues that "the association of the idea of progress with the environmental limitations of the earth" was, necessarily, a *post*-Enlightenment development (Glacken 1973, p. 654). The thinkers of the European Enlightenment, such as Condorcet, Godwin and Malthus, had all developed a primitive concept of "carrying capacity", but they did not explore the implications of environmental changes that were driven by human behaviour. In the late eighteenth century even the most radical thinkers assumed a stable physical environment, as the backdrop for human progress. The earth could be cultivated "like a garden" but Enlightenment thinking did not consider that "an environment deteriorating as a result of long human settlement, might offer hard choices in the future" (Glacken 1973, p. 654).

Later, Glacken makes his point even more forcefully, pointing to elements in the modern equation, which pre-nineteenth-century thinkers ignored. He writes:

> With the eighteenth century there ends in Western civilization an epoch in the history of man's relationship to nature. What follows is of an entirely different order, influenced by the *theory of evolution, specialization in the attainment of knowledge, acceleration in the transformation of nature.* (Glacken 1973, p. 705; emphasis added)

These three elements—evolutionary theory, scientific specialization, and economic development on an unprecedented scale, throughout the nineteenth century—define the context in which sustainability was to become important. They also define the context for Modernism and, I would argue, the human (or "inner") limits placed on the development of productive forces.

There has been considerable debate about what defines Modernism. For our purposes, Modernism is the view that ideas grounded in (essentially) Western philosophy and science can serve as the basis for social criticism and understanding. In the opinion of Post-Modernist writers like Lyotard, Modernism's mistake was to have recourse to "the grand narratives of legitimation" which are no longer credible (Lyotard 1984, p. 23). In terms of our discussion of sustainability, Modernism represents an attempt to deal with the problems of nature through reference to "natural laws": to "external limits" imposed on human societies. These laws were being developed throughout the eighteenth century, but it was not until the nineteenth century that scientific disciplines, and the successful application of science through technology, assumed the authority it has today. In a sense, then, Modernism sought to pit human ingenuity against the "external limits", in the Promethean spirit. Some thinkers, including Engels, were dimly aware of the costs attached to the advance of science, principally in terms of the difficulties in managing nature (Engels 1970). However, managing nature was quite a different thing from understanding it, and the Modernist position placed human beings above the environment from which they had sprung.

There are two key elements in the Modernist perspective on the environment. The first is tied up with the *idea of progress*, of Reason and Freedom. The second concerns the way in which Modernism *legitimates its own discursive practices*. Both elements take us some way towards understanding the essential ambiguity behind the way that sustainable development is invoked.

According to Sklair (1970) the nineteenth century represented a watershed in thinking about progress, because it was the period in which science became institutionalized, in which material progress was linked to new ways of thinking:

> By the middle of the nineteenth century those who wrote about society were in a position to elaborate a theory concerning the relations between scientific and social progress from an entirely different . . . point of view. (Sklair 1970, p. 33).

The centrality of science to society, has made it almost impossible to consider the idea of progress without thinking of its critique, which is by no means confined to Post-Modernist writing. Almost forty years ago Claude Lévi-Strauss, in his celebrated tract on *Race and History* (1958) pointed out that historicist conceptions of progress are ultimately flawed, "progress . . . is neither continuous nor inevitable; its course consists of leaps and bounds. . . . These . . . are not always in the same direction" (Lévi-Strauss 1958, p. 21). Later he goes on to write that advancing humanity is like a gambler throwing dice, and each throw giving a different score. "What he wins on one (throw), he is always liable to lose on another, and it is only occasionally that history is 'cumulative', that is to say, that the scores add up to a lucky combination" (Lévi-Strauss 1958, p. 23).

"Development" is a notion infused with the idea of progress, in itself an idea as powerful to the Left as to the modernizing Right. Notwithstanding the progress of science and technology, however, and the material improvements to which they helped give rise, "development" still has to confront a more deep-rooted difficulty. If human progress can only be achieved at the expense of destroying the environment, and ultimately the resources on which development depends, then a theory of development lacks legitimacy. Fraser and Nicholson (1990) note that Modernism "narrates a story about the whole of human history which purports to guarantee that the pragmatics of the modern sciences and of modern political processes—the norms and ends which govern these practices—are themselves legitimate" (1990, p. 22). For ideas to retain their power, they must be legitimated. Sustainable development is one such idea, which seeks to legitimate its own propositions by recourse to what are assumed to be universal values. By incorporating the concept of "sustainability", in an essentialist way,. within the account of "development", the discourse surrounding the environment is often used to strengthen, rather than weaken, the basic supposition about progress.

Sustainable development draws its programmatic character from this essentialist discourse. Development is read as synonymous with progress, and made more palatable because it is linked with "natural" limits, expressed in the concept of sustainability. Sustainable development then becomes a methodology, as well as a normative goal, a model for planning, a strategy involving purposeful management of the environment. Some of the approaches which recognize these political parameters, it must be added, are extremely useful within specific contexts. Michael Jacobs, for example, makes good use of the idea of "sustainability planning" in his case for more recognition, from the political Left, for the role of market interventions in environmental management (Jacobs 1990). As we shall argue later, sustainable development seeks to define an "ends/means" structure, based on a hierarchy of needs. As de Vries puts it, "planning for sustainable development assumes that a blueprint for Utopia can *and should* be made . . . a recipe for how to travel towards the end of the road" (de Vries 1989, p. 8). Other writers, notably Merchant (1980), find an echo in today's "managerial ecology" of earlier, seventeenth-century approaches, which also "subjected nature to rational analysis for long-term planning" (Merchant 1980, p. 252).

THE ALLOCATIVE PRINCIPLES BEHIND SUSTAINABLE DEVELOPMENT

If the idea of sustainable development is a product of Modernism, it also answers to the problems of Modernism, in a variety of ways. First, and here the comparisons with Marxism are particularly interesting, sustainable development *invokes the concept of "need", in the context of "development", to meet problems of resource allocation in time and space.*

Problems of allocation in time, between "now" and "later", between present and future generations, are central to the discourse surrounding sustainability. Intergenerational equity, in the way used by economists, is a concern to register the preferences and choices of future generations, as yet unborn. It has served to extend Neo-Classical theory, which would otherwise fail to fully reflect the supposed choices over the way the environment is valued. The fact that intergenerational equity considerations play such a large part in environmental economics, reflects the constraints under which the Neo-Classical paradigm is employed, as a tool of economic policy. Societies recognize questions of "intergenerational equity" in a variety of ways, and these concerns are reflected in a variety of social science disciplines, notably in anthropology, jurisprudence and philosophy.

Sustainable development also answers to problems of allocation in space: allocation of resources between "here" and "elsewhere". These are the problems of intragenerational equity, especially between different societies and between North and South, which are often taken for granted in the discussion. Instead attention has focused on the future costs of development to our own societies, as if the satisfaction of our future needs is the principal bone of contention, rather than the way we currently satisfy our needs at other peoples' expense.

The importance, indeed primacy, of intergenerational equity is vividly illustrated by the currency given to the definition of sustainable development used by the Brundtland Commission: "development that meets the needs of the present without compromising the ability of future generations to meet their own needs" (WCED 1987). This is an enticing definition, in many ways, but it begs at least as many questions as it purports to answer. First, this definition carries the clear implication that "needs" can be divorced from the development process itself, that they are not part of development, and can be arrived at independently.

The experience of the last two centuries in the industrialized world hardly bears out this proposition. Some would argue that needs can be viewed from a relativist position; that is, they are essentially historically determined. How needs are defined then depends on who is doing the defining. The knowledge we have of needs changes over time, and is linked to our ability to satisfy them. Each society "defines" needs in its own way, and has evolved quite complex mechanisms to reassure its members that their needs are being met. Others, including many within the contemporary Green movement, would argue that we need to discriminate between these mechanisms, as the "satisfiers" of needs, and the needs themselves, which are thought to be ahistorical.

Doyal and Gough (1991) point out that "needs" are different things to different people, and distinguish different ideological positions on human needs. Thus, to Neo-Classical economists needs are preferences; to the New Right needs are dangerous; to Marxists needs are historical; to anthropologists needs are group-specific; to radical democrats needs are discursive; and to phenomenologists needs are socially constructed (Doyal and Gough 1991). Again, a reflection of Lévi-Strauss is quite illuminating in this instance. He writes:

> cultures . . . appear to us to be in more active *development* when moving in the same direction as our own, and stationary when they are following another line. (Lévi-Strauss 1958, p. 25)

In other words, cultures only appear to be stationary because their ways of meeting their own needs are unfamiliar to us, often without meaning, and "cannot be measured in terms of the criteria we employ" (Lévi-Strauss 1958, p. 23).

SUSTAINABLE DEVELOPMENT AND THE PROBLEM OF LEGITIMATION

It was argued above that a distinguishing feature of Modernism was that it legitimates its own discursive practices. The discourse surrounding sustainable development was therefore a metadiscourse, in which the claims to provide insights could only be evaluated in terms of the discourse itself. In this respect the important point about sustainable development is that *the choice of a biological concept (sustainability) leaves open the possibility that it can be treated both as a model and as a point of legitimation.* The natural world is used, in other words, both as a model for systems based on human intervention and, ultimately, a constraint on human development. Sustainability appears to provide a point of reference outside the confines of human experience, which can also serve to guide human choices. We are dealing, then, with both the naturalization of social behaviour, and the legitimacy conferred on that behaviour by reference to natural laws. But, if sustainable development appears to provide a reference outside the confines of human experience, which is relevant to that experience, how seriously should we take this comparison? To what extent is the choice of biological systems one of metaphor, and to what extent is the natural environment treated as a point of reference? To answer these questions involves a short digression into the biological significance of "sustainability".

The concept of sustainability in ecology is an important one. Within plant ecology "sustainable" refers to the successional changes in plant communities which might serve as a model for the management of forests and rangeland. The key idea is that environmental management can benefit from referring to natural succession, from utilizing the knowledge we have acquired about natural, ecological systems. The principle of "sustainable yields" has become well established in certain fields of environmental management, particularly in fisheries management and forestry.

In ecological terms the most mature natural systems are those in which energy shifts away from production towards the maintenance of the system itself. The best example are tropical forests, which exhibit all the features of a "climax system", including enormous natural diversity, and in which the delicacy of the species is guaranteed by the complexity of system interactions. From an ecological point of view agricultural systems are always modifications, in which natural ecosystems have been interfered with by human beings, usually to enhance their productivity at the expense of their sustainability. To an ecologist, then, agricultural systems should demonstrate the capacity to renew themselves, to regenerate, in the face of disturbances in their natural evolution.

The ability of agricultural systems to withstand disturbances, stresses and shocks, is the principal characteristic of sustainable agricultural systems, according to Conway (1985). It was also the guiding principle which lay behind the first World Conservation Strategy, published in 1980, that of "sustainable utilization" (WCS 1980). In the hands of writers like Odum (1971) the ecologists' interest in "evolutionary adjustment", the idea that ecosystems only evolve successfully when they are protected from rapid changes, served as a guide to the way that power was exercised in human society. Ecology provided ideas about the way systems work, including systems subject to human intervention, at the same time highlighting the point beyond which such systems are no longer "sustainable".

The use of a concept drawn from ecology, rather than one of the social sciences, can be regarded as conveying several ambiguities:

(1) *It is often not clear when biological systems are being used as a metaphor, and when as a referent.*

(2) *Sustainable systems occurring in nature, were used as a model for environmental and resource management, without reference to the differences introduced by human needs and choices.*

(3) *Incorporating the ecological idea of sustainability represents a way of viewing the shortcomings, or contradictions, of "development". These shortcomings are usually seen as a "malfunction" of the system and, as such, one which can be addressed by human intervention.* For example, the Brundtland Commission reported that "as a system approaches ecological limits, inequalities (in access to resources) sharpen" (WCED 1987, p. 49). The implication is that distribution problems, of intragenerational equity, are made worse by the failure to adhere to sound ecological principles, which should inform global policy, as well as local environmental management.

The confusion surrounding our inability to behave according to biological injunctions, represented here by the absence of sustainability, is central to the appeal of sustainable development. It eases the passage from "scientific" uncertainty to political prescription. It provides a moral force, which we have seen as essential to Modernist discourse, which seeks to engage our emotions as well as our minds. As we shall argue later, this tendency to provide a normative foundation for allegedly "scientific" injunctions, reaches its clearest expression in relation to global climate change. The call to take measures to avert "global warming", and the suggestion that we have already reached unsustainable levels in our dependence on hydrocarbons, acquire moral, as well as scientific authority, from the profligacy of the current development model. Whereas the dilemma posed by the environmental lobby in the 1960s and 1970s was that the scarcity of resources posed "limits to growth", in the 1990s the principal threat to our survival is identified in the "externalities" (notably global warming and ozone depletion) of the growth model itself.

In the next section we examine the theory of value that underpins much of the discourse on sustainable development. If the concept of sustainable development represents an attempt to bring together ethical injunctions and scientific authority, the importance of the concept can be seen most clearly in the way it has come to inform economic policymaking. Environmental economics, we shall argue, proceeds by setting aside most of the problems associated with science as a social process, and the social authority of scientific knowledge. Recourse is made instead to nature, and the laws of "natural capital", providing increased legitimacy for the otherwise contested concept of "development".

ECONOMIC VALUES AND SUSTAINABLE DEVELOPMENT: PARADIGM REGAINED

Environmental economics has sought to extend Neo-Classical theory, by encompassing the environment, and attaching monetary values to losses in natural capital. The revisionist case, from within economics, begins with the observation that changes in wealth are only recorded in the national income figures *when they pass through the market*. This leaves changes in the stock of environmental capital outside the basis of calculation. There are two aspects of the "conventional" approach to environmental assets that are criticized:

(1) Conventional economic accounting frequently regards the destruction of resources as a contribution to wealth. For example, the destruction of tropical forests are recorded as an increase in Gross Domestic Product (GDP), in the national accounts.
(2) At the same time the cost of making good any environmental damage is recorded as a positive contribution to GDP. The costs of reducing pollution, for example, and of measures to prevent pollution, are registered as contributions to economic growth.

However, these two propositions lead to a paradox. If the costs of environmental redress are counted as a contribution to economic wealth creation, then logically pollution itself should be recorded as a cost against economic growth. We know, after all, at the intuitive level, that pollution (and other forms of resource degradation and depletion) actually reduce the value of the environment. Economics, in its conventional form, seems unable to recognize this fact.

Following our intuitive logic, nevertheless, carries problems. If we count pollution as a cost against natural capital, we must also argue that developed countries, which pay a considerable amount for environmental abatement, are poorer as a consequence. They are paying, in effect, to maintain the quality of their natural capital stock. Presumably countries which are unable to pay the price of environmental abatement, or choose not to do so, (including most developing countries) are therefore "richer" than those countries which attach importance to environmental abatement? This appears to lack logic, and to run counter to the experience of the real world, in which resource management in developing countries is increasingly unsustainable.

There is another problem, too. If we are to measure changes in environmental quality, such as air pollution, land degradation and the loss of species, how do we do it? There are two obvious answers which economists give to this question. First, we can measure the reduction in environmental quality by the cost of restoration. Second, we can calculate how much consumers are prepared to spend to maintain environmental quality (contingent valuation). In practice there are problems with both answers. Some environments, like that of the African Sahel for example, cannot be restored to their former quality, even if we knew precisely what it was. In addition, contingent valuation, for its part, is a very inadequate tool for measuring the value of environments to groups of people, as we shall see later.

It is clear, then, that problems with the definition, methodology and techniques of environmental economics, strike at the heart of the debate surrounding sustainable development. It is all the more important, then, that we are clear about the territory on which we seek to argue. Environmental economists like Pearce have advanced thinking within economics in a number of important ways, all of which retain importance for other social sciences such as sociology.

(a) They recognize that changes in natural capital stocks involve both costs and benefits. Unlike most conventional economics, environmental values are not determined by income flows alone, but by the stock of (natural) capital. Wetlands, for example, are converted, through drainage, for agricultural use. Similarly, the open seas are used as sinks for the disposal of wastes (Pearce *et al* 1989, p. 5).

(b) There is also a recognition that "non-use" values are important, as well as "use values". Environmental values include "existence values", which can be arrived at notionally, and a (theoretical) price attached to them.

(c) Environmental economics also recognizes uncertainty and irreversibility as principles in resource conservation, and as reasons for conserving the stock of natural capital, even if it is not "optimal" (Pearce *et al* 1989, p. 7).

(d) It is also recognized that "optimality" refers only to economic uses and efficiency, and effectively excludes any social goals for conserving resources. (This does not prevent Pearce from encountering a problem in "non-efficiency" goals, in that they might "be better served by converting natural capital into man-made capital" (Pearce 1989, p. 7).

The difficulty in fully incorporating social goals within the analysis of optimal resource utilization is, paradoxically, demonstrated by the principle which is used to defend it. Pearce declares that *we know natural capital is valuable because people are willing to pay to preserve it.*

> A simple conceptual basis for estimating a benefit is to find out what people are willing to pay to secure it. Thus, if we have an environmental asset and there is the possibility of increasing its size, a measure of the economic value of the increase in size will be the sums that people are willing to pay to ensure that the asset is obtained. *Whether there is an actual market in the asset or not is not of great relevance. We can still find out what people would pay if only there were a market (Pearce 1989, p. 8).*

It is clear from the foregoing discussion that environmental economists like Pearce have proved able to push back the boundaries of the Neo-Classical paradigm, and to accommodate environmental concerns in their analysis. However, this accommodation has come at a price. Essentially, the analysis has widened the bounds of consumer choice, enabling the individual's preferences to be expressed. In the next section we will examine the limitations of this approach. For the moment we need only register the fact that environmental economics leaves the Neo-Classical paradigm intact. Market values, or imputed market values, can be used to provide a fuller account of natural capital, and the benefits of sustainability. In seeking sustainable development, Pearce notes that "*what constitutes development, and the time horizon to be adopted, are both ethically and practically determined*" (Pearce 1989, p. 3). This observation should lead us to consider not only the political context in which decisions are taken about the environment, but also the circumstances under which environmental economics is used to help facilitate decisions. If "development" is subject to value judgements, and lies outside the compass of objective science, why is environmental economics not subject to the same value judgements? Is development to be subject to value judgements, but not the paradigm within which it is understood?

THE LIMITATIONS OF ENVIRONMENTAL ECONOMICS: PARADIGM LOST

We have already argued that environmental economics has succeeded in enlarging the Neo-Classical paradigm, with important consequences for the way that the environment is calculated. It remains to examine the assumptions of the paradigm itself.

The first problem with the paradigm is that it fails to recognize that monetary values are *always* exchange values, not use values. When Pearce refers to "use benefits" and "use values" he is referring to exploitation values. Use values do not attract monetary values because they exist outside the framework of market pricing. Environmental economists will argue that this is no impediment to using monetary values for them, and that the way that we arrive at these prices is a matter of methodological refinement. Economics has developed techniques to impute such values, in the form of shadow pricing, and contingent valuation. There are no barriers to attaching prices on environmental goods and services, it will be objected, merely misplaced ideological objections.

This is to miss the point. *Economists cannot value what the environment is worth; merely its value in monetary terms.* As Oscar Wilde maintained, it is possible to find a price for everything and the value of nothing. The point is that monetary valuations do not capture the worth of the environment to different groups of people. Giving increased value to environmental assets is not simply a question of attaching larger figures to assets in the course of cost–benefit analysis. As Elson and Redclift (1992) demonstrate, this means attaching *cardinal valuations* through monetary measures, such as prices and taxes, when *ordinal valuations* (more/less valuable) may be more appropriate, and useful. We can undertake valuation by establishing the thresholds that operate for real people in the real world, rather than through monetization.

Let us use women's labour in the forest communities of the developing world as an example. Men and women value the environment differently because of the different use they make of it. The value women attach to the environment is usually invisible to others because the use they make of it is not subject to market values. Nevertheless women's activities, such as collecting firewood, gathering plants and fetching water, for both use and exchange, are vital for the sustainability of poor rural households. Many of the environmental goods that women collect, and households use, are "free goods" in nature but vitally important for survival. Elson and Redclift (1992) note that one tribal community in Andra Pradesh could identify one hundred and sixty-nine different items of consumption, drawn from forest and bush land. Environmental accounting is ill-equipped to measure the real value of the environment to women, when these use values are part of direct household provisioning.

The second problem with the paradigm is that it claims "value neutrality", when environmental economics itself expresses the preferences and biases of the society in which it was developed. Values are a reflection of specific social systems, and express degrees of commitment to a specific social order, the order which espouses them. The values we place on nature, not surprisingly, reflect our priorities *not the value of nature itself*. Nature is a mirror to our system of values, and in seeking monetary values for environmental goods and services we are attempting to "naturalize" the environment.

Environmental economics provides a good illustration of the way we seek to socially construct the environment, through the mechanism of monetary valuation. Progress within the discipline aims to extend the paradigm, rather than to place it within its political and social context. Development projects, for example, such as large dams or irrigation schemes, are said to have "environmental consequences", which environmental economics is well-placed to address.

This is to ignore the fact that development projects are socially created and socially implemented. They already internalize a view of nature, in their methodology and practices. They also seek to acquire legitimacy for the idea of projects—another instance of the way they are socially constructed. Development projects have already internalized a view of nature *from which environmental consequences themselves spring.* (In the same way ecological projects have internalized a position on society; but this is a still more difficult nut to crack!) What is at issue, then, is the appropriatness of environmental economics, which does not recognize its own relativism, in evaluating projects which are themselves an expression of specific values, and interests in the social order.

There is a third area in which the Neo-Classical model can be faulted. It is that this model fails to recognize that *conventional economic analysis rests on a particular view of human nature and social relations.* It is important to establish the elements in this model of social relations which underlie the methodology of monetary valuation.

First, environmental economics sees social interaction as instrumental. That is, it is designed to maximize the individual's utility. As Hodgson writes, "(within environmental economics) the tastes and preferences of individuals are considered a given" (Hodgson 1992, p. 54).

Second, and related to this, environmental economics does not see social interaction as constituting value in its own right, because of the intrinsic value of human beings. Social interaction reveals the person as an "object", surrounded by other "objects", rather than a "subject person" (in Max-Neef's phrase (Ekins and Max-Neef 1992)) able and willing to behave in ways that do not correspond to short-term economic advantage. It is this failure to recognize human behaviour as culturally determined, and capable of a very wide range of variability, which cannot be easily married with the reductionism of economics.

The "rational, individual calculator" beloved of economists sits uneasily in cultures other than those which helped to develop the paradigm in the first place (and none too easily in many areas of behaviour within the developed countries). This individual is supposed to make choices, expressed as market preferences, within a "neutral" cultural context. Social and economic processes are never "rational" in a universal sense: rationality is always culturally grounded. In addition, the calculations of individuals are not the same as individual calculations.

The calculations of individuals are socially constructed, and can be best understood as the outcome of social processes, peculiar (and unique) to every society. Concepts like the "willingness to pay" concept, used by environmental economists, presuppose a set of cultural and ideological assumptions. Returning to the example we gave from Pearce earlier, although economists might look upon the North Sea as a "waste sink resource", fishing communities in the area would view it otherwise, as would holiday-makers, or artists, or any individual or group of individuals.

The problem for modern environmental economics is compounded by a fourth set of issues, which concern the degree to which the "individual, rational calculator" is fully appraised of the situation in which he is being asked to make choices. As Gleich puts it:

> Modern economics relies heavily on the efficient market theory. Knowledge is assumed to flow freely from place to place. The people making important decisions are supposed to have access to more or less the same body of information. (Gleick 1987, p. 181)

These objections to the paradigm on which environmental economics is founded, suggest that environmental economics has a certain technical competency, in attaching monetary values to environmental benefits and losses, but that this competence, important though it is, should not be confused with an adequate basis for environmental valuation. Indeed, we need to look at environmental economics within a wider context, in which we consider it as a product of society itself.

Before considering where this leaves our discussion of sustainable development, we should examine the wider policy context from another perspective, which builds on the points above. We need to look at the environment within the context of the way science itself is socially constructed.

THE ENVIRONMENT AND THE SOCIAL CONSTRUCTION OF SCIENCE

It is clear that the view we take of the environment is closely bound up with the view we take of science. Increasingly environmental problems are looked upon as scientific problems, amenable to scientific "answers". An example is the current policy prescriptions surrounding global environmental changes, particularly global warming. Since global warming is a "scientific" problem, it is assumed that it must have a scientific solution. The "greenhouse effect" is viewed as carrying social and economic implications, but scarcely as an "effect", in that the human behaviour which underlies global warming is rarely considered. More attention is paid to ways of mitigating the effects of global warming, than to its causes in human behaviour and choices, the underlying social commitments which make up our daily lives.

Part of the problem with this approach is that the modes of enquiry in the natural sciences are themselves *social processes, into which crucial assumptions, choices, conventions and risks, are necessarily built*. Once we regard science as outside ourselves it becomes impossible to take responsibility for its consequences. And so it is with global warming: relegated to the sphere of "consequences" we are able to avoid the environmental implications of our own behaviour, and that of our societies.

This process of disengagement from the consequences of our behaviour is well established in a variety of ways. The second World Conservation Strategy document, *Caring for the Earth (IUCN 1991)*, provides a useful example, in diagrammatic form, of the model through which we manage our resources (IUCN 1991, p. 76). The model portrays the way in which economic development, driven by fossil fuel resources, has taken society along a path which ignores the limits imposed by renewable solar energy (in all its forms). Instead our development model has channelled the material wealth which fossil hydrocarbons have helped to create, towards the creation of capital goods, themselves dependent on further fossil fuel exploitation. The model thus ensures a continued and spiralling demand for scarce and ultimately finite resources, which are fast contributing to global nemesis, by posing the ultimate, unsustainable, problem for the economies which consume them. Global warming, the loss of biodiversity, the problems associated with the "ozone hole", and other global environmental changes, represent the ultimate "externality", and point to problems in the growth model itself.

As *Caring for the Earth* points out, by concentrating investment of surplus value in order to maximize the accumulation of industrial capital, we have tended to neglect natural capital (environmental goods and services). Instead we have focused our support on the development of human capital, within a small intellectual elite, working within spheres of knowledge which are closely allied to new technologies and wasteful resource uses.

This illustrates the lack of congruity between technological and scientific knowledge, and the social implications of using that knowledge in specific ways. Wherever we look—nuclear power, toxic wastes, pesticides, air pollution, water quality—we see examples of our failure to grasp the social implications of the scientific knowledge we possess, and the costs which are passed on to the environment. We know that environmental science cannot make political choices, about the consequences of technology for the environment. At the same time environmental policy is nothing more than the formulation of one set of social and political choices, governing environmental uses, over another set of choices. It is hardly surprising that the discussion and practice of sustainable development is intimately linked to the social authority of our science and technology. In the North this authority is increasingly contested, especially by environmental groups and interested citizens. In the South it is frequently ignored, notably by development institutions whose model of "development" acknowledges no social authority but that of science. As we have argued, that is why development in the South is ultimately not socially and politically sustainable.

Where does this leave our discussion of sustainable development? It soon becomes clear that we cannot achieve more ecologically sustainable development without ensuring that it is also socially sustainable. We need to recognize, in fact, that our definition of what is ecologically sustainable answers to human purposes and needs as well as ecological parameters.

By the same token, we cannot achieve more socially sustainable development in a way that effectively excludes ecological factors from consideration. If the model for better environmental policy merely "adds on" environmental considerations to existing models it is not equipped to provide a long-term view. The strong sense of "sustainable development" emphasizes the sustainability of the interrelationship between biological, economic and social systems, rather than that of the component parts. Each system involves elements—social "needs", levels of production, biodiversity—which are subject to modification. It follows that any environmental social science is ill-equipped to address environmental problems that does not seek to rethink the development agenda.

We have argued that much of the writing on sustainable development takes its message from the natural sciences. In the past this has been a message of hope, as people have lived longer, and consumed more goods, especially in the North. Sustainable development, in this usage, is about seeking consensus and agreement, in the belief that we can manage the contradictions of development better. Sustainable development, we have argued, represents a renewal of Modernism.

A more critical perspective, it needs to be added, regards science as part of the problem, as well as the solution. It takes issue with the inevitability of economic growth, and its consequences for the aptly named "hydrocarbon society". It argues that the limits placed on development, are not merely limits in the resources available to us, as was believed in the 1970s. The limits today are "external limits", too, represented most vividly by the challenge of global warming. The more critical perspective suggests that environmental management, as a strategy to cope with the externalities of the development model, may well be found wanting.

If we are to meet the problems presented by imminent global nemesis, we need to go beyond the assertion that such problems are themselves socially constructed. We need to embrace a realist position, while recognizing and acknowledging the relativism of our values and our policy instruments. The challenge is to develop a "third view", which enables us to assume responsibility for our actions, while exploring the need to change our underlying social commitments. We need to develop a broader and deeper foundation for the formulation of a realist policy agenda, and one, unlike environmental economics, which does not abstract "interests" from its calculus. Sustainable development answers to problems initiated in the North, with our "global" development model. We have also understood sustainable development within a cultural context of our own—*our* view of nature, *our* problems with science and technology, *our* confidence in the benefits of economic growth. But sustainable development has become a "global" project, and our capacity to find solutions is seriously reduced by our inability to recognize that we are the prisoners of our history.

In subsequent chapters we examine what is meant by sustainable development in concrete cases, taking as examples first, the Philippines (Asia), then Northern Ghana (Africa) and Central Mexico (Latin America). The chapter on the Philippines provides a vivid example of the importance of the recent history of development in the South, is closing doors to greater sustainability. At the same time the adoption of the rhetoric of "sustainable development", by Philippine administrations, has done little to alter the real priorities of government policy, which lie in other directions. This analysis, essentially at the national level, is supplemented in the later chapters by examples drawn from local level experience. These demonstrate that rural people are well aware of the livelihood choices that determine their use of natural capital. As we shall see the management of the environment becomes, in many cases, closely linked to the livelihood systems adopted by the household economy.

Before we begin to "ground" our analysis in specific cases, however, we need to ask one fundamental question about sustainability that has been omitted from the discussion so far. The ultimate "driving force" behind development and environmental problems is demographic. Can our natural capital withstand the pressures of increased population and levels of consumption?

REFERENCES

Conway, G. (1985) "Agro-ecosystem analysis". *Agricultural Administration*, **20**, 31–55.
Cooper, D.E. and Palmer, J.A. (1992) *The Environment in Question*. Routledge, London.
Doyal, L. and Gough, I. (1991) *A Theory of Human Need*. Macmillan, London.
Ekins, P. and Max-Neef, M. (eds.) (1992) *Real Life Economics*. Routledge, London.
Elson, D. and Redclift, N. (1992) *Gender and Sustainable Development*. Overseas Development Agency.
Engels, F. (1970) "Introduction to the Dialectics of Nature". In *Selected Works* (one volume), K. Marx and E. Engels eds.), Lawrence & Wishart, London.
Fraser, N. and Nicholson, L.J. (1990) "Social criticism without philosophy: an encounter between Feminism and Postmodernism". In *Feminism/Postmodernism*, (Linda J Nicholson ed.), Routledge, New York.
Glacken, C. (1973) *Traces on the Rhodian Shore*. University of California Press, Berkeley, CA.

Gleick, J. (1987) *Chaos Theory*. Cardinal, London.

Hodgson, J. (1992) In Ekins and Max-Neef (1992).

IUCN (International Union for Conservation of Nature) (1991) *Caring for the Earth*. IUCN/UNEP/WWF, Gland, Switzerland.

Jacobs, M. (1990) *The Green Economy*. Pluto Press, London.

Lévi-Strauss, C. (1958) *Race and History*. Unesco, Paris.

Lyotard, J. (1984) *The Postmodern Condition*. University of Minnesota Press, St Paul, MN

Merchant, C. (1980) *The Death of Nature*. Harper & Row, New York.

Odum, H.E. (1971) *Environment, Power and Society*. John Wiley, New York.

Pearce, D., Barbier E. and Markandya A. (1989) *Sustainable Development: Economics and Environment in the Third World*. Earthscan, London.

Redclift, M.R. (1987) *Sustainable Development: Exploring the Contradictions*. Methuen, London.

Sklair, L. (1970) *The Theory of Progress*. Routledge & Kegan Paul, London.

Vries, H.J.M. de (1989) *Sustainable Development*. Groningen, Netherland.

WCED (World Commission for Environment and Development) (1987) *Our Common Future*. Oxford University Press, Oxford.

WCS (1980) *World Conservation Strategy*. IUCN/UNEP/WWF, Gland, Switzerland.

3 Population, Consumption and Sustainable Development

COLIN SAGE
Wye College, University of London, UK

INTRODUCTION

The relationship between population, consumption and environmental resources is increasingly recognized as an intellectually complex and politically difficult, as well as an ideologically polarized, area of debate. This was nowhere more apparent than during the UNCED process where the South refused to accept discussion of population growth without it being linked to action on poverty alleviation, food security and the reduction in levels of resource consumption in the North. For, notwithstanding the projected figures from UN sources that 90% of the expected 4.7 billion people that will be added to world population by 2050 will be born in the South, it is the industrialized countries that currently present the biggest threat to global environmental resources. Despite supporting only 24% of global population, the industrialized countries

> consume 85 per cent of the world's metals, 92 per cent of its cars, 85 per cent of its chemicals, 81 per cent of its paper, 78 per cent of sawn wood, 72 per cent of milk and 48 per cent of cereals. They also consume 82 per cent of gasoline, 72 per cent of diesel, 85 per cent of gas and 82 per cent of electricity. (Parikh 1992)

It is in this context that we need to reflect on the longstanding quarrel between Cassandras and Pollyannas (Hardin 1988): between those who argue that the growth of human numbers will inevitably outstrip the capacity of the earth to provide food and other vital support services (see Ehrlich (1968), and those who believe that the innate ingenuity of the human species will always provide the technical means to overcome resource constraints (see Simon (1981)). Certainly some of the writings of the arch-protagonists

Strategies for Sustainable Development: Local Agendas for the Southern Hemisphere
Edited by Michael Redclift and Colin Sage. © 1994 John Wiley & Sons Ltd

have occasionally struck an unusually defensive or spiteful tone (Simon 1990, Kasun 1988).[1]

Yet, given the importance of the population–consumption–resources equation within the context of the search for sustainable development and the need to slow global environmental change, it is vital to break away from fossilized positions in which population is viewed either as the single cause of impending planetary collapse or as the catalyst for ever-higher levels of material development. Whatever attempts are made will be beset by difficulties, not least in the way in which they tackle the contrasting circumstances and causes of environmental degradation in the rich industrialized countries (the "North") as opposed to the poorer and developing economies of the "South".[2] For, unfortunately, growing concern about the maintenance of biospheric system integrity has resulted in quite different international policy agendas.

While there is, as yet, little agreement and even less commitment amongst the rich countries of the North on formulating clear and effective policy responses to global climate change and loss of biodiversity, there is some convergence between them about the need to reduce the depletion of ozone and tropical forests—and the rate of population growth in the South. For many of the poorest countries, on the other hand, environmental problems have hitherto largely been treated as second-order issues that either derive as a necessary consequence, or mark the failures and distortions, of economic development. Their response to the North is that planning for a reduction in rates of population growth can only begin once economic growth has raised standards of living to "levels compatible with human dignity" (Latin American and Caribbean Commission 1990). This marked lack of congruence in the perspectives of North and South illustrates the need for innovative and imaginative approaches towards the analysis of population, consumption, resources and development.

It is, nonetheless, necessary to take heed of global demographic dynamics, for world population reached 5.3 billion by mid-1990 and is growing at a rate of 1.7% per year. Table 3.1 provides a summary of some demographic indicators for the major world regions. Asia accounts for the largest share of world population, with China (1.1 billion) and India (850 million) the most populous countries, although the fastest rate of increase is in Africa which is growing at an average rate of 3% per year (Sadik 1990). Meanwhile in the North fertility is generally below replacement levels and the intrinsic rate of population growth is negative (Alonso 1987). This bifurcation in the demographic trajectories of North and South has led some commentators to speculate on the international security implications of a world where today's hegemonic powers comprise a diminishing proportion of the total global population, although a high proportion of the world's aged population (Eberstadt 1991). Mapping such shifts in absolute and relative demographic

Table 3.1. Population indicators for major world regions

Region	Population millions 1990	Average rate growth (%) 1990–95	IMR per 1000 1990	Percentage urban 1990	Urban growth (%) 1990–95
World	5292.2	1.7	63	45	3.0
'North'	1206.6	0.5	12	73	0.8
'South'	4084.6	2.1	70	37	4.2
Africa	642.1	3.0	94	34	4.9
N. America	275.9	0.7	8	75	1.0
L. America	448.1	1.9	48	72	2.6
Asia	3112.7	1.8	64	34	4.2
Europe	498.4	0.2	11	73	0.7
Oceania	26.5	1.4	23	71	1.4
USSR	288.6	0.7	20	66	0.9

Source: Data derived from World Resources Institute (1990).

weights upon a changing resource base and deteriorating environment represents a vital ongoing task, for the demographic effects on international relations cannot be set against a constant environmental backdrop (McNicoll 1984).

Indeed, one of the few certainties from which to start is with demographic momentum for, irrespective of the efforts directed at reducing fertility, human numbers are set to grow to between 7.6 and 9.4 billion by 2025. In other words the world will still have to cope with between 44% and 62% more people by that date proving that the greatest policy challenge will be coping with the needs and pressures of the inevitable population rather than attempting to avoid the increment (ODA 1991).

It is not intended to rehearse here the main historical-demographic trends and trajectories that characterize the major world regions, a topic that is addressed by Demeny (1990) amongst others. Rather, the purpose of the chapter is to explore some of the underlying features and dynamics of population change, relating these to aspects of wealth and poverty, and to questions of land-use change and environmental degradation. Nevertheless, it is important from the outset to emphasize that the marked national diversity in demographic indicators is unparalleled in human history. Examples of such diversity include: natural growth rates of countries ranging from +4% to −0.2%; average family size from more than 8 to around 1.4; age structures that encompass the very youthful (half the population under 15 years) to the aged (less than 20% under 15); and levels of urbanization that range from 10% to 90% of total national populations. Given this extraordinary national diversity in demographic indicators—which are influenced by the complex interaction of economic activity, historical processes, social structures and cultural traditions—there is consequently an enormous variety of population–environment relationships. It is the purpose of this chapter to explore some of the features of this variety, and to evaluate the place of population within the complex of factors that fashion environmental change.

CONCEPTUALIZING POPULATION AND ENVIRONMENT

While cutting through the ideological accretions of recent years, it is still useful to embark upon an analysis of population–environment relationships with a juxtaposition of the positions of Thomas Malthus and Ester Boserup. More than 150 years separate their writings, yet they serve as twin pillars of a debate in which many interlocutors still find it necessary to place themselves within, or close to, one or other camp. Malthus was concerned with the relationship between population and food supply under conditions where technology and resources in land remained constant. He postulated that human numbers would outstrip the capacity to produce sufficient food and that "positive checks" such as poverty, disease, famine and war would impose downward pressure on the rate of population growth in the absence of fertility control. In contrast, Boserup argued that high population densities are in themselves a prerequisite for technological innovation in which agricultural systems continuously evolve into increasingly land-intensive forms. This process, she argues, has given rise historically to five distinct stages stretching from shifting cultivation with long fallow periods to multiple cropping (Boserup 1981).

It is important to remember that neither author was concerned with the environment other than as a resource for food production although they shared the assumption of diminishing returns to labour at a given level of technology (Lee 1986). Nevertheless, the central elements of change in their respective models—population growth for Malthus, technology for Boserup—has led to many of those involved in the environmental debate to support either a pro- or anti-Malthusian perspective on the cause of the world's ills. Thus, on the one side are those such as the Ehrlichs and Garrett Hardin who favour population control, while on the other a range of writers variously attribute environmental problems to inappropriate technology, overconsumption by the affluent, inequality and exploitation—everything, in fact, but population growth (Harrison 1990).

Developing a fresh conceptual approach toward understanding the linkages between population and environment means overcoming the dichotomy between the Malthusian and Boserupian models. Lee (1986) has attempted a most elaborate and sophisticated synthesis in order to understand the behaviour of population and technology, both as independent elements and in combination. He embarks upon his enquiry posing a number of penetrating questions such as: if larger populations encourage rapid technological progress, and if higher technological states induce more population growth, can a steady-state equilibrium exist? And does the Boserupian model of technological progress ultimately depend upon Malthusian features of positive checks? Lee's chapter finally demonstrates a high degree of convergence between the two models which is bolstered by some historical reflection.

Blaikie and Brookfield (1987) take a similar view in their discussion of population and land degradation, in which they challenge the inevitable outcome implicit in Boserup's model that population growth always produces agricultural innovation. They note that in many instances it is not innovation but environmental degradation which results and that the weakness of Boserup's model is that she isolates population as a single causal variable in a similar way to the neo-Malthusians. Two issues raised by Blaikie and Brookfield in the course of their argument are worth noting here. The first is their use of the notion, "pressure of population on resources" (PPR) which helpfully establishes a linkage without the need to specify critical thresholds embodied in the term "carrying capacity", a problematic concept which is entirely conditional on the level of technology and consistency of climatic factors. The second issue concerns the necessary distinction between intensification and innovation. While the former indicates increased output through the elimination of fallow and the use of inputs, it can also include the conditions of involution described by Geertz (1963) where more and more labour is used to squeeze marginal increments from Javanese rice paddies. Innovation, on the other hand, embodies the qualitatively new ways in which the various factors of production are employed. While intensification may act as a block to innovation, for example under conditions where high population densities are supported using simple technology, such conditions are also able to contain the consequences by which labour-intensive systems maintain terracing and other forms of landesque capital.[3] If labour is withdrawn from the maintenance of such a system the consequences, according to Blaikie and Brookfield, can be disastrous if it has become one of high sensitivity. Nevertheless, degradation is not an inevitable outcome of population pressure: it can occur, they argue, "under rising PPR, under declining PPR, and without PPR" (Blaikie and Brookfield 1987, p. 34).

If we treat population as an independent variable, then there are four general ways in which it can interact with environment:

(1) Population growth results in the expansion of the area under cultivation and leads to resource depletion and ultimately environmental degradation in the absence of institutional and technological change (the Malthusian scenario). Such circumstances may, for example, be found in areas of land settlement and frontier expansion.

(2) Population growth results in the intensification of production, involving increasing investments of human, natural and financial capital, and in innovation embodying the development of new technical means of production. While this technologically optimistic, Boserupian scenario represents, historically, the evolution of ever more sophisticated land management systems, non-sustainable outcomes may appear in the medium to longer term (e.g., groundwater pollution, declining soil fertility).

(3) Population growth is scale neutral in terms of the local resource base, either through the importation of food from elsewhere or as excess population outmigrates resulting in no demographic pressures for agricultural change. Such migrants must, naturally, be supported by resources elsewhere.

(4) Reverse effects or feedback loops, where changes in the productive potential of the local environment influence the determinants of population: fertility, mortality and migration.

These four simplified options are largely covered by Bilsborrow's threefold classification of responses to population pressures which he has labelled demographic, economic and, rather clumsily, demographic-economic. In the first category he refers to the variety of social responses available to reduce existing levels of fertility. The second category encompasses production responses in agriculture, while the third largely comprises migration (Bilsborrow 1987). Grigg has also generated a typology of responses comprising four categories, and while the first three conform to those listed above, he substitutes off-farm employment for feedback effects (Grigg 1980).

Nevertheless, while population is certainly one factor that acts to influence land-use changes, it does so in association with two other variables: technological capacity and levels of consumption. Thus, a given environmental impact (I) is derived from the multiplicative interaction of the three variables, population (P), per capita consumption (or affluence, A) and technology (T). This creates a useful shorthand expression, $I = PAT$, which is now widely used in the literature although originates in the writings of Paul Ehrlich. Nevertheless, its appeal may stem from the way it diffuses the singular responsibility of population, enabling it to be applied equally in the industrialized countries of the North and the largely rural economies of the South. A critic of inappropriate technology such as Barry Commoner has used a variant of the $I = PAT$ expression to calculate the total environmental impact of industrial pollution and to argue that it was primarily the technological factor rather than population which needed to be controlled (Commoner 1972).

Paul Harrison has recently reformulated Commoner's expression as environmental impact = population × consumption per person × impact per unit of consumption. To determine the "relative blame" for each factor over a period of time, he uses the following expression:

$$\text{Population impact (as percentage of total change)} = \frac{\text{Percentage change in population} \times 100}{\text{Percentage change in use of resource}}$$

Harrison distinguishes between upward and downward pressures on environmental impact by scoring them out of $+100\%$ and -100% respectively, for one or more of the three factors may be tending to reduce environmental impact. Working through the example of the expansion of arable land in developing countries, Harrison describes the process of calculation:

> Between 1961 and 1985, population expanded by 2.3 per cent a year . . . (and) agricultural production rose by 3.3 per cent. So production per person, which we can take as our consumption factor, rose by 0.9 per cent. Farmland, meanwhile, expanded by only 0.6 per cent a year. The farmland used per unit of agricultural production—the impact per unit of consumption—actually declined by 2.6 per cent annually, because yields were increasing. Technology in this case exerted a downward pressure on environmental impact, at least in

terms of land used. Only population and consumption exerted upward pressure. In this case we can say that population growth accounted for +72 per cent of the growth of farmland, and increase in consumption per person for +28 per cent. Technology gets a score of −100 per cent, since it was the only one of the three factors pushing towards lower use of farmland. (Harrison 1992, p. 308)

In developed countries, by contrast, population growth accounted for only 46% of the expansion of farmland and increased consumption per person for 54%, while technology again provides the only downward pressure. As a final illustration here, Harrison computes the causes of fertilizer use in developing countries and attributes 22% to population growth and 8% to increased consumption (measured by the growth in agricultural production per person), while the technology factor—increased fertilizer per unit of agricultural production—accounts for 70% of the increase.

So, to summarize we can say that in the case of developing countries, population appears to be a major driving force of land-use change according to the procedures outlined here. By using the simplest expression,

Farmed area = Population × Food consumption per person × Area per unit of food production

it is clear that if technology and food consumption do not change, population growth translates directly into land conversion for agriculture. Yet, as we shall see, there are other pressures upon land besides its use as a resource for food production. In the North pressures for land conversion derive from qualitative changes as well as quantitative increases in consumption. Some examples include the continuously increasing aspirations for personal mobility which involve road-building schemes; the ongoing suburbanization of the countryside; leisure interests most spectacularly illustrated during recent years by the conversion of farm and other land into golf courses (Pleumarom 1992), as well as the energy implications of all of this. Yet one detects more enthusiasm in much of the policy literature to isolate population as a factor for attention than to address either consumption or technology. For example,

For any given type of technology, for any given level of consumption or waste, for any given level of poverty or inequality, the more people there are, the greater is the impact on the environment. (Sadik 1990, p. 10).

While this is strictly correct, it hardly seems fair or meaningful to hold all factors other than population constant. Indeed, if for a moment we widen the terms of environmental impact beyond changes in land use and consider waste sinks as well as resources, it is clear that in the context of the North, it is changes in the factors of consumption (A) and technology (T) which have the greatest effect. The Ehrlichs (1990) conduct an exercise in which they employ per capita use of commercial energy as a surrogate statistic for A and T. They calculate that each baby born in the United States has an impact on the Earth's ecosystems three times that of one born in Italy, 13 times one born in Brazil, 35 times one in India, 140 times one in Bangladesh and 280 times one born in Chad, Rwanda, Haiti or Nepal. Such a range would seem to correlate very well with levels of per capita GDP.

Yet, while the size of the gross world product—the total of goods and services produced throughout the planet—has been growing at a faster rate than world population (the GWP tripled between 1960 and 1989) (Porter and Welsh Brown 1991), it has not been divided any more equally. In 1965 the high-income countries enjoyed 70% of global GDP, while the South took 19%. By 1989 the 16% of the world's population living in the North accounted for 73% of global GDP, while the 78% living in the South received less than 16% (Harrison 1992). The rising affluence of a stable population therefore poses as great a threat to the global environment if we consider waste sink services as well as resource use, and the oceans and atmosphere as well as land. However, while speculating on the relative contributory weight of population, consumption and technology at a global scale is a sobering exercise, it is not especially amenable to policy formulation, or to remedial action beyond abstract exhortations to reduce environmental impact.

Attributing this or that proportion of the blame to population size and birth rates is by itself a limited exercise. What is required is an understanding of other demographic variables, such as migration flows, the spatial distribution of population, and where people are in relation to the type and resilience of the ecosystem, which may be as important as total size or average density. Moreover, it is indispensable that we understand those factors, or proximate determinants, which give rise to population outcomes. This requires disaggregating the global picture in order to reveal the regional character of demographic change.

REGIONAL POPULATION TRENDS AND DYNAMICS

The rapid growth of world population in the post-war period is the result of a sharp decline in mortality levels due to interventions in public health and disease control. Crude death rates in the developing regions have fallen from 24 per thousand people in 1950–55 to 11 per thousand people in 1980–85, comparable to rates in the industrial market economies (Working Group on Population Growth 1986). Today, life expectancy at birth in the low- and middle-income countries has risen from 41 to 62 years over this period (World Bank 1990). The success of public health, sanitation and vaccination programmes is particularly apparent in reducing rates of infant and child mortality which, overall, fell by 36% between 1950–55 and 1975–80 (Hall 1989). However, infant mortality rates show much the greatest variation of the basic demographic variables as Table 3. 1 demonstrates.

While death rates are approaching their anticipated minimum, birth rates in the South are falling but lagging well behind mortality levels. This "delayed response" to changes in fertility has called into question the applicability of the theory of demographic transition based upon the experiences of nineteenth-century Europe to the developing world today.[4] Unlike mortality, which is highly responsive to improvements in economic development, fertility is a matter of individual and family decision, as responsive to cultural phenomena—gender relations, marriage contracts, inheritance of wealth and property—as to social and economic influences. However, such factors can have complex interactions depending upon the institutional context. It has been suggested, for example, that the currently high fertility rates in sub-Saharan Africa are believed to derive from shortened breast-feeding periods accompanying "modernization", in which post-birth sexual abstinence has been reduced from around three years to four months (Jones 1990). Consequently, given such complexity, there would appear to be little future in a single, universally applicable theory but, rather, a recognition that there are many possible demographic transitions, each driven by a combination of forces that are institutionally, culturally and temporally specific (Greenhalgh 1990a).

While fertility levels have generally stabilized at replacement levels throughout the North—the average is now down to 1.9 children per woman, 1.58 in Western Europe (Sadik 1990)—they have sharply diverged amongst the major regions of the South during the 1970s and 1980s. According to UN data, during the period 1960–65 there was little deviation from the mean of 6.1 births per woman, but by 1980–85 large regional differentials had appeared (Bongaarts *et al.* 1990). The largest decline occurred in East Asia where fertility fell to 2.4 births per woman, yet there is no single factor to explain such a decline. In China a powerful state apparatus assumed the right to impose fertility control, first through the "later—longer—fewer" (1971–78) programme and then the "one child" (1979–present) policy (Greenhalgh 1990b). In Korea, meanwhile, fertility rates fell by 44% between 1965 and 1982 as women married later and later during a period of rapidly growing economic prosperity and full employment. While fertility rates have continued to fall the decline has slowed as the average age of women at marriage tends towards a limit (Pearce 1991). In sharp contrast, however, fertility rates in Africa remain high, having fallen from 6.6 births per woman in 1960–65 to 6.2 in 1985–90. Yet this regional average disguises considerable and growing variation between countries.

A comparison of the total fertility rate (TFR) for 1965–70 and 1985–90 for 49 African states indicates a decline in 22 countries, an unchanged rate in 12, and an increase in the average number of births per woman in 15 countries. Included in this latter group are Tanzania, Malawi, and also Rwanda, where the TFR has risen from 8.0 to 8.3 in a country which has the highest population density on the continent. Those countries where the TFR remains unchanged include Kenya (8.1) and Côte d'Ivoire with 7.4 births per woman, the two remaining countries in Africa where average annual population growth rates still exceed 4%. In Nigeria, the most populated country in Africa with 113 million people, the TFR fell from 7.1 in 1965–70 to 7.0 in 1985–90 (World Resources Institute 1990).

Besides a complex raft of factors which underlay a constancy in the birth rate in Africa, population growth averaging 3% per year is also attributable to an infant mortality rate that has been cut by one-third since 1965 and life expectancy that has been raised by seven years. Such improvements derive from the introduction of state-directed health and education services following independence, which have primarily concentrated upon mortality prevention and only recently begun to take some action on fertility reduction. Yet such services have been introduced without reference to traditional systems of education and health care, or with regard to the social, environmental and political impact they might have. Gradually, the decline in infrastructure, growing bureaucratic costs and foreign exchange scarcity have made the maintenance and support of these services increasingly difficult. Where institutional decay has led these services to break down altogether, or be rejected by local people, there has been little with which to replace them as traditional systems have long since been eroded (Spooner and Walsh 1991).

With the collapse of economic capacity during the 1980s, widespread political insecurity, and the departure of skilled labour the ability of the state to deliver health and contraceptive services has been undermined. Indeed, it is questionable whether the state or the poor can have any real commitment to birth control under current circumstances of acute deprivation. For example, in parts of Africa children under the age of five years make up 20–25% of the population yet they account for 50–80% of the deaths. In Europe the mortality rate for the same group is 3% (World Resources Institute 1990). As long as child mortality remains so high and local survival strategies are ineffective, poor people will maintain high fertility rates to ensure child survival, and potential income and labour-generating options (Spooner and Walsh 1991).

The wide variations in fertility levels illustrate the importance of understanding such proximate determinants as marriage, post-partum practices, contraceptive use and abortion which are themselves fashioned by the socio-economic and cultural context. Traditional checks on fertility vary across sub-Saharan Africa: some societies practice controls on the starting pattern of fertility (delayed age at marriage, celibacy) while others employ spacing or stopping patterns (extended post-partum sexual abstinence, breastfeeding, reduced remarriage). Pathological sterility resulting from the spread of sexually transmitted diseases has also suppressed fertility rates in a broad area of Central Africa (Lesthaeghe 1986). Consequently, it should be noted that there is a highly uneven distribution of population in sub-Saharan Africa, stretching from the high densities of the cities, along the coast, and in the highlands, where population pressures have contributed to environmental degradation, to areas in the interior where low population densities serve as a brake on agricultural development (Hewitt and Smyth 1992).

Nevertheless, in any of these regions, how far are the proximate determinants of fertility responsive to economic, social or environmental conditions? It is often noted that Africa, compared to Europe of two centuries and more ago, is characterized by the early and universal marriage of young women (Grigg 1980). Cain and McNicoll (1988), in an article exploring the institutional determinants of population growth and the consequences for agrarian change, argue that in the case of Africa there are not the same kinds of economic, family or community controls on fertility as existed in pre-industrial North-West Europe and Japan. They partly attribute the insulation of marital fertility from economic change to the lineage system in which husbands and wives share differential costs and benefits. This echoes a parallel debate in the economic anthropology literature regarding the economic value of children and incentives for higher levels of fertility.[5]

A major factor supporting the differential benefits of children is the importance of male-labour migration which is a feature of many of the Sahelian and Southern African economies. With prolonged periods of spousal separation, women rely heavily upon their children as their major productive assets and, consequently, there are low levels of contraception (Lesthaeghe 1986). The organization of labour and domestic (residential) units is thus a vital area influencing the proximate determinants of fertility. Relatedly, there are two other universal variables that play an important part. The first is the character of the specific relations of gender which will determine women's status, the level of participation by women in agriculture and other economic activities, and the degree to which they are able to exert control over their fertility. The second is the social class position of the household, or its location according to indicators of economic wealth and control over means of production. Here, there is often a striking correlation between wealth and household size, very much in line with Chayanov's notion of demographic differentiation. Lockwood draws upon three studies in different parts of Northern Nigeria which each show that richer households have more dependants but also meet more of their grain needs than poorer households. Under the system of dryland agriculture in the region, larger households (including more wives) mean more labour to engage in soil improvement measures, irrigation and tree planting. In other words, improved environmental management is more easily achieved amongst the richer farmers because they can bear the costs and obtain the benefits in terms of enhanced food security (Lockwood 1991).

This illustrates the importance of approaching the issue of population growth through the proximate determinants of fertility at the micro-level. But it also highlights the need to consider the range of structural factors that influence population dynamics through mortality rates and mobility. For this reason a political economy of fertility has been proposed that would comprise a hierarchical, multi-levelled analysis capable of examining household behaviour and community institutions in structures and processes operating at regional, national and global levels, besides the historical roots of those macro–micro linkages (Greenhalgh 1990a). Such an approach might begin from examining the dynamics and rationale of reproductive behaviour and work upwards toward the larger forces shaping institutional change. Alternatively, it could start from an analysis of the way the world market shapes local demographic regimes and work down to individual fertility behaviour. Direction, however, is less important than integrated, multi-levelled analysis combining an understanding of both structure and agency (Greenhalgh 1990a).

ECONOMIC GROWTH, INCOME CHANGE AND CONSUMPTION

Rising levels of per capita income, as part of a process of economic development, is a major variable of land-use change, as we have seen in relation to the $I = PAT$ formula. Yet rising income displays a varying elasticity of demand according to the derived goods and services. In the industrialized countries of the North, for example, the income elasticity for food is low and approaching zero, whereas it is high and positive for such functions as recreation and housing (Pierce 1990). In the South, by contrast, rising per capita incomes stimulate relatively large increases in demand for basic food goods, although as incomes rise this creates a change in the composition of demand (Crosson 1986). Thus traditional grains and tubers gradually give way to higher protein sources and acquired dietary tastes, such as livestock products, imported cereals and processed foods.

Consequently, it is through the changing effective demand for food that rising levels of income exert different pressures upon the agricultural resource base. For shifts to higher protein diets and the increased demand for livestock products requires expanded production of animal feeds. This, in turn, will involve an increase in the indirect per capita consumption of plant energy in a developing country with rising incomes. Given that an estimated 40% of net primary production (NPP) of land-based photosynthesis is currently utilized for food production, this has led some authors to express some real Malthusian concerns: "For an expanding population with a rising income the demands on the agricultural system (will be) nothing short of monumental" (Pierce 1990, p. 102).

Rising income also creates other far-reaching changes in relation to land use, for example by increasing demand for living space, transport and recreational uses especially amongst urban populations. Through rural to urban migration and a growing share of the total population based in urban areas, aggregate demand is also increased as urban dwellers invariably have higher average levels of income and consumption. The consequences are to produce more food for direct consumption by the urban population, as well as cash crops for export to pay for imported food also largely consumed by urban dwellers. The need to engage in export production of land-intensive commodities for high-income countries places a further demand on resources in the South. According to Bilsborrow and Geores (1990), the two main factors responsible for changes in the level of resource depletion are increasing per capita incomes in the North and increasing populations in the South. However,

> (W)ith per capita incomes in low-income countries one-tenth those of developed countries, even with four-fifths of the population residing in low-income countries the bulk of the growth in effective demand upon resources in low-income countries in recent decades is attributable to *increases in the high levels of consumption of developed countries.* (Bilsborrow and Geores 1990, p. 35; my emphasis)

This argument is underpinned by the Ehrlichs who make reference to The Netherlands in developing their case about worldwide overpopulation. They argue that The Netherlands can support a population density of 1031 people per square mile,

> only because the rest of the world does not. In 1984–86, the Netherlands imported almost 4 million tons of cereals, 130,000 tons of oils, and 480,000 tons of pulses. It took some of these relatively inexpensive imports and used them to boost their production of expensive exports—330,000 tons of milk and 1.2 million tons of meat. (Ehrlich and Ehrlich 1990, p. 39)

The functional roles of different groups of countries within the world economic system according to the principles of comparative advantage has led many critics to argue that unequal terms of trade prejudice the prospects of the poorest countries to achieve economic growth. Certainly the total size of the world economy has grown at a faster rate than population, increasing from $5 trillion to $17 trillion over the period from 1960 to 1988, at an average annual rate of 3.64%. The relative growth rates of different world regions are, however, quite uneven. While the developed market economies of the North have grown at a rate of 3.5% over the period, rates in the South have been quite divergent, ranging from 2.53% in sub-Saharan Africa, to 3.84% in Latin America to just over 6% in South and Southeast Asia over the period from 1960 to 1988. Yet it is during the 1980s that these differences have widened, for in Africa and Latin America per capita incomes have fallen while they have continued to rise steadily in Asia. Moreover, the overall gap between the rich North and poorer South continues to widen as measured by the ratio of per capita output which grew from 13.42 in 1980 to 14.7 in 1990 (UN General Assembly Document 1991).

The relationship between rich and poor countries, as between classes within countries, is ultimately determined by superior economic power expressed in the market place which provides the necessary signals and incentives to the sphere of production. Supported by structural economic reforms to remove "distortions", the market has heralded a growing trend in many developing countries where basic food staples have given way to export crops and feed-grain production for Northern end-consumers, resulting in an increasingly segmented structure of agricultural markets in the South (Helwege 1990).

The role of export crop production as a means of generating economic growth has a long and often controversial history where, since colonial times, it has been suggested that such crops enhance food security through the exploitation of natural comparative advantage. Critics argue, however, that export crops dominate areas of high agricultural potential and enjoy a disproportionate use of natural resources as well as credit and other inputs. Local food staples are then displaced into areas of low agricultural potential subject to greater uncertainty of climate, and often lack comparable access to credit and other subsidized inputs. As Leonard observes, the greatest disparities within rural areas of the South are often those between areas of high agricultural potential which have benefited from agricultural modernization and those areas of low potential which have been neglected (Leonard 1989). This raises important questions regarding the location of the poor, especially whether there is a clear tendency for many of the poorest people to be found in areas of low potential subject to climatic hazards and resource degradation. Before examining this issue, it is necessary to raise some practical considerations regarding the measurement of poverty, especially through the use of income, and whether it constitutes a variable of land-use change.

First, a large proportion of goods and services are produced and consumed within the household, or exchanged through barter or reciprocal arrangements, so that there is no record and little evidence on which to collect income and expenditure data (Anderson 1991). Secondly, production and any derived income can fluctuate considerably within and between years, so that notional figures may refer to unspecifiable periods. For this reason consumption may be a better general measure of well-being than income, although by the same token *current* levels of consumption may not be an accurate measure of a household's typical standard of living (World Bank 1990). Attempts to develop a set of social indicators as an index of the level of development and welfare within a society led to the emergence of the notion of basic needs. Yet this has largely fallen into disrepute, criticized as attempting to universalize Western cultural values when needs are, in practice, socially constructed and culturally specific (Doyal and Gough 1991).

While there are still efforts invested in attempting to develop a more sophisticated universal measure of well-being, such as UNDP's Human Development Index, an often-used rule-of-thumb measure of poverty is the FAO/WHO estimates of daily calorie intake as a percentage of requirements. Using the first measure of insufficient calories to prevent stunted growth and serious health risks (ie below 80% of FAO/WHO requirements) some 340 million people fall below the poverty line. A second measure at 90% of FAO/WHO requirements, the minimum amount needed for an active working life, covers some 730 million people. Of these some 40% are children below the age of ten, 75% are rural dwellers and 80% of their income is spent on food (Pearce 1991). These figures are very crude for they do not take account of maldistribution between classes and other groups within a country, and between members of households, which results in an underestimate in the relative malnutrition of women (Doyal and Gough 1991). Moreover, as Kates and Haarmann demonstrate, the use of different poverty indicators, including both absolute and relative measures, can result in estimates varying by up to 750 million in the numbers of poor and hungry people (Kates and Haarmann 1992). Nevertheless, using the incidence of hunger as an indicator of poverty clearly illustrates the extent of food insecurity, which is a problem of access rather than a lack of availability (Pearce 1991).

The incidence and extent of food insecurity as a measure of inadequate incomes through insufficient purchasing power—the incapacity to express demand through the market demonstrating the limited entitlements to food by the hungry (Sen 1981)—might then be linked to the question of location. For it is generally widely assumed that a majority of the poor are located in the most ecologically fragile, low resource areas marked by limited arable land of low potential, and subject to the risks of natural hazards and environmental degradation. The livelihoods of the poor in such areas are consequently believed to be highly insecure, and exacerbated by the strongly seasonal demand for agricultural labour and the limited opportunities for off-farm employment. But to what degree is there a correlation between social and environmental poverty? Do economically marginal people live in ecologically marginal places?

According to Leonard, a total of 470 million people, or 60% of the developing world's poorest according to his criteria, live in rural or urban areas of high ecological vulnerability—"areas where they are highly susceptible to the consequences of soil erosion, soil infertility, floods and other ecological disasters" (1989, p. 19). Of this total, some 70% live in the squatter settlements and areas of low agricultural potential in Asia, 17% in sub-Saharan Africa and 13% in Latin America. Yet these 63 million people living in the ecologically vulnerable areas in Latin America comprise 80% of that region's poorest. Consequently, Leonard believes that poverty in many developing countries is becoming ever more concentrated into definable geographical areas which lack, yet most need, appropriate infrastructure and technology, making increasing numbers of the poorest people vulnerable to environmental hazards and degradation.

Kates and Haarmann cast doubts on the quality of data employed by Leonard but then observe that, even on his calculations, 43% of the poorest live in areas of high agricultural potential. They argue that it is not appropriate to equate areas of low potential with high ecological vulnerability:

> In many parts of the world, land of low agricultural potential is little used, is appropriately used for pastoralism, or is forested. Although subject to erosion, desertification, and deforestation, these areas are not necessarily more vulnerable than are intensively used lands of high agricultural potential that are also subject to erosion, flooding, and, in the case of valuable irrigated lands, salinization and waterlogging. (Kates and Haarman 1992, p. 7)

While they believe it is difficult to map poor people directly onto threatened environments, Kates and Haarmann do examine whether poor countries have more than their share of drylands, highlands and rain forests, three major environments which occupy more than half the world's land area and support one-quarter of its people. They find that low-income countries do indeed possess a disproportionate share of savannah grasslands, while the very poorest countries which account for 20% of the land area in the South possess 63% of its drylands. Moreover, some 71% of tropical moist forests are concentrated in the low-income countries, although not in the very poorest, while highland environments are more equally distributed among poorer and wealthier developing countries.

The main thrust of Kates and Haarmann's article, however, is with identifying particular pathways, or spirals, of impoverishment and degradation. Through a review of a number of case studies taken from the literature, they find a remarkable consistency in the analysis of ways poor people lose their entitlements to environmental resources leading to these downward spirals. Driving these spirals are forces acting in combination, two of which are external to the locality (natural hazards, and development and commercialization) and two which are internal to the community (population growth and poverty). While all the driving forces are implicated in the forms that the spiral sequences assume, Kates and Haarmann suggest that two tend to dominate in each of three major spiral sequences which they label "displacement", "division" and "degradation". While the case-study environments differ in the particular combinations of driving forces, impoverishment and degradation sequences, and in the ameliorative responses undertaken, they are nevertheless able to group together these studies into the three principal environmental categories of drylands, highlands, and rain forests. This permits some fairly generalized, but useful, descriptions of the way people are displaced, whether by population pressure, resource expropriation, or natural hazards, leading to expansion into areas of lower potential and excessive or inappropriate use resulting in degradation and impoverishment. This exercise reveals the importance of understanding the different combination of driving forces acting in concert according to local circumstances and dynamics, and the need to develop policy responses across a broad front.

POPULATION AND ENVIRONMENTAL RESOURCES: CONCLUDING COMMENTS

The caution and circumspection that feature in the paper by Kates and Haarmann when describing the combination of driving forces, including population growth, which form the three impoverishment–environmental degradation spiral sequences is most appropriate for a universally applicable approach. For frequently, efforts to establish a statistically significant relationship between population growth and environmental degradation founder on the preceding prioritization of human numbers and on the extraordinary regional heterogeneity of demographic characteristics which undermines the relevance of global correlations. Moreover, it has been found that the time scales of population variability are asynchronous with environmental change. Consequently, it has been argued that "no simple correlations can be established between population and environmental transformations" and that there is a "need for caution in using population as a simple surrogate for environmental transformation" (Arizpe *et al.* 1992, p. 62; Whitmore *et al.* 1990).

One of the principal areas where population has been treated as the major driving force of land-use change is in relation to deforestation. In some respects this may be because the data for forest clearance are better than for, say, the conversion of pasture or the falling out of production of arable land, besides occurring on a greater scale worldwide.[6] Allen and Barnes (1985) have proposed a statistically significant correlation between population growth and deforestation for a sample of countries from Africa, Asia and Latin America, yet avoid any location-specific analysis or explanation. In a wide-ranging review of literature, Bilsborrow and Geores (1990) propose a more circumstantial linkage between population growth and land extensification involving tropical deforestation, although these authors are anxious to incorporate intermediate and explanatory factors such as land fragmentation, patterns of land-ownership and migration.

Myers and Tucker (1987) go one stage further and emphasize the significance of tenure systems and the unequal distribution of land as central to an understanding of the dynamics of deforestation in Central America. They assert that the rise in sheer population numbers is not by itself the cause of rapid environmental degradation in the region. Other authors are even more forthright in their defence of human actions, deflecting the cause of deforestation away from demographic increase. Barraclough and Ghimire (1990), for example, state that it is tautological, a mere truism, and a generalization lacking in rigour to blame growing rural populations, which are characterized as the source of the "hordes of slash-and-burn cultivators". Meanwhile, in true agrarian populist style, they argue that it is increasing urban populations which stimulate demand for agricultural and forest products, although in many parts of Africa and Latin America they may actually be fed by food imports and food aid from abroad.

Barraclough and Ghimire argue that current rates of deforestation

can be much better comprehended by assuming that they are the outcome of complex historical processes taking place in interacting social and natural systems and sub-systems. (1990, p. 15).

In other words, it is necessary to adopt a regionally specific analysis of the factors creating forces for change. In the context of Africa the authors highlight the expansion of export crops, which have either replaced forest directly or indirectly through the displacement of food crop production encouraging encroachment by subsistence farmers on to forest land. Meanwhile, in Latin America, it has been the expansion of commercial cattle production which has been the major cause of deforestation: the State of Tabasco, Mexico, for example, has lost 90% of its forests during the last four decades to cattle pastures (Barraclough and Ghimire 1990). Browder (1989) supports this argument, stating that pasture development has been responsible for 60% of the total tropical forest area converted in the Brazilian Amazon, which until recently was encouraged by substantial government subsidies.

In Indonesia the major dynamic of forest clearance has been the transmigration programme designed to relieve high population densities in Java and Bali through resettlement on the outer islands. However, the management of many of these cleared forest areas has proved extremely difficult for farmers accustomed to rich volcanic soils, as they attempt to sustain production on two-hectare farms in the face of low fertility, high acidity, susceptibility to erosion and the dominance of invasive grasses, most notably *Imperata cylindrica* (Blaikie and Brookfield 1987). *Imperata* is estimated to occupy 10% of the former extent of forest in the outer islands. It severely retards natural succession and the replenishment of soil fertility under shifting cultivation, while on small farms it is extremely difficult to work because of its extensive rhizomes. Consequently, many small-farm households are forced to choose one of the following options: adopt capital-intensive, high-input solutions; make increasing use of off-farm employment for income generation; or abandon their degraded land and move elsewhere in search of fresh stocks of soil fertility under forest cover. In Lampung Province, Southern Sumatra this has led to extremely high levels of relocation (*"transmigrasi lokal"*), so that in addition to the more than 200 000 people officially resettled in reserved forest areas from the early to the late 1980s, there are many thousands of spontaneous migrant families occupying land let as logging concessions or retained as public forests and watershed protection in environmentally critical areas (World Bank 1988; Pain et al 1989).

Thus, in the context of land settlement in Indonesia and almost certainly elsewhere, the clearance of tropical forests is not being replaced by stable, productive, sustainable or equitable systems of production, key indicators of agricultural performance proposed by Conway and Barbier (1988).[7] Rather, forest is giving way to an intermediate and extensive form of land use which is expanding more rapidly by deforestation than it is being reduced by the introduction of successful systems of management (Blaikie and Brookfield 1987). This, however, demonstrates the vital importance of examining trends in the different categories of land use (which are fraught with definitional and measurement difficulties) and how these might correlate with demographic and economic indicators. Yet an exercise in complex data analysis should not preclude attention to other variables that mediate between population and resource use: technology most certainly, but also the socio-political structures that help us to understand the conditions and dynamics of transmigrant settlement, and the circumstances of poverty that influence household livelihood and demographic strategies. Consequently, "we need to develop a much deeper understanding of the relationships between human populations, their technologies, cultures, and values, and the natural capital (renewable and non-renewable natural resources) they depend on for life support if we are to achieve sustainability" (Arizpe et al 1992, p. 61).

While employing a hierarchical, multi-levelled framework helps us to remain alert to the ways these components interact at different scales, it is also becoming more widely appreciated that non-linear behaviour might prevent simple aggregation and extrapolation. Increasing recognition of the limits of scientific explanation and causation (Mearns 1991), problems of indeterminacy and uncertainty, and of plural rationalities (James and Thompson 1989) is not to herald a retreat from rigorous, applied research and the search for solutions to pressing environmental problems. It is, however, to beware of a preoccupation with sheer numbers of people and mathematical "limits to growth" and rather to focus upon the relationships between individuals, regions and nations, their institutions, technologies and patterns of resource consumption. These are the objects of analysis in the next four chapters which offer case studies that illustrate the degrees of convergence between household livelihood systems, national policy frameworks and the prospects for achieving sustainable development.

NOTES

1. The Julian Simon (1990) volume is a collection of writings which includes previously published exchanges with Paul Ehrlich as well as the transcription of a vituperative debate with Garrett Hardin.
2. While Kates and Haarmann (1992) are strictly correct to argue that the main differences in national incomes accord to a latitudinal, tropical–temperate divide, the terms North and South are used here because they embody and convey, through conventional usage, a historical and political relationship which "tropical" and "temperate" simply do not.
3. The term "landesque capital" describes those investments in land with an anticipated life beyond that of the present crop cycle which help ensure the future maintenance of land capability and the productivity of labour (Blaikie and Brookfield 1987).
4. Demeny (1990) interprets "demographic transition" at one level as a broader frame of reference for organizing the mass of historical experience yet, at another level, as

   a set of propositions incorporating generally valid relationships that can be extracted from that experience. . . . Such relationships can be used to discern and predict the direction of change in demographic growth and its proximate determinants (or) even quantitative features of such changes. (1990, p. 45).

5. A sense of the issues raised by this debate can be garnered from two extracts that take different perspectives:

   Under general conditions of rural poverty, it may be economically rational for all families to reproduce at a biological maximum due to the economic value of children. But actual family size may vary according to class position, which reflects differences in infant and child mortality rates resulting from variations in household incomes. In addition, the economic value of children may differ according to class position. (Deere *et al* 1982, p. 101).

In contrast to this position, Youssef proposes an approach to fertility that:

   stresses a linkage to women's workload (both home and productive activities) . . . (uses) the mother as the basic unit of analysis (as opposed to the household), and allows for the specification of differential interests in children among household members, since it grounds fertility behaviour in *the women's rational calculation of perceived benefits.* (Youssef 1982, p. 190).

Youssef's belief that women place a high value on children as substitutes for the workload assigned to them by the labour-allocation process within the household is challenged by studies from elsehere, for example in Bangladesh where women express a preference for smaller family size (Kabeer 1985).

6. However, data dealing with estimates of rates of deforestation is not without its technical difficulties or political controversy, as the World Resources Institute has discovered in its attempt to calculate a Greenhouse Index (see McCully 1991; Agarwal and Narain 1991).

7. Conway and Barbier here define agricultural sustainability as the ability of a system (field or farm) to maintain productivity in the face of stress or shock. It is clear that where farmers in transmigrant settlements face *Imperata* domination, their agricultural systems are generally unable to sustain arable production under traditional technology. However, *Imperata* can prove extremely useful as a source of fodder in relatively intensive smallholder livestock systems.

REFERENCES

Agarwal, A. and Narain, S. (1991) *Global Warming in an Unequal World: A Case of Environmental Colonialism*. Centre for Science and Environment, New Delhi.

Alonso, W. (ed.) (1987) *Population in an Interacting World*. Harvard University Press, London.

Allen, J.C. and Barnes, D.F. (1985) "The causes of deforestation in developing countries". *Ann Ass Am Geog*, **75**, 163–184.

Anderson, V. (1991) *Alternative Economic Indicators*. Routledge, London.

Arizpe, L., Costanza, R. and Lutz, W. (1992) "Population and natural resource use". In *An Agenda of Science for Environment and Development into the 21st Century* J.C.I. Dooge *et al* (eds). Cambridge University Press, Cambridge, pp. 61–78.

Barraclough, S. and Ghimire, K. (1990) The Social Dynamics of Deforestation in Developing Countries: Principal Issues and Research Priorities. Discussion Paper 16, United Nations Research Institute for Social Development, Geneva.

Bilsborrow, R.E. (1987) "Population pressures and agricultural development in developing countries: a conceptual framework and recent evidence". *World Development*, **15**, 183–203.

Bilsborrow, R.E. and Geores, M.E. (1990), "Population, environment and sustainable agricultural development". Draft monograph prepared for FAO.

Blaikie, P. and Brookfield, H. (1987) *Land Degradation and Society*. Methuen, London.

Bongaarts, J., Mauldin, W.P. and Phillips, J.F. (1990) "The demographic impact of family planning programs". Population Council Research Division Working Papers, No. 17. Population Council, New York.

Boserup, E. (1981) *Population and Technology*. Blackwell, Oxford.

Browder, J.O. (1989) "Development alternatives for tropical rain forests". In *Environment and the Poor: Development Strategies for a Common Agenda* H.J. Leonard and contributors (eds). Overseas Development Council, Washington DC, pp. 111–133.

Cain, M. and McNicoll, G. (1988) "Population growth and agrarian outcomes". In *Population, Food and Rural Development* R.E. Lee *et al* (eds). Clarendon Press, Oxford, pp. 101–117.

Commoner, B. (1972) *The Closing Circle: Confronting the Environmental Crisis.* Jonathan Cape, London.

Conway, G. and Barbier, E. (1988) "After the Green Revolution: sustainable and equitable agricultural development". *Futures*, **20**, 651–670.

Crosson, P. (1986) "Agricultural development: looking to the future". In *Sustainable Development of the Biosphere* W.C. Clark and R.E. Munn (eds). Cambridge University Press, Cambridge.

Deere, C.D. Humphries, J. and Leon de Leal, M. (1982) "Class and historical analysis for the study of women and economic change". In *Women's Roles and Population Trends in the Third World* R. Anker *et al.* (eds). Croom Helm, London, pp. 87–114.

Demeny, P. (1990) "Population". In *The Earth as Transformed by Human Action* B.L. Turner II (ed.). Cambridge University Press, Cambridge, pp. 41–54.

Doyal, L. and Gough, I. (1991) *A Theory of Human Need.* Macmillan, Basingstoke.

Eberstadt, N. (1991) "Population change and national security". *Foreign Affairs*, **70**, 115–131.

Ehrlich, P. (1968) *The Population Bomb.* Ballantine Books, New York.

Ehrlich, P. and Ehrlich, A. (1990) *The Population Explosion.* Hutchinson, London.

Geertz, C. (1963) *Agricultural Involution: The Processes of Ecological Change in Indonesia.* University of California Press, Berkeley.

Greenhalgh, S. (1990a) "Towards a political economy of fertility: anthropological contributions". *Population and Development Review*, **16**, 85–106.

Greenhalgh, S. (1990b) "State-society links: political dimensions of population policies and programs with special reference to China". Population Council Research Division Working Paper No. 18.

Grigg, D. (1980) *Population Growth and Agrarian Change: A Historical Perspective.* Cambridge University Press, Cambridge.

Hall, R. (1989) *Update: World Population Trends.* Cambridge University Press, Cambridge.

Hardin, G. (1988) "Cassandra's role in the population wrangle". In *The Cassandra Conference: Resources and the Human Predicament* P. Ehrlich and J. Holdren (eds). Texas A&M University Press, College Station, pp. 3–16.

Harrison, P. (1990) "Too much life on earth?" *New Scientist*, 19 May 1990.

Harrison, P. (1992) *The Third Revolution: Environment, Population and a Sustainable World.* I.B. Tauris, London.

Helwege, A. (1990) "Latin American agricultural performance in the debt crisis: Salvation or stagnation?" *Latin American Perspectives*, **67**, 57–75.

Hewitt, T. and Smyth, I. (1992) "Is the world overpopulated?" In *Poverty and Development in the 1990s* T. Allen and A. Thomas (eds). Oxford University Press, Oxford, pp. 78–96.

James, P., and Thompson, M. (1989) "The plural rationality approach". In *Environmental Threats: Perception, Analysis and Management* J. Brown (ed.). Belhaven London, pp. 87–94.

Jones, H. (1990) *Population Geography.* Paul Chapman Publishing, London.

Kabeer, N. (1985) "Do women gain from high fertility?" In *Women, Work and Ideology in the Third World* H. Afshar (ed.). Tavistock, London, pp. 83–106.

Kasun, J. (1988) *The War against Population: The Economics and Ideology of World Population Control.* Ignatius Press, San Francisco.

Kates, R.W. and Haarmann, V. (1992) "Where the poor live. Are the assumptions correct?" *Environment*, **34**, 4–11; 25–28.

Latin American and Caribbean Commission (on Development and Environment) (1990) *Our Own Agenda*. Inter-American Development Bank and United Nations Development Programme, Washington DC

Lee, R.D. (1986) "Malthus and Boserup: a dynamic synthesis". In *The State of Population Theory* D. Coleman and R. Schofield (eds). Blackwell, Oxford, pp. 96–130

Leonard, H.J. (1989) "Overview". In *Environment and the Poor: Development Strategies for a Common Agenda* H.J. Leonard and contributors (eds). Overseas Development Council, Washington DC.

Lesthaeghe, R. (1986) "On the adaptation of Sub-Saharan systems of reproduction". In *The State of Population Theory* D. Coleman and R. Schofield (eds). Blackwell, Oxford, pp. 212–238.

Lockwood, M. (1991) "Food security and environmental degradation in Northern Nigeria: demographic perspectives". *IDS Bulletin*, **22**, (3), 12–21.

McCully P. (1991) "Discord in the greenhouse: how WRI is attempting to shift the blame for global warming". *The Ecologist*, **21**, 157–165.

McNicoll, G. (1984) "Consequences of rapid population growth: an overview and assessment". *Population and Development Review*, **10**, 177–240.

Mearns, R. (1991) "Environmental implications of structural adjustment: reflections on scientific method". Institute of Development Studies Discussion Paper 284.

Myers, N. and Tucker, R. (1987) "Deforestation in Central America: Spanish legacy and North American consumers". *Environmental Review*, **11**, 55–71.

ODA (Overseas Development Administration) (1991) "Population, environment and development". An issues paper for the Third UNCED Preparatory Committee.

Pain, M. Benoit, B. Levang, P. and Sevin, O. (1989) *Transmigrations and Spontaneous Migrations in Indonesia*. ORSTOM, Paris.

Parikh, J.K. (1992) "Restructuring consumption patterns for sustainability". *The Network*, **20**, 3.

Pearce, D. (1991) "Population growth". In *Blueprint 2: Greening the World Economy* D. Pearce (ed.). Earthscan, London, pp. 109–137.

Pierce, J.T. (1990) *The Food Resource*. Longman, Harlow, Essex.

Pleumarom, A. (1992) "Course and effect: golf tourism in Thailand". *The Ecologist*, **22**, 104–110.

Porter, G. and Welsh Brown, J. (1991) *Global Environmental Politics*. Westview Press, Boulder, CO.

Sadik, N. (1990) *The State of World Population 1990*. United Nations Population Fund, New York.

Sen, A. (1981) *Poverty and Famines: An Essay on Entitlement and Deprivation*. Oxford University Press, Oxford.

Simon, J.L. (1981) *The Ultimate Resource*. Martin Robertson, Oxford.

Simon, J.L. (1990) *Population Matters: People, Resources, Environment and Immigration*. Transaction Publishers, New Brunswick.

Spooner, B. and Walsh, N. (1991) "Fighting for survival: insecurity, people and the environment in the Horn of Africa". Consultants' report prepared for IUCN Sahel Programme.

UN General Assembly Document (1991) "Cross-sectoral issues. The relationship between demographic trends, economic growth, unsustainable consumption patterns and environmental degradation". A/CONF 151/PC/46.

Whitmore, T.M., Turner II, B.L., Johnson, D.L., Kates, R.W. and Gottschang, T.R.

(1990) "Long-term population change". In *The Earth as Transformed by Human Action* B.L. Turner II (ed.). Cambridge University Press, Cambridge, pp. 25–40.

Working Group on Population Growth (and Economic Development) (1986) *Population Growth and Economic Development: Policy Questions*. National Academy Press, Washington DC.

World Bank (1988) *Indonesia: The Transmigration Program in Perspective*. Washington DC.

World Bank (1990) *World Development Report 1990*. IBRD, Washington DC.

World Resources Institute (1990) *World Resources 1990–1991*. Oxford University Press, Oxford.

Youssef, N. (1982) "The interrelationship between the division of labour in the household, women's roles and their impact on fertility". In *Women's Roles and Population Trends in the Third World* R. Anker *et al.* (eds). Croom Helm, London, pp. 173–201.

4 Recent Philippine Political Economy and the Sustainable Development Paradigm

AMADOR REMIGIO
Quezon City, the Philippines

An account of the historical development of the Philippine political economy is indispensable to an understanding of the dynamics of how development and environmental concerns have interfaced in Philippine society and the state. It also provides the broader political and economic context against which such natural resource and environmental policy formulation and implementation have been undertaken, inasmuch as the underlying and structural causes of natural capital degradation have historic roots that are not merely confined to the Marcos and Aquino governments, the focus of this chapter.

THE POLITICAL CONTEXT[1]

During the colonial era (after the penetration of the Philippine economy and society by the Spanish and American colonizers), the concept of economic growth and development foisted upon the Philippines was coterminous with rapid economic expansion through corporate production and the diversification of agricultural exports (Dixon and Parnwell 1994). The political system grafted on to this economic base during the early part of the twentieth century was largely patterned after the US liberal-democratic form of governance. The agrarian, landholding elite were in effective control of both the economy and the polity (with the elite in the state virtually synonymous with this economic elite). This elite which largely dominated Philippine politics had its economic base in the production of agricultural products for export

---

[1]Much of this section has drawn liberally from Hawes (1987), to whom the interested reader is directed for a more comprehensive treatment.

Strategies for Sustainable Development: Local Agendas for the Southern Hemisphere
Edited by Michael Redclift and Colin Sage. © 1994 John Wiley & Sons Ltd

to the US market. Such a predominantly agro-export orientated economy was functionally dependent on the US market owing to the colonial nature of the Philippine–US economic relationship.

Such a dependency relationship shaped the nature of the struggle for Philippine political independence and has, despite political independence in 1946, exerted a prominent influence on the kind of development model that the Philippines was to pursue in later years.

Just as Cardoso and Faletto (1979) recognized, the historical specificities of the linkage of dependency between Third World economies (in Latin America) and the world market brought about by the colonization process, so the linkage of the Philippines to its colonizers during its colonial era exemplified this relationship of classic dependence of the colony upon its colonial master. The country then became a launching pad for cheap raw material exports and the willing importer as well as consumer of manufactures produced by the colonizer (Constantino, 1985; Dixon and Parnwell 1991). From the economic standpoint therefore, the Philippines was forcibly incorporated into patently colonial trade patterns that were vitally determined by the interests of colonizer and significant segments of the collaborating domestic elite. As Roxas observes, "development under colonial rule consisted of the establishment of enclaves of modern enterprise within the traditional society of the Philippines: plantations, mines, logging and lumber mills, and the financial, trading, insurance and other ancillary industries that served these export-import enclaves" (Roxas 1989, p. 59).

After the destruction of the Philippine economy during the Second World War and the imminent bankruptcy of the nation's treasury that followed, import and exchange controls were imposed. Such controls then led indirectly to a short-lived experiment with import-substitution industrialization. Resultant changes in Philippine social structure followed soon after, as foreign investors allied themselves with local joint-venture partners and middle-class managers. It also signalled the rather considerable infusion of domestic capital, until then confined to the agricultural sector, into the industrial sector. As the number of workers in the modern sector increased, greater urbanization pressures arose in the large urban centres and primate cities (such as Manila) owing to the increasing number of workers that were needed by industry.

The consequent boom in the production of manufactured goods by import-substituting industries for the domestic market engendered favourable conditions for political conflict, as questions arose over issues such as the degree of foreign control in the economy. Even the government itself was often polarized between the supporters of agricultural and export-led growth and those who favoured a more nationalist, populist path to economic growth and development through the pursuit of further import-substitution industrialization. All these led to a decline in elite cohesion and an upsurge in popular political participation and nationalism that resulted in political indecisiveness and economic stagnation. Consequently, the Philippines began the transition to export-oriented industrialization much later than the Asian Newly Industrialising Countries (NICs) (such as South Korea and Taiwan).

Thus, the breakdown in elite cohesion, the poor economic performance of the late 1960s, and the increase in nationalistic sentiment among large segments of the population inclined many to question the legitimacy of the political system and the continued rule of an elite segment led by President Marcos. Attempts by Marcos to consolidate his rule and to usher the nation toward a more open economy, in which foreign investment would play a bigger role, failed. A combination of factors militated against this projected course of action, including an entrenched group of import-substitution manufacturers, the growing nationalist reaction to foreign domination of the Philippine economy, and the continued power of the rural elites who were reluctant to allow any further centralization of power.

Marcos breached the policy stalemate in 1972 by declaring martial law on the bases of perceived threats to national security from an active leftist movement aimed at overthrowing the government and the worsening Muslim–Christian conflict in the Southern Philippines. Invoking his power as commander-in-chief of the armed forces, he padlocked the Philippine Congress or legislature and subordinated the judiciary to the executive by making all judges resign (and appointing only those that were friendly to his regime). He also manoeuvred the drafting and ratification of a new constitution that allowed him to remain in office indefinitely. Further, emergency constitutional provisions equipped the martial law regime with the power to intimidate alternative political leaders and to control dissident political elements.

It was also clear that this lurch towards authoritarianism in 1972 was linked to a marked preference for the development path of export-oriented industrialization. And treading this new path required the assembly of a fresh political coalition that included the vast majority of foreign investors, their local partners (such as the technocrats in the Marcos cabinet), the business community linked by political interests to the President, local politicians who remained in office because of their allegiance to Marcos, and the military officers who enforced martial rule. The martial-law government and the export-orientated development model it had adopted came to be financed with increased foreign loans, aid and investments that were all attracted because the regime had the imprimatur of the World Bank, the International Monetary Fund and the US Government (Bello et al. 1982).

As Marcos's martial rule continued, the thrust toward a more open economy based on export-orientated industrialization began to yield economic fruit. Despite some growth in manufacturing exports, the Philippines was unable to generate sufficient employment to accomplish the gradual improvement of wage rates and living standards (as well as a lowering of economic inequality) which should have accompanied export-orientated industrialization (as was true of NICs such as South Korea and Taiwan). Rather, the inequalities in the economy and society were exacerbated, as the regime faltered in its efforts to effect what it touted then as structural policy reforms of its New Society programme (such as agrarian reform). Thus, rising levels of poverty and inequality parallelled increasing political discontent as the Philippines floundered in its efforts to replicate the economic breakthroughs attained by East Asian NICs.

Growing domestic opposition to the rule of Marcos, plus increased international pressure from the World Bank and the US government to undertake reforms in the military, political and economic domains, foreshadowed the demise of the Marcos regime. The precipitous economic decline caused by slumping commodity prices, rampant mismanagement, corruption and fraud, the unavailability of new short-term credit, massive capital flight from the Philippines and intensifying political restiveness finally culminated in the regime's downfall in 1986.

The Aquino government which came to power was also committed to an export-orientated model of development (with a greater emphasis on agricultural productivity) and generally adhered to a redemocratization of the political process so thoroughly subverted by the previous President. What has emerged in the Philippines since 1986, though, is the reincarnation of another variant of the elite democracy that existed prior to the declaration of martial law.

Mrs Aquino introduced several important policy reforms: the ending of agricultural monopolies that were used by the Marcos political machine to extract huge amounts of "economic rent" from the countryside; the liberalization of trade; the privatization of state capitalist institutions; the rescheduling of debt; and the pursuit of an agrarian reform programme. But the enormous foreign debt has also meant that the country has relinquished substantial economic sovereignty to its international creditors (such as the multilateral development banks and private commercial banks). Also, in retrospect, such economic policies have not produced the intended distributional impact on an economy and society that is fundamentally feudal and still characterized by gross structural inequalities.

This brief account of the prevailing political realities in the Philippines, then, underlines the fact that deforestation, urban pollution and other major environmental problems can be described as government failures in the development and environment fields. Such failures have definite political roots insofar as the fractured character of the political economy of the Philippine state is concerned. For the state has been so much riven in the past by partisan vested interests that have successfully penetrated it to exert accordingly an inordinate influence on the state policymaking and implementation apparatus, thereby rendering such policymaking and implementation pliable to the pursuit of their respective interests (Putzel 1992a, 1992b). When viewed against the backcloth of the continuing political and socio-economic marginalization of the poor in both the uplands and in the lowlands (particularly the urban poor) and the resultant asymmetrical power relations that govern the relationship of the poor to more powerful societal agents, it will be easier then to appreciate the political roots of the progressive deterioration of the natural capital bases in both the upland and urban ecosystems. As Walker (1989) has observed, the elite, as it exerted substantive influence over the modern state, has often intensified the exploitation of the natural resource base.

ECONOMIC TRENDS

Relative to the other Southeast Asian countries, the growth of the Philippine economy over the past two decades (1971–90) has been relatively constrained, with an annual GNP growth rate average of 4.12%. This period can be analysed in two phases: (a) the debt-driven phase (from 1971 to 1980), with an average annual GNP growth rate of 6.4%; and (b) the debt-constrained phase (from 1981 to 1990), with an abysmally low GNP growth rate averaging 1.8% per year.

The debt-driven growth phase was heavily reliant upon massive foreign borrowing contracted by the Marcos regime, purportedly to support its development projects and to address mounting pressures on the balance of payment accounts (Dohner and Intal 1989). Whatever economic growth occurred during these years could be attributed to investments that were primarily sourced through foreign loans, with industry accounting largely for the growth of real GNP during this period by contributing 2.7% compared to 2.2% from services and 1.4% from agriculture.

While there was still economic growth during the debt-constrained phase (during the last five years of the Marcos regime—from 1981 to 1985—and the first five years of the Aquino government from 1986 to 1990), economic growth and development efforts were severely curtailed by the necessity of servicing the massive foreign indebtedness incurred principally by the Marcos regime. Such debt-servicing led to severe budgetary limitations (as a substantial share of the budget had to be devoted to the servicing of debt) that led to reduced government expenditures. Such reduced expenditure exacted its toll in terms of the reduced delivery of social services (that were of most benefit to the poor), the delayed building (as well as poor maintenance) of needed infrastructure and the overall macroeconomic growth deceleration effect of high interest rates due to the government's huge budgetary deficits. Moreover, it must be recalled, too, that the external macroeconomic environment facing developing countries in the 1980s has been rather hostile in terms of deteriorating terms of trade (as manifested in unstable commodity prices and the growing protectionism in developed market economies) and stagnating flows of aid (Macneill 1989).

The Philippine economy registered its highest growth rate in 1973 when its real GNP grew by 9.26%. In contrast, the lowest growth rate of −7.07% for real GNP was experienced in 1984, owing to the contraction of economic output occasioned by the political and economic crises of 1983 and 1984. It was only in 1986 that the economy's recovery began, as can be gauged from the positive growth rate that it registered that year. The succeeding years from 1987 to 1991 saw real GNP growth to be positive, although such growth has been declining, with later developments (in terms of attempted coup d'états, natural disasters such as the 1990 earthquake, typhoons and the 1991 Mt Pinatubo volcanic eruptions and low investment levels) tending to dampen the positive growth trend.

In the 1970s, the Philippines deliberately shifted from an import-substitution industrialization strategy to an export promotion strategy. Exports that were previously disadvantaged by the tariff system were encouraged as well as granted incentives. Foreign exchange restrictions were loosened in order to encourage foreign investments. However, while export activities have responded positively to these shifts in economic strategy and inducements, the growth in exports over the past two decades (at an average annual rate of 12.4%) has not been enough to cover the trade deficit (as imports increased annually at an average of 14.9%, and resolve the country's perennial balance of payments problem.

Also, there was a marked shift from 1971 to 1990 in terms of the nature of products that were being exported, as traditional exports (that is agriculture and natural-resource based, e.g., forestry, mineral, sugar and coconut products) began declining in importance relative to the non-traditional exports (e.g., garments, semiconductors, footwear, furniture, copper metal and fixtures). As a percentage of total exports, traditional exports accounted for 85.2% of all exports in the 1971–75 period while constituting only 22.2% of all exports in the 1986–90 period. For non-traditional exports, it dramatically increased its share of total exports from 14.1% in the 1971–75 period to 76.3% in the 1986–90 period.

As far as income distribution is concerned, analysing the percentage shares of total income accruing to various income deciles for the period from 1971 to 1988 yields a picture of the highly unequal distribution of income in the Philippines. In both 1971 and 1988, the top 20% of the various income deciles accounts for over 50% of total income while the lowest 20% accounts for only 3.6% of total income in 1971 and 5% of total income in 1988. Intal (1990) characterizes this income distribution picture as the worst among the countries of the Association of South-East Asian Nations (ASEAN).

Coupled with this rather unequal income distribution picture is a persistent and disturbing long-term economic trend: the growth in the absolute number of families living below the official poverty line from 1975 to 1988, that has continued even during years when the Philippine Gross National Product satisfactorily reflected increased growth rates (Roxas 1989)

Parenthetically, it may also be observed that the underlying strategy for Philippine national planning and development in the Marcos and Aquino governments has been predicated on Western Neo-Classical economic theory and ideology (that emphasized an atomistic philosophy of individualism). Interestingly, its historical introduction into the Philippines dovetailed with the adoption of late-nineteenth-century European liberal ideas that informed Philippine revolutionary fervour then against Spanish colonial rule (Roxas 1989). Such ideas, so readily imbibed by the elite, were to be reinforced further when the Americans (insofar as they epitomized the unfettered pursuit of individualism) replaced the Spanish as the new colonizers of the Philippines.

THE CURRENT STATUS OF THE NATURAL RESOURCES AND ENVIRONMENTAL BASE OF THE PHILIPPINES: AN OVERVIEW

Compared to other developing countries, the Philippines has been relatively well endowed with a substantial natural resource and environmental base that has historically generated a substantial share of national income and wealth. But, it must be noted that the dramatic changes in the natural capital base (illustrated, for example, by deforestation, soil erosion, and urban environmental pollution) are but part of the various broad patterns of environmental transformation mirrored elsewhere in both the developed and developing countries (Clark 1989). These environmental transformations must also be understood in relation to the following components of the growth and globalization of human activity that have had the greatest impact on the environment: agriculture, energy and manufacturing (Clark 1989).

Currently, there are only six million hectares of forest remaining in the Philippines, of which less than one million hectares is primary growth forest. There are about 3.8 million hectares of secondary growth forest with the remainder comprising mangrove and pine forests. All these forests now occupy just around 20% of the total land area of the Philippines, a dramatic decline from the 1960s when it was reckoned that forests covered almost 15 million hectares (or one-half of the total land area). The country has now become a net importer of its wood requirements, as recently established industrial tree plantations have been projected in an Asian Development Bank study as being unable to supply much of the domestic wood consumption needs until after the year 2000 (EMB, 1991). The loss of such forest resources has also definitely entailed disturbing distributional consequences, as the upland rural poor depend on these forests for their food, fuel and other material needs.

Serious environmental problems due to deforestation have been observed in various parts of the Philippines, such as in the Ilocos, Central and Bicol regions of Luzon and in Cebu and Bohol in the Visayas as well as in some areas of Mindanao (Boado 1988). In the island of Cebu, with a population of 3 million, potable water shortages have become widespread. Floods during the rainy season have become more serious in terms of devastating consequences such as the heavy loss of life (as exemplified by the November 1991 Ormoc, Leyte flood that killed more than 5000 people) and extensive damage to property, crops, livestock and infrastructure. Conversely, during the dry season, severe droughts in various places that have been deforested and in downstream areas (resulting in crop losses) have been likewise reported. Such deforestation has also been contributory to massive soil erosion, in conjunction with other factors such as steep gradients (with slope being over 18% in one-half of the total Philippine land area and where topsoil layers are rather thin), seasonally concentrated and heavy rainfall intensities and the pursuit of other upland activities such as shifting cultivation and grazing that have effectively removed vegetative cover. Such soil erosion definitely signifies soil fertility losses (with their equivalent economic opportunity costs) in vast tracts of upland areas that could be alternatively used for crops or tree plantations as well as coastal resource damage due to heavy siltation. Of 73 Philippine provinces, 25 have between 40% and 85% of their surface area subjected to severe soil erosion (World Bank 1989). Forest loss, therefore, exacts severe ecological and economic costs on human and social welfare in terms of lost watershed protection, lost genetic material, local (and global) climate change, threatened species extinction and lost coastal resources and fishing grounds (World Bank 1992, p. 6).

The country is also highly mineralized, with a 1988 estimate of metallic and non-metallic ore reserves amounting to 31.65 billion metric tons. While the mining industry has been contributing a significant share to the Gross Domestic Product in the past two decades, it has also been implicated in the environmental degradation of upland and lowland ecosystems that are in the vicinity of these mining activities and/or are located downstream of these large-scale mining activities (such as the Baguio Mining District, the Bued and Amburayan rivers, Lingayen Bay in Pangasinan and Calancan Bay in Marinduque).

The Philippines consists of 7107 islands with a long and irregular coastline of 18000 kilometres that is shared by 80% of the country's provinces and about two-thirds of all its towns and municipalities.

Coastal fisheries produced 62% of total fish output in 1987 and supplied most of the protein requirements of the rural population. While total fisheries production has been increasing in the last 35 years, the trend in recent years has been towards a levelling off and decline of production that has been partly ascribed to destructive fishing methods employed by some municipal fishermen and the extensive degradation of marine and terrestrial ecosystems.

For instance, about 75% of the country's coral reefs that contribute to the biological productivity of coastal and nearshore waters have been found to be in poor condition (EMB 1991, pp. 1–25). This has been caused by: siltation and sedimentation, blast fishing, use of cyanide for fisheries catch, muro-ami fishing and coral mining and harvesting. Other examples of the widespread deterioration of marine and terrestrial resources that have affected the livelihoods of coastal communities (where more than half of the total national population lives) include physical and chemical damage to coral reefs, the disruption of benthic habitats through seabed bottom trawling, mangrove clearing, the pollution of freshwater lakes, swamps and rivers and the degraded quality of coastal waters through sedimentation and other pollutants.

In the case of mangrove swamps that form the foundation of the food chain for coastal fisheries, only 139 725 hectares of these remained in 1990, compared to the original estimate of approximately 500 000 hectares in 1918 (EMB 1991). These remaining stands can now be found concentrated in the islands of Palawan, the east and southwest coasts of Mindanao and eastern Visayas and Bohol. Such rapid decline in the areal extent of mangrove resources has been attributed to harvesting for fuelwood and charcoal production, its clearing for fishpond establishment and the expansion of coastal communities.

In a recent study (DENR and DTI 1991) the net effects of the deterioration of the natural resource and environmental systems due to urbanization in Metro Manila (which supports 15% of the total national population) were identified, as follows:

(a) the increasing deterioration of public health, especially among the poor;
(b) direct and indirect economic costs (including the loss of "free" environmental services such as unpolluted groundwater and surface water); and
(c) unquantifiable adverse effects on quality of life and mental health.

Moreover, air and water pollution are very evident signs of environmental deterioration in large urban centres in the Philippines. The quality of inland and coastal waters in most urban centres has been mostly affected by domestic wastes, although the discharge of untreated wastewater is also a significant factor. Laguna de Bay, the country's largest lake located beside Metro Manila, has already reached critical levels of biological oxygen demand levels and faecal coliform counts. Environmental quality parameters for the major river systems of Metro Manila and its outlying areas also indicate heavy pollution. Environmentally related diseases such as upper respiratory infections and gastro-intestinal ailments already constitute a large proportion of morbidity cases in Metro Manila.

Table 4.1. Health and productivity consequences of environmental mismanagement

Environmental problem	Effect on health	Effect on productivity
Water pollution and water scarcity	More than 2 million deaths and billions of illnesses a year attributable to pollution; poor household hygiene and added health risks	Declining fisheries, rural household time and municipal costs of providing safe water; aquifer depletion leading to irreversible compaction; constraint on economic activity because of water shortages
Air pollution	Many acute and chronic health impacts excessive urban particulate matter levels are responsible for 300 000–700 000 premature deaths annually and for half of childhood chronic coughing; 400–700 million people, mainly women and children in poor rural areas, affected by smoky indoor air	Restrictions on vehicle and industrial activity during critical episodes; effect of acid rain on orests and water bodies
Solid and hazardous wastes	Diseases spread by rotting garbage and blocked drains. Risks from hazardous wastes typically local but often acute	Pollution of groundwater resources
Soil degradation	Reduced nutrition for poor farmers on depleted soils, greater susceptibility to drought	Field productivity losses in range of 0.5–1.5% of Gross National Product (GNP) common on tropical soils, off-site siltation of reservoirs, river-transport channels, and other hydrologic investments
Deforestation	Localized flooding, leading to death and disease	Loss of sustainable logging potential and of erosion prevention, watershed stability, and carbon sequestration provided by forests
Loss of biodiversity	Potential loss of new drugs	Reduction of ecosystem adaptability and loss of genetic resources
Atmospheric changes	Possible shifts in vector-borne diseases; risks from climatic natural disasters; diseases attributable to ozone depletion (perhaps 300 000 additional cases of skin cancer a year worldwide; 1.7 million cases of cataracts)	Sea-rise damage to coastal investments, regional changes in agricultural productivity; disruption of marine food chain

Source: World Bank (1992).

In this respect, it would be useful to view these environmental damages as imposing the following costs to current and future human and social welfare (World Bank 1992): human health costs, reduction of economic productivity and losses in "amenity" values, ie, reduction in satisfaction obtained from an unspoiled environment. Table 4.1 presents the principal health and productivity consequences of environmental mismanagement.

Preliminary results from recent natural resource accounting studies (DENR 1991b) covering forest resources indicate that the Philippine net national product (NNP) growth rate for the past two decades (from 1970 to 1989) will have to be adjusted by an average ranging from $-$ 0.22% (using the asset value method) to $-$ 6.6% (using the net price method) to arrive at a modified NNP growth rate estimate that takes into account forest resource depletion and degradation. Such an exercise, however wide the variance of the initial estimates are (due to methodological and information difficulties), would be nonetheless useful when extended to the other natural capital bases in the Philippines. Its utility lies in its provision of tentative and imperfect quantitative estimates of the rough economic costs that are bound to be incurred by economic activities on natural capital bases. When such economic costs are considered with the social and political costs of natural capital depletion and degradation, it would be only reasonable that this should lead to an interrogation of the sustainability of Philippine development.

This short discussion, then, of the substantive pressures on the natural resource and environmental base of the Philippines and the widespread depletion and degradation of natural capital, viewed in conjunction with the discussion of the environmental problems of deforestation and urban pollution, leads to the question of whether past and current rural and urban growth in the Philippines has been and is ecologically sustainable. At the heart of this question, too, are the issues of what kind or nature of future environment do Filipinos in this current generation desire and what kind or nature of future environment can be secured, given the current social, economic and political realities and development efforts as well as environmental and natural capital trends? The answers to this question and the issues that it raises will be determined by social choices, as reflected in the political preferences of the various stakeholders, and the dynamics of the relations of power governing the interaction of these numerous stakeholders.

THE HISTORICAL AND INSTITUTIONAL CONTEXT OF PHILIPPINE NATURAL RESOURCE AND ENVIRONMENTAL POLICY AND MANAGEMENT

While the preceding section outlined the broader policy canvas of the Philippine political economy and the relevance of a qualified sustainable development paradigm, the specific historical and institutional circumstances of

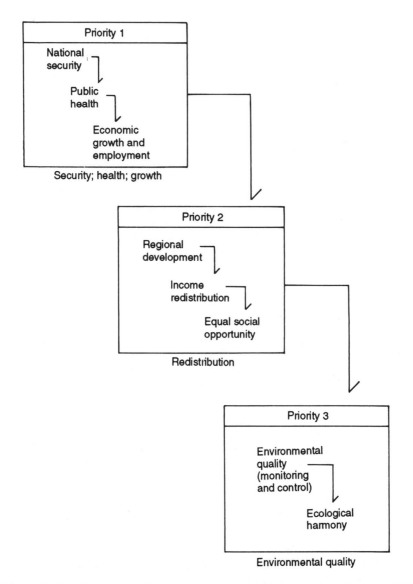

Figure 4.1. The hierarchy of national goals (reproduced by permission of Pion Limited, London, from O'Riordan, T. (1976) *Environmentalism*, p.20)

Philippine natural resource and environmental policy will be the locus of discussion next.

Prior to 1972 (when the first UN Conference on the Human Environment was held in Stockholm), many Third World countries hardly viewed the problems of natural resource deterioration and the degradation of air, water and land quality as grave enough to merit a serious policy response. Their preferred mix and relative weights of national policy objectives such as economic growth and development, equitable distribution of income, regional and rural development, national self-sufficiency, environmental quality, and maintenance of the productivity of natural systems unmistakably show what their national development priorities were (Hufschmidt et al. 1983). O'Riordan (1976) graphically depicts these as illustrative of a hierarchy of goals reflective of national policy priorities and objectives (Figure 4.1).

While natural resource and environmental quality problems have been elevated as a concern since then in the national goal hierarchy of most Third World countries, great emphasis is still assigned to the policy objectives of economic growth and development, the promotion of exports, the reduction of poverty and the fulfilment of basic human needs (Hufschmidt, et al 1983).

In the Philippines, the economic policy of import substitution industrialization in the late 1950s and early 1960s began to reap the unwanted impact of negative externalities (readily visible as air, water and land pollution in urban areas such as Manila). As an early example of environmental NGO (non-government organization) lobbying, the Philippine Society of Sanitary Engineers then battled for the enactment of legislation on pollution control pending before the Philippine Congress. On 18 June 1964, Republic Act No. 3931 (the enabling law which created the National Water and Air Pollution Control Commission) was promulgated to prevent and abate pollution from industrial activities. While this law was immediately implemented, the low level of budgetary funding (with the Commission receiving only token actual funding of P50 000 during the first year, even though P12 5 million was its authorized budgetary appropriation) indicated that pollution control was not a priority government activity.

Also, this law was largely ineffective because it never vested any penal powers and sanctions which the Commission could directly employ in regulating the activities of pollutive establishments. Moreover, there were deficiencies in the law that militated against its effectiveness (e.g., the administrative machinery for the issuance of pollution control permits for the construction and/or operation of industrial establishments revolved around district and city engineers who were not then necessarily knowledgeable in the technical aspects of pollution). In retrospect, the passage of relatively weak environmental legislation during this period could possibly be attributed to the success of the strong and dominant legislative representation of industrial interests and capital in diluting the demands of environmental lobbying then.

In the 1960s, it can be recalled that environmentalism in the United States drew a wide spectrum of public support from the pioneering and crusading efforts of its intellectual high priests (such as Rachel Carson, Rene Dubos and Barry Commoner). Such American-inspired environmentalism eventually migrated across the Pacific to Philippine shores (Rogue 1986), so aptly symbolized in the early 1970s when Charles Lindbergh visited the Philippines to champion the cause of endangered wildlife species such as the tamaraw and the Philippine monkey-eating eagle.

By 6 July 1976, an inter-agency committee for environmental protection (composed of representatives from 18 environment-related agencies in the government) was created by Presidential Letter of Instruction No. 422 to assess the existing environmental situation as well as extant government policies on environmental protection. It was placed under the coordinative direction of the Department of Natural Resources (previously organized in 1974 when the then Department of Agriculture and Natural Resources was reorganized into two separate departments). Among the findings of the inter-agency committee were the marked lack of coordination in the implementation of environment-related activities and programmes of 22 government agencies and the absence of a procedural mechanism and systematic process for the assessment of the environmental impacts of development projects.

Subsequently, the committee recommended the rationalization and integration of disparate environmental policies and programmes and the consideration of three alternative institutional mechanisms for effecting such policies and programmes:

(a) the creation of a central environmental agency;
(b) the creation of an inter-agency organization for environmental protection; or
(c) the strengthening of existing agencies (such as the Department of Natural Resources) with specific sectoral responsibilities that have environmental quality implications.

Alternatives (a) and (c) were scotched because of the anticipated difficulty of having one government department regulate the other government departments insofar as environmental matters were concerned. Alternative (c) also presented the difficult problem of reconciling in one department the apparently contradictory objectives of environmental protection and the exploitation/utilization of natural resources. Clearly, alternative (b) became the preferred institutional option.

By August 1976, the almost ineffectual National Water and Air Pollution Control Commission was strengthened when its enabling law (R.A. 3931) was amended by Presidential Decree No. 984, which clothed it with broader and stronger regulatory powers. This later law also renamed it as the National Pollution Control Commission.

On 18 April 1977, the inter-agency committee on environmental protection was reconstituted into the National Environmental Protection Council (the Cabinet-level coordinating body on environmental protection chaired by President Marcos) through Presidential Decree No. 1121, after the committee recommended the creation of an agency at the policy level that would undertake the formulation of new environmental policies and the implementation of environmental programs in an integrative fashion. The Council was then tasked with the rationalization of the functions of environment-related agencies through an effectively coordinated government-wide system for environmental protection efforts (principally achieved by the establishment of inter-agency committees dealing with particular environmental administration concerns, such as environmental impact assessment, toxic and hazardous waste management and coastal zone management) and the implementation and enforcement of environmental laws.

Landmark environmental legislation were subsequently enacted on 5 June 1977. These were the environmental policy law (as embodied in Presidential Decree No. 1151) that institutionalized the environmental impact assessment system and the Philippine environment code (Presidential Decree No. 1152) which codified separate environmental legislation into a single law and provided management standards for air and water quality, land use, natural resources management and conservation and waste management. Close examination of these laws, especially P.D. No. 1151 on Philippine environmental policy, reveals its unabashedly American-inspired character. For instance, Section 4 of P.D. No. 1151 required all agencies and instrumentalities of the national government as well as private corporations "to prepare, file and include in every action, project or undertaking which significantly affects the quality of the environment", a detailed statement on:

(a) the environmental impact of the proposed action;
(b) any adverse environmental effects which cannot be avoided should the proposal be implemented;
(c) alternatives to the proposed action;
(d) the relationship between local short-term uses of the human environment and the maintenance of long-term productivity; and
(e) any irreversible and irretrievable commitments of resources which would be involved in the proposed action, should it be implemented.

It is evident then that this content requirement for a detailed environmental impact statement is merely a documentational replication of Section 102 (2), paragraph (c) of the 1969 US National Environmental Policy Act.

Even the design of the initial environmental impact assessment system was accomplished with American assistance (particularly consultancy services provided by the US Agency for International Development).

Perhaps, it was more than just symbolic that this rather uncritical "cuddling" of American environmentalism by the Marcos leadership came to be epitomized in the chairing by Imelda Marcos, a prime proponent of what was then *au courant* (such as environmentalism) in developed countries, of the National Environmental Protection Council by the late 1970s. This cabinet-level council met only once (in 1979) and was never convened again.

Admittedly, the period between 1976 and 1981 (when the last environmental policy guideline of consequence was issued through presidential fiat under the Marcos regime) has been unusually productive in terms of environmental policy formulation, albeit undertaken via unorthodox and undemocratic means. Most of the extant environmental policies that were legislated into being by the late 1970s through presidential fiat had their origins in the multi-agency task force (previously referred to as the inter-agency committee on environmental protection and subsequently transformed into the National Environmental Protection Council) convened and coordinated by the Department of Natural Resources. It was primarily a legal-technocratic exercise in policy formulation that scarcely considered any inputs from other segments of the body politic. The recommendations of both the task force and the Council were then translated into the form of presidential issuances which, when promulgated under the martial-law powers of President Marcos, had the full force of law. The Secretary of Natural Resources then endorsed these presidential issuances to Malacanang Palace (where they were given the final scrutiny by presidential staff before the President signed them into law). In the latter part of martial law rule, the Cabinet Standing Committee (later known as the Cabinet Executive Committee) began to increasingly assume this task of sifting and recommending to the President preferred policy directions. Not surprisingly, the Cabinet (and its members) became the arena of struggle among the various dominant elite segments battling for control of the national policy apparatus.

The parallel existence and operation of the Ministry of Natural Resources (the natural resource policy formulation and implementation agency), the National Environmental Protection Council or the NEPC (as the environmental policy formulation and coordination body) and the National Pollution Control Commission or the NPCC (as the implementing agency for pollution control regulations) as the major natural resource and environmental agencies in the Philippines was the institutional hallmark that characterized natural resource and environmental administration in the Marcos regime.

The overthrow of the Marcos regime in 1986 was to usher in new changes in natural resources and environmental administration. In January 1987, the

Ministry of Natural Resources was reorganized into the Department of Environment, Energy and Natural Resources (DEENR). Adding further impetus to the Aquino governments' emerging agenda to increasingly address both developmental and environmental concerns was the 1987 publication and dissemination of the World Commission on Environment and Development's "Our Common Future" report. In June 1987, the DEENR was again reorganized into the Department of Environment and Natural Resources (DENR) by Executive Order No. 192 and was tasked to "ensure the sustainable use, development, management, renewal and conservation of the country's forests, mineral lands, offshore areas and other natural resources, including the protection and enhancement of the quality of the environment". Both the NEPC and the NPCC (that were then operating under the Department of Human Settlements and Ecology) were abolished, with many of their functions and powers effectively absorbed into the DENR's newly created Environmental Management Bureau.

Under the new organizational set-up, the DENR is currently composed of the Department proper, the staff offices, the staff bureaus and the field offices (as comprised by the regional, provincial and community natural resources offices). Line functions of the DENR (that include the implementation of natural resource and environmental laws, policies, plans, programmes and DENR rules and regulations) are now performed by its field offices. Also, most of the former line bureaux of the defunct Ministry of Natural Resources were transformed into sectoral bureaux tasked to perform staff functions, as indicated below:

(a) Forest Management Bureau (the merger of the Bureau of Forest Development and the Wood Industry Development Authority);
(b) Lands Management Bureau (formerly the Bureau of Lands);
(c) Mines and Geo-Sciences Bureau (the merger of the Bureau of Mines and Geo-Sciences, the Minerals Reservations Development Board and the Gold Mining Industry Development Board);
(d) Environmental Management Bureau (the merger of the National Environmental Protection Council and the National Pollution Control Commission);
(e) Ecosystems Research and Development Bureau (the merger of the Forest Research Institute and the National Mangrove Committee of the DENR); and
(f) Protected Areas and Wildlife Bureau (formerly the Division of Parks and Wildlife and the Marine Parks Program of the Bureau of Forest Development).

With respect to NPCC's former regulatory functions on pollution control, these were transferred to the DENR's regional offices in deference to the

Aquino government's initiatives to decentralize the powers of the national government to the regional and local levels. Also, the previous quasi-judicial functions and powers of the NPCC over the adjudication of pollution cases were likewise moved to DENR's Pollution Adjudication Board, the secretariat of which is in the Environmental Management Bureau.

From these recent institutional developments, a new pattern of natural resource and environmental administration can be inferred. The shift or trend has been for DENR to transform what were previously integrated staff and line agencies (e.g., Bureau of Forest Development, National Pollution Control Commission) into those that are now either purely staff agencies (e.g., Forest Management Bureau) or purely line agencies (e.g., DENR Regional Offices) or an admixture of both (e.g., Environmental Management Bureau). Thus, the enforcement of natural resource as well as environmental laws (primarily environmental quality standards as well as pollution control rules and regulations) has been made the exclusive prerogative of the DENR regional offices, while the administration of the environmental impact assessment system has been lodged with the Environmental Management Bureau (which now exercises both staff and line functions).

In retrospect, the abolition by the Aquino government of the National Environmental Protection Council was a strategic error that marginalized the Department of Environment and Natural Resources in terms of much-needed inter-agency support and coordination. As a line department, it was not structured nor equipped at all in terms of effecting a government-wide coordination system for policies, programmes and projects to be anchored on a more ecologically sustainable basis. Clearly, the institutional outcome (and political cost) was predictable: its efforts to institutionalize the Philippine Strategy for Sustainable Development have been only peripherally successful, with few government agencies following in DENR's "wake" in the effort to operationalize the PSSD's strategies in terms of concrete programmes and projects.

According to Roque (1986, p. 161), the following factors in the prevailing historical, economic and social milieux of previous Philippine governments also circumscribed to a large extent the effective implementation of environmental policies:

(a) the culture of poverty (in an economic landscape of socio-economic dualism) that ensured the inexorable application of short-term survival logic by the poor rural majority (which pursued livelihood opportunities that tended to destabilize further ecologically sensitive upland areas);

(b) the political disenfranchisement and disarticulation of the masses under an authoritarian political climate;

(c) social and bureaucratic inertia;

(d) low levels of social discipline;

(e) colonial legal and administrative traditions; and
(f) a trade and industrial policy regime that abetted the rapid degradation and deterioration of the country's natural resource base (owing to the previous dominance of resource extractive-based exports, such as logs and minerals).

Likewise, there have also been critical operational factors that have had adverse repercussions on the effectiveness, efficiency and soundness of the enforcement and implementation system for environmental policies and institutions, such as (Roque 1986):

(a) difficulties in the operationalization of key environmental concepts (such as sustainability);
(b) ill-timing of implementation;
(c) the lack of political clout of environmental agencies;
(d) the relative dearth of resources for environmental agencies owing to persistent government budgetary deficits, owing to heavy foreign debt servicing;
(e) weak enforcement of regulatory controls; and
(f) the dispersion and diffusion of authority over many environment-related agencies.

PHILIPPINE SUSTAINABLE DEVELOPMENT: A STRATEGIC FOCUS

Rural and urban growth and development have not been sustainable insofar as the natural capital bases of both kinds of growth and development have been depleted and degraded, with substantial economic, social and political costs involved. In this regard, it is rather lamentable that, as Goodland and Ledec (1987, p. 38) note, "when natural capital is liquidated, the revenues are typically invested in man-made capital stock, which is frequently oriented towards supplying the luxury demands of the present generation". In the Philippine case, there is some evidence that has linked such liquidation of natural capital to private foreign asset accumulation on the part of certain elite segments that have been closely identified with the previous political leadership (Boado 1988, Vos 1992). Indubitably, the effect of these has been to exacerbate issues of intragenerational and intergenerational justice: the further worsening of what has already been and continues to be a highly skewed pattern of income (and probably asset) distribution coupled with the legacy of a depleted and degraded natural capital base discussed earlier.

Given these developments, it should not be considered surprising, then, that the major thrust of past and existing development models, which have put so much primacy on economic growth and development (involving natural resource destruction) and the consequent inequitable distribution of its benefits (marked by increasing rural disenchantment fanning the escalation of insurgency) has been and is being questioned (Roxas 1989). In the following sections, policy responses of both the Marcos and Aquino governments to the increasingly vigorous questioning of traditional development patterns are discussed and analysed.

Since the 1970s, there have been attempts by the Marcos government to view natural resource and environmental problems, issues and concerns in the Philippines from an integrated and holistic perspective. This can be gleaned from various technical reports dating from this period, such as the Population, Resources, Environment and the Philippines Futures Study, studies on the environment undertaken by the Task Force on Human Settlements of the Development Academy of the Philippines, and the inclusion of environmental considerations in the government's development plan formulation process.

It was only in the 1978–82 national development plan that environmental problems (e.g., metropolitan pollution, the environmental effects of mining activities, diminishing fisheries yield) were accorded serious government attention (EMB 1991, pp. 1–5). Generally, it prescribed an approach advocating natural resource exploitation and utilization and their protection and replenishment that was to be followed by all the succeeding development plans (viz., the 1983–87 development plan as well as its updated version in the 1984–87 plan) of the Marcos regime. In contrast, the Marcos regime's first development plan which preceded all these (i.e. the 1974–77 development plan) had a narrow environmental focus, with forest resource conservation as its primary concern. Several common themes can be identified as characterizing these plans:

(a) the recognition of the private sector's role as the initiator and prime mover of development;
(b) the reliance on market forces to organize economic activity;
(c) the focus on the agricultural sector and the objective of achieving food self-sufficiency; and
(d) the promotion of exports.

All these preliminary attempts in the 1970s to address natural resource and environmental problems from a policy perspective were to lay the groundwork for the more institutionalized undertaking of further studies on the Philippine environment in the late, especially by the National Environmental Protection Council (NEPC). Its mandate under Presidential Decree No. 1121, which included the preparation of national environmental quality status reports on an annual basis and the coordination of environment-related activities on a government-wide basis, propelled initial efforts to formulate an integrated framework for environmental planning and management. Such government efforts then were aimed at providing for a systematic rationale for confronting the increasingly urgent and critical environmental issues that were being identified by such national environmental quality status reports.

Such an attempt to formulate a National Environmental Enhancement Programme (NEEP) was initiated by the NEPC in December 1979. The final version of the NEEP was adopted in 1984, after a lengthy process of multi-sectoral consultation. [Parenthetically, it may be noted that the National Economic and Development Authority then also drafted a National Environmental Management Action Plan (1983). However, this NEDA draft plan was not officially adopted by the NEDA's board.] The NEEP, which was among the initial attempts by the government to integrate its varied environmental projects into a comprehensive national programme, had the following emphases: the protection and management of coastal and estuarine ecosystems, environmental education, groundwater salinity intrusion control and the establishment of a national information system for environmental quality management. But the NEEP, however useful it may have been at that time for programme coordination purposes, was to find eventually its utility circumscribed by the voluntary nature of compliance by government agencies, with its attendant goals, objectives and strategies. By 1986, when the Marcos regime was overthrown, it had become a moribund document that was updated periodically but no longer commanded the priority and loyalty of agencies that were supposed to be instrumental in its execution.

As for the Aquino government, its adoption of the 1987–92 medium-term development plan (together with its revised version, the 1990–92 updated development plan) embodied a countryside agro-industrial development strategy. Also, it embraced a community-based approach to natural resources management that actively encouraged the participation of the community in the planning and implementation of natural resources projects. This approach considers local communities as the actual managers of these natural resources, with government developing and implementing programme that provide natural resource users with the incentives and the know-how for the proper management of these resources.

When the Department of Environment and Natural Resources (DENR) was created by Executive Order No. 192 in June 1987, Section 16(h) explicitly stated the need for a National Conservation Strategy. (It was also during this period that "Our Common Future", the World Commission on Environment and Development's report on sustainable development, was gaining wider currency after being released in April 1987.) Thereafter, in recognition of the legal mandate and the growing influence of the WCED report, the Environmental Management Bureau of the DENR convened a multi-sectoral national workshop in May 1988, which recommended that the

President and the Congress should adopt and implement a Philippine Strategy for Sustainable Development (PSSD). On November 1989, the executive branch of the Aquino government finally heeded this workshop recommendation by adopting the Conceptual Framework of the PSSD through Cabinet Resolution No. 37, with the following qualifications (DENR 1990, p. iv):

(a) The PSSD shall address specifically the adverse impact of growth and development such as, but not limited to, pollution from factories, pesticide build-up from agriculture and the depletion and degradation of natural resources due mainly to misuse and over-exploitation.
(b) Its conceptual framework shall consist of a set of general strategies to resolve and reconcile the diverse and sometimes conflicting environmental, demographic, economic and natural resource use issues arising from the country's development efforts as well as sectoral strategies identified after a review of the current efforts being undertaken in the sectors of population, environment and natural resources, agriculture, industry, infrastructure and energy.
(c) All pertinent government agencies are directed to review their respective development programmes and projects for consistency with this conceptual framework.

The primary goal of the PSSD is the achievement of economic growth with adequate protection of the country's biological resources and its diversity, vital ecosystem functions and overall environmental quality (DENR 1990, p. 4). Its ancillary objectives for attaining this primary goal are:

(a) to ensure the sustainable utilization of the country's natural resources such as forests, croplands, marine and freshwater ecosystems;
(b) to promote social and intergenerational equity in the utilization of the country's natural resources;
(c) to develop management programme to preserve the country's heritage of biological diversity;
(d) to achieve and maintain an acceptable quality of air and water;
(e) to promote and encourage an exploration programme for economically important minerals;
(f) to promote the technologies of sustainable lowland agriculture and upland agro-forestry through the encouragement of research and development (R&D) and the demonstration of the results of these in pilot projects;
(g) to promote R&D in environmentally sound and economically efficient processing of the country's mineral and energy resources;
(h) to enhance the foundation for scientific decision making through the promotion and support of education and research in ecosystems;

(i) to promote and support the integration of population concern (including migration variables and family welfare considerations) in development programmes with special emphasis in ecologically critical areas; and

(j) to expand substantially the family planning programmes and responsible parenthood programme.

While the PSSD explicitly adopts the WCED definition of sustainable development as "meeting the needs and aspirations of the people without compromising the ability of future generations to meet theirs", it recognizes the need to flesh out this general definition in operational terms. The following set of guiding principles are then embraced as well to serve as a framework to evaluate the sustainability of (and direct) policy interventions to be proposed in the PSSD (DENR 1990, p. 5)

- a systems-oriented and integrated approach in the analysis and solution of development problems;
- a concern for meeting the needs of future generations;
- a concern for equity in the access of the people to natural resources;
- a concern not to exceed the carrying capacity of ecosystems;
- living on the interest rather than on the capital or stock of natural resources;
- maintenance or strengthening of vital ecosystem functions in every development activity;
- a concern for resource use efficiency;
- the promotion of research on substitutes, recycling, exploration, etc from revenues derived from the utilization of non-renewable resources;
- a recognition that poverty is both a cause and consequence of environmental degradation; and
- the promotion of citizen's participation and decentralization in implementing programme.

For the realization of its primary goal and objectives, the PSSD employs the following general implementing strategies:

(1) The integration of environmental considerations in decision-making.
     What this means is that the process of development should be viewed from the outset as a multipurpose undertaking (rather than as single sector planning exercises) that includes an explicit and defined concern for the quality of the environment. To effect this desired shift in economic decision-making and to accommodate the social and environmental consequences of the misuse of the nation's natural capital in economic calculations, the use of tools such as natural resource accounting, environmental impact assessment and land use planning is advocated.

(2) Proper pricing of natural resources and the environment.

The treatment of natural resources as truly scarce is touted as a good means for improving the management and utilization of natural resources through the proper pricing of natural resources based on their cost of replenishment, the increase of their supply and/or the provision of appropriate substitutes. Thus, this approach aims to correct the gross underpricing of natural resources (e.g., logs, minerals) that lies behind the wasteful extraction and utilization of these resources. It should also involve charging polluters a social price on environmental resources (e.g., air, water) that have been usually regarded as free and have been therefore indiscriminately polluted.

(3) Property rights reform.

To preclude the over-exploitation of "open access" resources that characterizes the "tragedy of the commons", the assignment of secure access rights (or the grant of private ownership status) to responsible individuals and communities over these resources is favoured, as these agents are presumed to hold a long-term stake in the protection and management of the resource for sustained productivity, once they establish a stable relationship with the resource.

(4) Conservation of biodiversity and the establishment of an integrated protected areas system.

As the stability of ecosystems is dependent on the maintenance of the diversity of genes and species, protected areas should be established for the conservation of wildlife and unique ecosystems in order to safeguard genetic resources for scientific, educational, cultural and historical values.

(5) Rehabilitation of degraded ecosystems.

Such rehabilitation of degraded ecosystems should address the massive magnitude of both past as well as current environmental degradation owing to the increasing demands for natural resource-based raw materials and products. It should be linked as well to ecosystem protection programmes and policy reforms that deal with the socio-economic roots of ecosystem degradation.

(6) The strengthening of residuals management (pollution control).

The espousal of this more comprehensive framework for viewing pollution problems is grounded on the recognition of the limitations of "end of pipe" pollution control systems. Thus, resource recovery, recycling and less material and energy-intensive product design are encouraged. However, the strengthening of the enforcement of appropriate pollution control laws, economic incentives and conciliatory forms of pollution regulation are also viewed as complementary approaches.

(7) Integration of population concerns and social welfare in development planning.

The emphases of the country's population programme must not be confined to the control of fertility alone but should encompass improvements in education and health and the formation of values. Measures
to manage population distribution and mobility and effect balanced
regional development are likewise proposed to address the rapid population growth in large urban centres due to rural-to-urban migration.

(8) Inducing growth in rural areas.
   It is hoped that economic growth and recovery in the rural areas will
   bring increased employment and incomes in the rural areas. Such
   increased incomes are then assumed to lead to lessened dependence
   from (and decreased pressure on) the natural resource base by the rural
   poor.

(9) The promotion of environmental education.
   This has two objectives: (a) to enable citizens to understand and
   appreciate the complex nature of the linkage between environment and
   development and to develop social values that are strongly supportive
   of environmental protection (in terms of mobilizing the necessary political will and commitment); and (b) to develop a knowledge base on the
   local natural resource and environmental systems through the institu-
   tionalization of tertiary and graduate courses in ecology, environmental
   science, resource management and resource economics at the formal
   educational level.

(10) The strengthening of citizen's participation and constituency building.
   As the failure or success of development/environment-orientated projects hinges on the participation and support of citizens, the citizens'
   active participation in such projects should be therefore encouraged.

In this connection, it has been observed that despite the passage of Cabinet Resolution No. 37, mandating the line agencies to integrate the PSSD
into their plans, programmes and budgets, the pacing and rate of adoption
and uptake by such agencies have been rather glacial. While the Department
of Environment and Natural Resources (DENR), as the lead agency for the
implementation of the PSSD, has admittedly achieved vertical coordination
on environmental management extending from the national to the regional
and local levels of government, horizontal coordination (or the actual integration of environment-related programmes) between DENR and other
environment-related agencies as well as within these agencies themselves has
been minimal and sometimes elusive (Tolentino 1991, p. 10).

Interestingly, the legislature also never acted on the legislative equivalent
of the PSSD in terms of adopting it in the form of a law, which would then
embody the official national policy regarding sustainable development. Such
a policy hiatus, which was never resolved by the legislature during Mrs
Aquino's government, effectively meant that Cabinet Resolution No. 37

(Series of 1989) merely invested the PSSD with an adhoc character, the life-span of which was coterminous with that of the Aquino government. Also, under the Aquino government, insofar as the National Economic and Development Authority (as the national economic planning agency) was concerned, the PSSD has been mistakenly incorporated into the updated Medium-Term Philippine Development Plan as an adjunct strategy confined to and with misjudged relevance only to the Plan's natural resource sector.

In terms of its content, the PSSD can be viewed as a positive development in the history of development planning in the Philippines, as it recognizes the bankruptcy of previous national economic and development planning strategies that were predicated on the unbridled pursuit of economic growth and development objectives, irrespective of their adverse natural resource and environmental consequences and negative distributional outcomes. Also, to the extent that it tries to address natural resource and environmental problems in a systematic manner and from both the macro and national and micro and sectoral perspectives, it has been a useful exercise in strategic development and environment planning. While its goal to effect a radical sea-change in national development policy and planning thinking by attempting to reorientate the same towards more sustainable development modes is admirable, there are substantive inadequacies that effectively militate against its successful execution, as discussed in the following sections.

The strategy of integrating environmental considerations into decision-making unnecessarily restricts its application to the economic decision-making sphere. The use of tools such as natural resources accounting, environmental impact assessment and land-use planning confines the impact of this strategy to economic planning, project planning and physical planning. Now, natural resources accounting does have useful functions in economic planning in terms of more accurate "scorekeeping" relative to the consideration of the environmental dimensions of development in the national income accounts, and a "management" function that enables planners and decision-makers to keep track of the constantly changing nature and dimensions of the "stock" as well as "flow" of natural capital. However, the character of its theoretical underpinnings makes it clear that these techniques are grounded on some postulates governing Neo-Classical welfare economics that are not necessarily tenable nor conceptually relevant to developing country situations. Clearly, these postulates can be seen in the assumptions that environmental asset values are determined according to the preferences of this current generation, rather than of the future generation and/or to the summation of the individual utility valuations from the use of natural and environmental resources that characterizes standard cost–benefit analyses, rather than addressing the possible independent value that society might invest in such resources (Peskin 1991, p. 190).

As for environmental impact assessment in the Philippine context, it has been generally applied to ensure that micro-planning at the project level does take on board environmental factors. However, it has never been applied to macro-planning at both the programme and policy levels (when it has become abundantly clear that development policies and programmes are not necessarily benign). Also, inasmuch as development policies, programmes and projects are not just sectoral but multi-sectoral as well, such policies, programmes and projects exert environmental impacts not just on a sectoral level but on a cross-sectoral basis, too.

Even land-use planning has had its utility circumscribed by the rapidity of physical changes in urbanizing areas of developing countries, such as the Philippines. For such countries, the brisk rate and complex pattern of multi-farious development activities in large urban areas has simply overwhelmed the institutional capacity of the state to effectively institute land-use planning controls that are anticipatory in nature, rather than being ad hoc, reactive responses to the escalating barrage of demands for multiple, and often conflicting, land uses.

It is argued therefore that the integration of environmental considerations into decision-making should not be confined to the economic sphere alone but should encompass the other relevant political, social and cultural domains where the incorporation of environmental dimensions are equally relevant, too. In this respect therefore, treading the path of sustainable development implies that the cognitive consciousness of the significance of protecting, maintaining and improving natural resource and environmental capital must employ operational means that will then suffuse and influence planning and decision-making structures, processes and activities, not just in the economy *per se* but in the society, culture and polity as well.

As for the proper pricing of natural resources, this will entail fundamental policy changes that will have to be enshrined in law. While the Aquino government undertook ad hoc measures to redress the problem of gross undervaluation of natural resources (e.g., increasing forest user charges) the challenge is how to establish this policy stride on a more permanent footing in the face of powerful vested interests in the current Ramos government determined to frustrate efforts to curb excessive "rent-seeking" behaviour relating to public natural resources. Even optimistically assuming in the near future that this legislative barrier will be hurdled, the state must then ensure that it will also have the technical and institutional capacity to undertake this pricing exercise across the whole range of natural capital bases (especially those that are amenable to the monetization of environmental values) that are currently threatened by degradation and deterioration.

The reform of property rights in the uplands is an even more daunting task, as has been illustrated by the experiences of both the Marcos and Aquino governments. As both governments have not been successful in their agrarian reform programmes in the lowlands and the uplands (Putzel 1992a,

1992b), it is clear then that the pursuit of both a lowland and an upland agrarian reform programme in the current Ramos government will be an uphill struggle that will require the mustering of enough political will and the mobilization of the necessary resources for effecting structural policy changes. These would need to include the reversal of policies that have tended to encourage the alienation and disposal of public forest land to redistribute it to the rural poor because of the fear of all post-war governments in the Philippines to reform the highly feudal structure of agricultural land ownership and concentration in the rural areas.

While biodiversity conservation and the establishment of a protected areas system are definitely worthwhile implementing strategies of the PSSD, what is crucial is the consideration of how feasible and survivable such strategies would be in the face of tremendous economic pressures to exploit the resources in these areas, given prevailing conditions of endemic poverty, unemployment and under-employment in the rural areas and a weak government's incapacity to ensure that these strategies are indeed fully implemented.

Although there is indeed a need to rehabilitate degraded ecosystems with diminished natural capital bases, there should not necessarily be a headlong rush to affirm the current bias (and to earmark most of the limited available money) towards reforestation programmes and projects. There must be a careful evaluation of what the government's natural resource and environmental priorities should be (and the trade-offs entailed) in the light of timely, available and accurate information before the substantial commitment of financial resources that have pressing alternative uses. For instance, is the current policy of repairing damage to forest ecosystems through reforestation an adequate policy response that also takes into account the socio-economic, political and cultural roots of forest depletion and degradation? Or, would a preventative approach that primarily stressed the tackling of the structural roots of forest degradation (such as the encouragement and provision of livelihood opportunities created by environmentally appropriate kinds of rural economic growth and development) be equally cost-effective as, or more cost-effective than, a remedial approach? Or, would spending scarce financial resources on reforestation that yields its benefits over relatively long time-frames be really more productive of human welfare compared to expending such resources on urban environmental problems where the human welfare effects of such interventions are immediately translated into realized, palpable human health and productivity improvements? These are questions that have not been (and should have been) clearly answered before the embarkation of the Aquino government on massive ecosystem rehabilitation programmes. As currently formulated, it appears that this PSSD implementing strategy was hastily crafted to rationalize DENR programmes that were already existing prior to the conceptualization of the PSSD.

The strengthening of residuals management, will definitely require the quantitative and qualitative enhancement of the currently inadequate technical cadre of environmental manpower and expertise in the country and assumes that the current educational system can then be geared to produce the specific kinds of environmental professionals that an urban environmental quality management programme demands. It will also necessitate positive changes in government budgetary priorities that will ensure that such a programme will be backstopped with adequate financial resources.

Also, the emphases on integrating population concerns and social welfare in development planning (to include health/educational improvements and value formation and not just fertility control) is noteworthy. But the ancillary measure of managing population distribution and mobility to address rapid rural-to-urban migration does appear to be rather utopian, given the citizen's right (enshrined in the 1987 Constitution's Bill of Rights) to freely choose his/her abode under the veneer of political democracy that has been restored since 1986. And, however shrill the plea and polemic has been for balanced regional development, the prevailing bias towards the development of large primate cities will be difficult to overcome without fundamental structural changes.

It can be observed then that reliance by the Philippine government solely on this PSSD does not guarantee that development efforts in the Philippines will necessarily be sustainable. In addition to these formidable structural obstacles that have to be overcome, there are other aspects of unsustainable development which will have to be addressed as well. These are the previous flight of massive amounts of capital in the Marcos regime (Dohner and Intal 1989, 172; Boyce 1992, pp. 335–349) and the paucity of such productive capital, savings and investment in the Aquino government, even as a substantive "pool" of Philippine money and capital (conservatively estimated at $4.5 billion in 1991) continues to be placed in offshore foreign currency deposits because the reward for holding it in pesos is not commensurate with the risks. Also, the country's overall debt increased from US$28.3 billion in 1986 to US$30 billion in 1991, that foreign debt-servicing is still a burden (Chua 1992, p. 14), with debt-service commitments in 1991 consuming 20.7% of foreign exchange earnings from the exports of goods and services (Tiglao 1992b, p. 62). Moreover, there has been an excessive drain of highly skilled and trained Filipino human capital to developed countries (Sivaramakrishan and Green 1986, pp. 76–77) and to lands where economic opportunities are relatively more available because jobs in the local economy are scarce (Bello and Formby 1990, p. 180). It is noteworthy that none of these factors have been mentioned in the PSSD and/or the Medium-Term Philippine Development Plan of the Aquino government.

The fateful decision to accumulate human capital (through education and technological advance) or man-made physical capital in exchange for running down natural capital is an inherently political decision. Such a momentous social choice is usually deemed politically and economically acceptable by those who believe that these kinds of capital are substitutable for the improvement of human welfare (Serafy 1991) and with the proviso that the overall productivity of the accumulated capital (in terms of its impact on human health, welfare and incomes) should more than compensate for any loss from the depletion and/or degradation of natural capital. In the Philippine case, it has become evident that the costs of the depletion and/or degradation of natural capital (as manifested in declining resource stocks and worsening urban pollution) has not been clearly offset by the overall productivity of the accumulated capital (because of the inequitable asset and income distribution picture prevailing in the Philippines and the substantial leakage of human and financial capital in both the Marcos and Aquino governments). Moreover, natural and other kinds of capital (such as man-made capital) are substitutable in both the intragenerational and intergenerational contexts only to a certain extent because the destruction of particular kinds of natural capital is oftentimes equivalent to irreversible environmental damage (the estimated and actual monetized values of which are a poor surrogate in terms of its total social and economic value).

Moreover, what is happening to the Philippines is almost distressingly akin to what recent commentators (Meadows et al. 1991, pp. 138–139) have described as conditions characterizing a population–economy–environment system in an "overshoot" and unsustainable mode. These conditions obtain when:

(a) capital, resources, and labour must be diverted from final goods production to exploitation of more scarce, more distant, deeper, or more dilute resources;
(b) capital, resources, and labour must be diverted from final goods production to activities that compensate for what used to be free services from nature (for example, sewage treatment, air purification, flood control, restoration of soil nutrients, etc);
(c) capital, resources, and labour are used to protect, defend, or gain access to resources that are increasingly concentrated in just a few remaining places;
(d) natural pollution—clean mechanisms begin to fail;
(e) capital depreciation is allowed to exceed investment, or maintenance is deferred, so there is deterioration in capital stocks;
(f) investment in human resources (such as health care, shelter) is decreased in order to meet immediate consumption needs or to pay debts;
(g) debts become a higher percentage of annual real output; and
(h) conflicts increase, especially conflicts over sources or sinks. There is less social solidarity, greater gaps between haves and have-nots, etc.

These conditions have already occurred in the Philippines. During the Marcos regime (from the mid-1960s to the mid-1980s eighties), approximately one-third of Philippine forest hectarage became deforested. Comparatively, the total Indonesian hectarage subjected to deforestation, for the same period as the Philippines, was equivalent only to 2% of its forests (Panayotou 1989). Timber resources have definitely become more scarce with the recent decline of the export performance of the forestry sector being indicative of such scarcity (Intal 1990). Also, depreciation in such natural capital has been allowed to exceed investment and maintenance. Meanwhile, large amounts of capital, resources and labour are being expended for reforestation and afforestation activities in order to protect these resources that are increasingly concentrated in just a few sites. Similarly, a consideration of the urban environment in the lowlands indicates that natural pollution-cleanup mechanisms in the large metropolitan centres have already begun to fail.

Furthermore, it has become apparent that because of structural factors in the political and economic spheres (such as the debt service "overhang" that has claimed high percentages of annual real output), investments in human resources (such as government budgetary expenditures for health services for both the rural and urban poor) have decreased relative to debt-servicing (Tan 1991, p. 53). In the ASEAN region, the Philippines has become the laggard in the rate of improvement of its health system and the health status of its population (Intal 1990, pp. 2–3). These have had the effect of certainly exacerbating the smouldering social conflicts in the Philippines (just as socioeconomic inequity has been a crucial factor for the leftist-led insurgency still raging in the countryside).

The accession of the Ramos government to the political helm after the June 1992 elections could possibly lend a distinctively military bias to national development policy (in view of his long association with the Philippine military during the Marcos and Aquino governments as a senior general and defence minister and the impending withdrawal of the US military presence in the Philippines). With the US military role in Philippine military affairs diminished, insofar as it has historically served in being the prime source of military hardware and assistance for the Philippine armed forces, there is the strong likelihood that the resources that the Philippine military will need in fulfilling its national security role will now have to be sourced solely from the annual budgetary appropriations of the Philippine government. The resulting scramble and intense competition for limited budgetary funds by so many government agencies will probably tax the budgetary prioritization process and result in possibly dire implications on the budgetary funding prospects of the other non-military sectors (e.g., the social sector, under which the emerging development and environmental financing agenda is usually considered). To these could be added the consideration of the latent and apparent tension and contradictions involved between the technocentric, sector-biased, short-term economic gain perspective of national planners/decision-makers/leaders, coupled with their restricted spatial and temporal decisional horizons imposed by democratic political processes in contrast to the ecocentric, holistic, long-term perspective needed to implement sustainable development strategies. These almost certain political prospects do not augur well for the protection, maintenance and improvement of the remaining natural capital bases, in particular, and sustainable development, in general, for the immediate and medium-term futures.

Recent Philippine experience suggests that the economic and political inheritance of indebtedness, and the wholesale exploitation of natural resources, eclipses any serious attempt to develop sustainability. Under Marcos, natural resources, especially forests and fisheries, were "mined" to pay for the exorbitant costs of unsustainable development. The export-led model undermined the conservation of natural resources and increased indebtedness. At the same time the poor were increasingly marginalized from any benefits in the development model. The resources on which the poor depended were more vulnerable in rural areas, while in urban areas it was the poor who suffered most from the "externality" effects of growth, such as pollution, urban congestion and poor waste disposal. After 1987 the *idea* of sustainable development gained currency in the Philippines and (after November 1989) a Philippine Strategy for Sustainable Development (PSSD) was established. This national "strategy" however, made no reference to debt servicing and proved unable to enforce legal guarantees.

The natural capital stock of the Philippines, especially the forests, was considerable until the 1960s. However, these resources have been exploited to the point where their very existence lies in the balance. What was needed was long-term planning to implement an alternative model of sustainable development. However, techniques such as Environmental Impact Assessment were at best no more than technical measures applied to planning choices and at the local level. At the macro level no assessment was made of the environmental objectives the Philippines should address. In the absence of competent political action there has been nothing to guide policy towards greater sustainability.

In this chapter we have largely considered macro-policy, and the extent to which natural resources are brought into play to meet economic objectives. These economic goals are themselves a function of a country's insertion within wider systems of trade and economic relations. The approach we have adopted is to identify the chain of cause and effect, which links the international system to national elites and micro-decision-making.

The next chapter is concerned with a very different geographical milieu, whose natural capital is also under threat. In Northern Ghana the resource base is extremely fragile and land degradation is advanced. In the absence of policies which support agricultural producers in their efforts to manage their environments sustainably, local people have become more dependent on adaptive strategies for meeting livelihood obligations. These strategies might, if strengthened, form the basis of more sustainable development, but the management of risks in semi-arid regions is given low priority by government. As we shall see, the preservation of natural capital is lacking from public policy, not only because of the stake which elite groups have in their country's economy but because of the ignorance shown towards local knowledge and local practices.

REFERENCES

Angeles, M.S. de los and Lasmarias, N. (1990) "A Review of Philippine Natural Resource and Environmental Management: 1986–1988. Working Paper Series No. 90–08. PIDS, Metro Manila.

Bello, W. and Formby, P. (1990) "South–South integration: southern locomotives". In *Third World Guide 91/92* R. Bissio (ed.). Instituto del Tercer Mundo, Montevideo.

Bello, W., Kinley, D. and Elinson, E. (1982) *Development Debacle: The World Bank in the Philippines.* Institute for Food and Development Policy and the Philippine Solidarity Network, San Francisco, USA.

Boado, E. (1988) "Incentive policies and forest use in the Philippines". In *Public Policies and the Misuse of Forest Resources* R. Repetto and M. Gillis (eds). World Resources Institute, Washington DC, pp. 165–203.

Boyce, J. (1992) "The revolving door? External debt and capital flight: a Philippine case study". *World Development,* **20**, (3), 335–349.

Cardoso, F. and Faletto, E. (1979) *Dependence and Development in Latin America.* University of California Press, Berkeley.

Chua, R. (1992) "Aquino's successor will inherit country beset with problems". *The Straits Times,* 11 May 1992, 14.

Clark, W. (1989) "Managing Planet Earth". *Scientific American,* **261**, (3), 19–26.

Constantino, R. (1985) "The Philippines: history". In *The Far East and Australasia 1986.* Europa Publications, London.

DENR (Department of Environment and Natural Resources) (1990) "DENR investment program: 1990–1995". DENR, Philippines.

DENR (Department of Environment and Natural Resources) (1991a) "Four-year accomplishment report: 1987–1990". DENR, Philippines.

DENR (Department of Environment and Natural Resources (1991b) The Philippines natural resources accounting project (Phase 1) final report, Vol. 1: "Main report". DENR, Philippines.

DENR and DTI (Department of Environment and Natural Resources and the Department of Trade and Industry) (1991) "Industrial efficiency, pollution control program and environmental management strategy project—inception report". DENR and DTI, Philippines.

Dixon, C. and Parnwell, M.J.G. (1991) "Thailand: the legacy of non-colonial development in South East Asia". In *Colonialism and Development in the Contemporary World* C.J. Dixon and M.J. Heffernan (eds). Mansell, London, pp. 204–225.

Dohner, R. and Intal, P. (1989) "Debt crisis and adjustment in the Philippines". In *Developing Country Debt and the World Economy* J. Sachs (ed.). University of Chicago Press, Chicago, pp. 169–192.

EMB (Environmental Management Bureau) (1991) "A report on Philippine environment and development: issues and strategies". DENR, Philippines.

Fay, C. (ed.) (1989) "Our threatened Heritage: the transcript, recommendations and papers of the solidarity seminar on the environment". *Solidarity*, **124**, October–December.

Goodland, R. and Ledec, G. (1987) "Neoclassical economics and principles of sustainable development". *Ecological Modelling*, **38**, 19–46.

Hawes, G. (1987) *The Philippine State and the Marcos Regime: The Politics of Export*. Cornell University Press, Ithaca.

Hufschmidt, M., James, D., Meister, A., Bower, B. and Dixon, J. (1983) *Environment, Natural Systems and Development: An Economic Valuation Guide*. Johns Hopkins University Press, Baltimore.

Intal, P. (Jr.) (1990) "Macroeconomic policies". In *Economic Policies and Sustainable Development Research Project*, Philippine Institute for Development Studies (PIDS) and Asian Development Bank (ADB). PIDS and ADB, Metro Manila.

Macneill, J. (1989) "Strategies for sustainable economic development". *Scientific American*, **261**, (3), 104–113.

Meadows, D., Meadows, D. and Randers, J. (1991) *Beyond the Limits: Global Collapse or a Sustainable Future*. Earthscan, London.

National Environmental Protection Council (NEPC) (1977, 1978, 1980, 1982, 1983, 1984, 1985) Philippine Environmental Quality Reports. NEPC, Metro Manila.

O'Riordan, T. (1976, 1981) *Environmentalism*. Pion, London.

Panayotou, T. (1989) *Natural Resources and the Environment in the Economies of Asia and the Near East: Growth, Structural Change and Policy Reform*. Harvard International Institute for International Development, Cambridge, MA.

Peskin, H. (1991) "Alternative environmental and resource accounting approaches". In *Ecological Economics* R. Costanza (ed.) Columbia University Press, New York, pp. 176–193.

Putzel, J. (1992a) "Agrarian reform, the state and environmental crisis in the Philippines". Catholic Institute for International Relations (CIIR). Papers from CIIR Seminar on 22 January 1992 on Agrarian Reform and the Environment in the Philippines and Southeast Asia. CIIR, London, pp. 73–83.

Putzel, J. (1992b) *A Captive Land: the Politics of Agrarian Reform in the Philippines*. Catholic Institute for International Relations, London.

Roque, C. (1986), "Factors influencing environmental policies in developing countries". Asian Development Bank (ADB) Environmental Planning and Management. ADB, Manila.

Roxas, S. (1989) "Social and environmental consequences of national economic planning". *Solidarity*, **124**, 157–170.

Serafy, S. El (1991) "The environment as capital". In *Ecological Economics* R. Costanza (ed.) Columbia University Press, New York pp. 168–175.

Sivaramakrishan, K. and Green, L. (1986) *Metropolitan Management: The Asian Experience*. Oxford University Press, Oxford.

Tan, M. (1991) "Sustaining health and development: retrospect and prospects". *Countryside Development Journal*, **1**, (2), 45–64.

Tiglao, R. (1992) "Invisible hand: money at work". *Far Eastern Economic Review*, July, 58.

Tolentino, A. (Jr.) (1991) "Options for legal reform in the environment sector".

Paper prepared for the 1991 Pollution Control Association of the Philippines Annual Convention, Makati, Metro Manila, Philippines.
Vos, R. (1992) "Private foreign asset accumulation, not just capital flight: evidence from the Philippines". *Journal of Development Studies*, **28**, (3), 500–537.
Walker, K. (1989) "The state in environmental management: the ecological dimension". *Political Studies*, **37**, 25–38.
World Bank (1989) *Philippines: Environment and Natural Resources Management Study*. World Bank, Washington DC.
World Bank (1992) *World Development Report*. World Bank, Washington DC.

5 Land Degradation and Society in Northern Ghana

University of Science and Technology, Kumasi, Ghana

LOCAL PEOPLE'S PERCEPTIONS AND RESPONSES TO ENVIRONMENTAL DEGRADATION

In the analysis of land degradation, planning and design of desertification abatement programmes, experts have often used a range of sophisticated mathematical techniques (FAO 1979, Bruk 1985, Stocking 1987, Lal 1988, ICASLAS 1988), while grossly underestimating local opinion, perceptions and other experience-based measurements. As a result of the profound neglect of local opinion, perceptions and adaptive strategies and the failure to enlist local support in project planning and implementation, many agricultural projects in arid and semi-arid areas have been expensive and ineffective (Ellis 1987). Several observers, particularly Norman *et al.* (1979) have stressed both the richness of local perceptions and the need to take them into account in any development planning. This chapter examines local perceptions of, and responses to, land degradation and the strategies local people employ to deal with accelerating land degradation. The research was conducted in North West Ghana between 1988 and 1990.

At the First African Ministerial Conference on the environment, the Executive Director of UNEP noted that:

> There is no doubt that the renewable resources of this continent are being dismembered at an alarming rate, but as yet there is insufficient awareness both within and outside Africa as to the magnitude of the problem. (Tolba 1985)

The growing public and political demands for explanation and quantification of the extent and type of desertification mean that the clearest evidence can be obtained from resource users themselves. Local people's perception of what is happening to the micro-environment (i.e., soils, vegetation, water

Strategies for Sustainable Development: Local Agendas for the Southern Hemisphere
Edited by Michael Redclift and Colin Sage. © 1994 John Wiley & Sons Ltd

and wildlife) may serve as an indicator of land degradation (Dregne 1983) because it is at this level that the most fruitful causal explanation lies. Moreover, achieving cooperation and local participation in desertification control and environmental rehabilitation require the study and analysis of local people's beliefs, knowledge, interests and perceptions of the environment and resources (Earle *et al.*, 1981). This chapter seeks to measure local people's level of awareness and their perceptions about the environment.

PERCEIVED AWARENESS OF DESERTIFICATION ASSOCIATED PROBLEMS

There are differing and contradictory beliefs, opinions and perceptions about land degradation and desertification (McNamara 1985, Pearce 1988) because there are many elements in the processes some of which are subtle, site-specific and not readily visible (Nowak 1983). The United Nations Conference on Desertification (UNCOD 1977) and many writers consider both soil erosion and vegetation deterioration as evidence of land degradation and processes which result in desertification (Lamprey 1975, Tucker 1985); others include salinization and alkalinity, drying up of water resources, fuelwood shortage, loss of wildlife, loss of habitat, and drought. Milner and Douglas, for example, believe that "continued abuse of the land has made Africa more vulnerable to drought. Drought, in turn, has accelerated the processes of land degradation" (Milner and Douglas 1989).

Since Marsh (1864) and Hardin's insights, people have typically characterized human beings as self-centred individuals attempting to maximize their well-being (Hardin 1968). The classic explanation for degradation has been to blame depletive resource use, land mismanagement and a general resistance to change and innovation on conservatism, ignorance and irrationality of peasant farmers (Blaikie 1985, Manshard 1986). For example, some studies show that rural people, especially farmers, are not as concerned about environmental quality as urban dwellers. While initiatives for environmental protection come mainly from urban dwellers (Van Liere and Dunlap 1980), farmers resent being blamed for land degradation, misperceive and underestimate soil erosion on their farms, and resist change (Nowak 1983).

However, Stocking (1987), believes that blaming the ignorance of rural land-users for land degradation is more the result of government and their advisers' own ignorance of the social and economic reasons why rural people continue to degrade the environment. Biswas and Odero-Ogwel (1986) have noted that the reason is not the farmer's ignorance but that policies are based on inadequate understanding of the concerns behind the farmer's land-use decisions. If human misuse of the physical environment as a result of the farmers' ignorance is the cause of Africa's environmental problems, bad policies which ignore indigenous technical knowledge (ITK) is the driving force. (Biswas and Odero-Ogwel 1986). In the analysis of local people's awareness about the environment in North West Ghana, two scenarios were proposed:

(1) People will perceive environmental degradation and desertification on the basis of their socio-economic interest. That is, farmers, would be more aware and concerned about environmental damages which affect agricultural productivity such as soil erosion than non-farmers.

(2) Local people will attempt to control their degradation behaviour when they know that their physical environment is deteriorating (Watske *et al.*, 1972). That is, they will be willing to accept blame, change their behaviour and support desertification control programmes if they are aware that their actions are harmful to others and the environment (Heberlein 1972).

To determine the level of awareness of desertification and associated problems, two exploratory questions were asked: (a) whether local people perceive environmental degradation in their villages and the region, and (b) whether local people recognize the magnitude or the severity of the desertification problem. Respondents were simply asked if they were aware of any environmental damage to land, crops, livestock, air, water and vegetation. If they responded affirmatively, they were then asked to mention and comment on the damage of which they were aware, indicating the most critical problems in a rank order, their perception of environmental changes during the last decade, and the expected changes in the next five years.

FARMER'S PERCEPTION OF PRODUCTION RISKS AND ENVIRONMENTAL CONSTRAINTS IN AGRICULTURE

Risk in agriculture can be broadly classified into: (a) natural/environmental; (b) social/institutional; and (c) economic/financial. Natural risks are mainly those of bad weather conditions, pests and disease. Pronounced droughts, for example, not only affect the years in which they occur but they also affect incomes and farming in subsequent farming seasons.

The importance of agriculture and livestock rearing in the regional economy, and the fact that the area falls within the "hunger crescent" where a period of 150 days of precipitation allows rain-fed agriculture of risk during years of drought (UN 1987), ensured that the discussion was centred on the environmental problems facing agriculture.

The answers to the question "What are the most critical problems facing agriculture in your village?" are shown in Table 5.2, according to locality within the survey area.

The responses in Tables 5.1 and 5.2 show that rural people were aware of

Table 5.1. Perceived awareness of desertification associated problems

Category of problem	Responses Farmers ($n=$ 329)		Non-farmers ($n=211$)	
	(%)	(Number)	(%)	(Number)
Aware of crop loss and famine	100.0	329	42.2	89
Aware of land degradation, ie salinity and alkalinity	55.6	183	64.4	136
Aware of air pollution	12.7	42	45.9	97
Aware of drought and water shortage	96.6	318	100.0	211
Aware of deforestation	93.0	306	100.0	211

Source: Field survey (Nsiah-Gyabaah 1991).

the environmental problems facing them, especially those that affected their farm earnings and rural energy supply and those that resulted in more visible landscape changes such as deforestation, drying up of village drinking water and soil erosion. For example, weather is an important variable in agriculture and farmers are so dependent on the weather that they often have an intimate knowledge of their nature, based on practical experience of long-term personal observation. It is therefore not surprising that the majority of respondents agreed that the environment is being degraded because of declining rainfall.

A common opinion that the environment was being degraded ranged among "serious" or "much worse now than a decade ago" (55.7%); "minor problem" (29.2%); and "not a problem" (15.1%). Old people noted that the soils in the area were very fertile and many areas were more wooded prior to independence than today. During that period there was no talk of water shortage or desertification. Most farmers had the choice to avoid the onchocerciasis-affected areas of the Kulpawn and Sisili rivers because of land surplus in other areas.

DISCUSSION AND RESULTS

In the early 1970s, the government introduced the Operation Feed Yourself (OFY) and Operation Feed your Industries (OFI), programmes which encouraged absentee farmers to bring more land into cash crop farming, especially rice, tobacco and cotton. The non-beneficial effects of mechaniza-

Table 5.2. The most critical environmental problems facing agriculture in the survey villages

Problem	Gwollu	Tumu	Babile	Nandom	Busie	Dorimon	Dafiama	Han	Ducie
Physical/weather	26	42	19	43	3	5	7	8	5
	48	*45*	*50*	*54*	*50*	*62*	*38*	*38*	*42*
Institutional	8	8	4	7	1	0	0	4	1
	15	*9*	*11*	*9*	*7*	*0*	*0*	*9*	*8*
Input price	6	7	5	9	1	1	3	3	2
	11	*8*	*13*	*11*	*17*	*13*	*17*	*14*	*17*
Pest/disease	2	4	2	6	0	0	1	0	0
	4	*4*	*5*	*8*	*0*	*0*	*6*	*0*	*4*
Finance	12	32	8	14	1	2	6	6	4
	22	*34*	*21*	*18*	*17*	*25*	*39*	*29*	*33*
Total response	54	93	38	79	6	8	18	21	12
									(329)

Italicized numbers reprəsent percentages of responses.
Physical/weather refers to soil conditions, climate, rainfall. Institutional problems refer to poor producer prices and lack of marketing facilities.
Source: Survey data (Nsiah-Gyabaah 1991).

tion on agricultural land use were considerable, especially when the cultivation of soil-nutrient demanding cash crops, such as cotton and tobacco, were favoured.

Crop yields decreased through declining soil fertility owing to continuous cropping without adequate fallow periods and drought. Although, from a technological point of view, the application of chemical fertilizers is a central measure in the solution of soil fertility problems, poor distribution, increasing cost of fertilizers and low rural incomes are practical reasons limiting its use by small farmers.

Local people were themselves quite aware that the productivity of grassland was dwindling annually. Pasture was becoming qualitatively and quantitatively poorer, as a result of bush fires and prolonged drought, and it was becoming more difficult to feed and fatten animals, especially in the dry season. Farmers expressed awareness that crop losses had contributed to famine, which has plagued the region since 1968 and has continued to affect local people, particularly during the *harmattan* season.

Among the different types of risks and uncertainties in agriculture, the most frequently occurring problems in all the villages studied relate to bad weather, rainfall variability and drought and infertile soils. Overall, farmers believed that bad weather and erratic rainfall, which affected animal and crop production, vegetation and soil moisture, were the two most critical environmental problems facing agriculture.

Farmers who worked the poor lateritic and easily eroded soils at Babile, Dorimon, Nandom and Busie felt that crop failure, due to soil erosion and the resultant loss of soil fertility, was the second most critical problem. When asked about yields, farmers complained that they had suffered a decrease over the last five years, although the decrease is estimated to be only 20–30% below the highest yields they had attained at first cultivation. There was a general consensus of opinion that yields increased immediately new land was brought under tractor cultivation, but such yields were short-term. This turned into a disadvantage after continuous cultivation without fertilizer application.

When a sub-sample of 329 farmers were asked why they thought the environment was deteriorating, 151 farmers (46%) mentioned the spread of spear grass (mostly associated with poor infertile soils) on their farmlands. Another 121 (36.7%) of the farmers mentioned the general decline in tree cover and the invasion of drought-resistant species characteristic of dry climates.

In contrast to areas worked by hand or animal traction (AT) technology, the tractor-ploughed areas showed a higher rate of general decrease in crop yield after continuous cropping and showed greater evidence of eroded surfaces.

While bush fire was a serious problem to rice farmers, pest and disease attacks were of less concern to farmers because they were infrequent and severe cases were rare. Farmers' knowledge of the environment extended to when and where to plant crops. Through trial and error, farmers had gained experience which helped them to distinguish fertile areas from infertile land. They were aware of ecological associations of plants according to characteristic soil type. They were also aware of the variations in soil fertility and natural vegetation. The importance of local knowledge of the environment has been acknowledged among the Kusasis (Benneh 1971) and the Mbereere in Kenya (Brokensha and Riley 1988).

Social risks were of minor importance in the survey area. Cattle theft occurred only during the dry season when cattle roamed unattended for pasture and water. In the more fertile, wetter areas, farmers believed that the greatest problem was lack of credit facilities. After a drought year small farmers faced an acute problem with planting material in the following season, as a result of reduction in cash income. In cases of drought, farmers often took several years to recover from losses.

There is no doubt that in a region where household incomes are low, lack of credit facilities and incentives to small farmers can stifle the initiative to work hard, produce and undertake conservation and land improvements on small farms.

IDENTIFICATION AND RANKING OF THE MAJOR ENVIRONMENTAL PROBLEMS FACING THE UPPER WEST REGION BY LOCALITY

As a result of extreme variability, both spatially and temporally, and diverse perceptions of people on the causes and processes of land degradation, it was hypothesized that local people would recognize environmental problems which result from their own and others disruptive activities, but the type of perceived damage would differ between different villages, given the extreme variability of land-degradation processes.

By asking respondents whether they thought their village was suffering from the various elements and processes of land or environmental degradation which were identified by them, it was possible to rank the damage according to whether it constituted (a) "a problem", (b) "a minor problem" or (c) "a serious problem". The responses were then grouped according to village-specific problems, to reveal inter-village variations in factors affecting degradation and the localized areas at risk of degradation.

Drought and water shortage

About 73% of the respondents reported that water shortage and droughts constituted serious environmental problems in the region. Many experts have thought of drought as a temporary anomaly but local people believe that what they have observed in the last decade is not temporary.

Local people reckoned that rain should fall at the end of April, but it appears not only that this pattern fails to repeat itself in at least one year out of three, but also that the amount of rain varies considerably. Ultimately, droughts reduce local crop yields and, if prolonged, result in complete crop failure.

Since surface and groundwater are more directly related to precipitation, the unreliability of rainfall proves catastrophic for community water supply. In the dry season, water shortage constitutes one of the most serious environmental problems for rural agriculture and livestock production, especially at Gwollu, Tuopari, Babile, Ducie and Dorimon. Water shortage is acute in villages where wells and local drinking sources dry up.

The effect of drought and water shortage on women has been described extensively by Redclift (1987). Between two and three hours may be spent on a round trip and if this time is doubled, as rural women fetch water in the morning and in the evening, the loss of productive or leisure hours spent on water collection can be considerable.

Although distances and travelling time have been reduced in some towns and villages by the provision of hand-dug wells and water pumps, the high demand for water results in long queues which make water collection a time-consuming exercise.

The provision of small-scale irrigation facilities, hand pumps and dams are necessary preconditions for agriculture and plant growth. However, water projects which are planned without pasture improvement schemes contribute substantially to the growth of livestock populations beyond the available feed stock and destruction around watering points (Grainger 1990). Therefore the supply of water must be accompanied by village pasture improvement schemes.

Bush fires

Herders burn off dry vegetation to make room for tender, green forage readily available to animals, while hunters burn to flush out game. Pasture research has confirmed the positive effect that burning has on the productivity of grasses (Nye and Greenland 1960, Innes 1972). However, frequent and uncontrolled burning is harmful both to vegetation and soils. Owing to its scale and repetition, local people believe that indiscriminate bush burning has become one of the primary causes of environmental degradation in the Upper West Region.

Although complete statistics for the occurrence and impact of bush fires are not available at the local level, Ghanaians generally believe that uncontrolled bush fires destroyed about 35% of crops during the 1982–83 season alone. The patchy records of the incidence of bush fires indicate that in the northern savannah zone, about 145 bush fire outbreaks were reported in 1984–85 alone (Ampadu-Agyei 1986). The average farms affected were about 50 hectares, with the largest covering about 10 square kilometres (Ampadu-Agyei 1986).

Most of the areas affected by frequent bush burning show evidence of stunted growth of vegetation and where the regenerative power of the soil has been destroyed, grass has failed to grow.

In parts of the Lawra, Burufu, Sabulu, Jirapa/Lambussie and Wa areas, the combined effects of over-grazing, fuelwood collection, over-cultivation and bush fires have destroyed vegetation and tree cover, leaving only economic trees (e.g., Shea nut and "*dawadawa*") standing on crop lands which give the impression that they have been the only trees in the past. This confirms the findings of a 27-year trial in the northern savannah zone which compared early and late burning with complete protection and found a number of useful trees by X5 (early), and X10 (late), and the number of species was 73, 53, 44 (Mann 1989). Indiscriminate bush burning, a long-standing practice among local people in the entire savannah zone constitutes one of the most serious threats to the fragile ecology of the region.

The vast majority (91%) of local people think that indiscriminate and uncontrolled biomass burning depletes grazing resources to the detriment of livestock and wildlife. Respondents who consider that bush fires constitute a serious problem in their localities argue that fire pressures have intensified throughout the region during the last decade, resulting in destruction of standing crops (e.g., rice), vegetation and the woody protective cover of the soil.

An important consequence of bush fires identified by 58% of the respondents (313), relate to burning of trees which result in a more open grassland vegetation or parklands in previously wooded areas. This finding confirms other studies in northern Ghana which demonstrate that protected plots contained 73 species compared to 52 on early- and 44 on late-burnt plots. Field evidence of recent burning protected areas and farmlands showed that fire had been damaging and economic trees such as *Parkia butyrospermum* (Shea nut) and "*dawadawa*" (*Parkia clappertoniana*), which have long been protected because of their economic value, have become less frequent on intensely burnt plots.

Although indiscriminate burning is damaging to trees and other vital land resources, the incentives for burning were quite evident. Villagers felt that the critical issue was the relative lack of pasture for livestock and the desire to hunt for meat when food supplies were limited. The permissive attitudes of local people towards burning would, undoubtedly, make the implementation of burning regulations and legislative controls difficult. Legislative controls must therefore take cognizance of local custom and such control mechanisms must be designed with local people and implemented by them. The need for integrating local hunters and farmers into the conservation effort becomes clear.

Deforestation

The detrimental effects of deforestation on the regional ecology is believed to constitute a problem in the absence of effective soil conservation measures in all regions of Ghana (Foggie and Piasecki 1962, Mann 1989). In 1939, the volume of wood exported from Ghana was 42 450 cubic metres. By 1987, it had risen to 1 471 600 cubic metres per annum (a 34-fold increase). The forest which had produced this volume of timber is now less than one-fifth of what it had been in 1923. In 1986, about 12 977 trees were extracted from 1622 hectares of forest reserves and for every tree harvested, between 200–300 metres of vegetation was destroyed. This means approximately 5 acres of vegetation is destroyed for every large tree logged. In the forest reserves there are approximately three trees per acre and between one and two trees per acre in non-forest reserves. Logging activities tend to be more intensive in the non-forest reserves than in the forests. The rush for timber which started in the early 1980s has intensified since.

The export of lesser-known species began in the early 1980s and exporters have left themselves open to accepting whatever logs are produced and brought to the port for export. This has aided and abetted the current wanton destruction of Ghana's forest resources. Although trees in the Upper West Region are short, small and not suitable for export as timber, almost all local building materials such as poles for fencing, roofing, carving, handles of farm tools, yam props, and especially fuelwood for energy supply, come from the savannah woodland and forests.

The expression of local opinion in Ghana generally, and in the Upper West Region, is comparable to that contained in official reports by the FAO (1971) and Mann (1989) on the long-term consequences of deforestation on the hydrology, rainfall, flood and erosion (Omaboe and Neustadt 1962). According to the household interview, about 82% (445) of the respondents consider deforestation a serious environmental hazard in the region, with female respondents emphasizing that fuelwood collection was taking an increasing proportion of their time.

Deforestation due to increased fuelwood collection was reported to be a growing problem around Wa and the densely settled areas of Lawra, Jirapa and Nandom where fuelwood sources have moved so far away from settlements that people have to travel long distances and spend several hours in order to get their daily supply.

Field observation and interview responses show that the areas close to heavily populated centres are severely denuded of trees and are experiencing fuelwood shortage. Deforestation and biomass burning also affect animal health, population and nutrition. Although only 32% (172) of the respondents expressed serious concern over the loss of wildlife and destruction of wildlife habitat, the majority of respondents (95%) recognized the importance of wildlife and genetic resources as valuable sources of protein, medicine and revenue during off-farming seasons.

The inefficient management of reserves, game and wildlife resulting from technical, institutional and financial problems facing the Departments of Forestry and Game and Wildlife were responsible for wildlife destruction in the region. Natural resources, especially forests and their ecosystems, are the basis of local livelihood and successful management is central to reducing famine, drought and desertification vulnerability.

Soil erosion

About 51% (275) of the farmers interviewed believed that soil erosion was a serious problem, compared to 8% (41) who did not consider soil erosion to be a problem in their villages. Respondents from the relatively more wooded, sparsely settled and little disturbed environments of the onchocerciasis-freed zone of the Tumu district thought that soil erosion was not a serious problem. As run-off during the rainy season is very high, water impoundment or rain harvesting programme would be a feasible water development option for the region's socio-economic development.

Salinization and Alkalinization

The responses show a great divergence of opinion about the severity of salinity and alkalinity. The majority of respondents did not consider the presence of excessive amounts of sodium chloride (NaCl) on farm and irrigated lands as constituting serious environmental hazards.

While salinity problems undoubtedly exist in the irrigated fields of the region, the rather imperceptible nature of the processes, accounted for the lack of recognition of salinity and alkalinity as serious problems. Moreover, the lack of knowledge and understanding of the relationships between soil, water and plants may explain the lack of emphasis on salinity and alkalinization as environmental hazards in the region.

Air pollution

Air pollution problems which were identified by respondents related to those resulting from burning and infrequent dust storms which were both experienced during the dry *harmattan* weather. Unlike the industrialized countries, where pollution from industrial establishments and agriculture constitute the greatest environmental problems, the lack of air-polluting industries and chemical fertilizers owning to supply problems explain local opinion on air pollution as constituting little or no problem in the area.

Over-grazing

Animal grazing of vegetation has both positive and negative effects. Moderate grazing stimulates the growth of many savannah species (Pearson 1965, Edroma 1981), but excessive grazing results in pasture deterioration. The faeces of livestock fertilize the rangeland and seed dispersal can be enhanced (Warren and Maizels 1977). The less desirable effects of grazing, reviewed by Warren and Maizels (1977), are due mainly to trampling and browsing which destroy sensitive plant species and increase soil exposure to wind and water erosion. Selective grazing for palatable species reduces the number of species with nutritional value of the rangeland (Dyksterhuis 1949) and results in the invasion of hardy and less palatable species.

Anthropologists have argued that grazing on communal lands has historically been tightly regulated by local communities and that the common property nature of the rangeland is at best an incomplete explanation of rangeland degradation. In the Upper West Region where local regulations are not effectively enforced, abuse is common and the incentive to over-exploit resources in order to meet private immediate needs is paramount.

Interviews with local people revealed that over-grazing has resulted in both qualitative and quantitative degradation of soil cover and of woody vegetation, especially around watering points. In many areas, the most palatable plant species have been eaten up and the invasion of less desirable species (e.g., *Imperata* grass and thorny bushes) have accelerated the process of degradation.

In many areas heavy grazing and extensive rangeland damage occurred during the Sahelian drought when Fulani pastoralists from Burkina Faso invaded the rangelands of the region with cattle which resulted in considerable damage to the land. The movement of cattle into the region from Burkina Faso erupted into a political conflict which was ended by a diplomatic solution. The government was too slow to act and by the time the Burkinabes moved out of the region, considerable damage had already been caused to the land and vegetation.

Confronted with worsening conditions at Nandom, Gwollu and Babile, where the effects of the Fulani invasion was most felt, local people were inclined to see the problem as the unavoidable result of over-grazing in the last decade.

Although the processes leading to over-grazing are well understood by the respondents, they unanimously objected to the suggestion that households must reduce herd size to ensure ecological balance. Respondents objected to a reduction of livestock size because animals are a source of income and a status symbol. Rather, respondents expressed a positive commitment to increasing animal size in each household.

With a growing population consisting of independent households each trying to maximize the use of free pasture on the communal land to private advantage, over-stocking is unavoidable and over-grazing the long-term consequence. Therefore, effective management systems and adequate regulatory mechanisms are required to avoid stress on communal rangelands.

Over-cultivation

Over-cultivation is another problem identified by respondents. Over-cultivation inevitably exposes the soil to erosion and encourages crust development (Mensching 1980). In some arid regions such as Northern Nigeria, over-cultivation of millet and sorghum cultivation have been blamed for sand remobilization (Ibrahim 1979, Mainguet and Cossus 1980).

A view held by half of the respondents was that over-cultivation and the spread of crops onto marginal areas is accelerating environmental degradation in their localities. The problem is serious at Nandom, Jirapa, Topari, Babile, Lambussie, Lawra, Dafiama and Ducie and in the areas where actual populations have exceeded the land's carrying capacity under traditional systems of farming.

Local responses and field observations are in agreement with Boudet (1972) that destructive agricultural techniques for cash crop production have led to irreversible trends in the carrying capacity of the land. They have led to soil erosion, land degradation and depletion of sub-surface water content on the one hand and removal of land cover resulting in higher albedo on the other. These conditions have contributed to increasing aridity and the threat of desertification in the region.

Organic fertilizers (manure) are necessary for soil fertility restoration on over-cultivated farmlands. They are cheap to obtain and small farmers should be encouraged to exploit the potential for organic fertilizing. The cultivation of leguminous crops with a high nutrient value and the parallel fixation of nitrogen must be promoted among small farmers to increase both food production and soil fertility.

Land degradation and incipient desertification

The view that the desert is encroaching southwards on marginal lands as a result of human influence (Kassaa 1970a, Thompson 1970b, et al., 1988; Harrison 1987) is at the root of proposals that are made from time to time for the establishment of desert stopping belts and was the origin of the demarcation of pastoral zones in some French-speaking countries prior to independence.

Using the FAO guidelines (FAO 1983) for measuring desertification, respondents were asked to comment on the *nature* of the desertification process in their localities. Local people were unable to distinguish clearly between drought and desertification. When desertification was defined in terms of prolonged drought, decreased land productivity and crop failure, about two thirds were of the opinion that land productivity was decreasing rapidly throughout their localities. Respondents attributed the declining productivity to inadequate rainfall and the lack of fertilizers. However, when respondents were asked whether degradation had reached an "irreversible stage' in their localities, 85% of the respondents answered in the negative because they believed that if the land was well managed and allowed to rest, it could recover when the rains returned.

After the Sahelian drought many writers observed a direct relationship between dust storm occurrence and desertification as a result of increased concentration of wind-blown aerosols of Sahelian origin in the Caribbean in the same way as atmospheric turbidity in Sudan (Prospero and Nees 1977). According to Klaus (1981), dust storm occurrence and their remote effects are good indicators of drought and accelerated desertification.

Although meteorological stations in the region do not provide reports on dust storms, considering the importance of the dust storm phenomenon as a major indicator of desertification, respondents were queried on the frequency of occurrence and severity of wind-blown sand. Local people thought that localized dust storm was infrequent and ranged between one and two events per month during the *harmattan* season. They were observed on crop lands after harvest and linked to a negative soil-water balance and removal of vegetative cover such as standing crops. Thus, they were limited to the *harmattan* season and were curtailed when soil water storage was high and vegetation (grass) was well developed after rains.

The principal findings summed up from local opinion correspond to field observations which show that degraded land often occurs in the densely populated areas of the region, and often far away from the desert front. These are small, scattered areas with desert-like conditions in areas of intense human activity. Rather than an "advance of the desert southwards on a broad front", there is a development of a Von Thunen's concentric-like circles which begin at areas of human disturbance and spread outwards to marginal areas. The degraded areas are, in fact, not deserts but degraded cultivated and grazing land.

Allocation of responsibility for environmental degradation

Small farmers are widely recognized as agents of resource degradation. Consequently substantial emphasis has been placed on projects which influence their interaction with the environment. Although this emphasis is sometimes

Table 5.3. Allocation of blame for environmental degradation

Problem area	Gwollu	Tumu	Babile	Nandom	Busie	Dorimon	Dafiama	Han	Ducie	Total
Over-cultivation	16	42	10	32	3	3	6	6	8	126
	24	*25*	*17*	*25*	*20*	*21*	*27*	*18*	*27*	*23*
Over-grading	18	37	24	36	4	2	4	6	7	138
	26	*22*	*40*	*28*	*27*	*14*	*18*	*18*	*23*	*26*
Fuelwood collecting	22	46	14	28	4	4	7	9	8	142
	32	*27*	*23*	*22*	*27*	*29*	*32*	*27*	*27*	*26*
Burning/hunting	12	46	12	31	4	5	5	12	7	134
	18	*27*	*20*	*24*	*27*	*36*	*23*	*36*	*23*	*25*
Total	68	17	60	12	15	14	22	33	30	540

Italicized numbers represent percentages of responses.
Source: Computed from survey data (Nsiah-Gyabaah 1991).

misplaced, because the actors in land degradation processes are many and varied, it is believed that farmers cannot accept responsibility for their actions until it is known where to lay the blame for environmental destruction. Therefore, an important dimension of the study was to investigate how local people apportioned blame for environmental degradation by asking: "What do you think is the primary reason for environmental degradation and accelerated desertification in your village?" The responses were categorized according to type of activity, that is whether respondents mentioned fuelwood collection, hunting, farming or over-grazing. The responses are shown in Table 5.3.

Although strong kinship ties often prevent people from blaming kinsmen whose actions damage the environment, kinship ties did not significantly affect the results. Contrary to popular belief, local people were quick to apportion blame and to accept the consequences of their own actions on the environment.

From Table 5.3 it is clear that there is no single person or group of persons who can be blamed for environmental degradation. Farmers, herders, charcoal burners, fuelwood collectors are all important actors in the process. Although fuelwood is the main source of rural energy and all households are responsible for damage to trees, respondents blamed "Pito" brewers and charcoal burners as the greatest offenders and the activities most destructive of tree cover. Recently, the contributions of farmers and hunters have become important in rapidly altering the landscape.

The important policy consideration which emerges from this, is that the solution of land degradation problems in the villages necessarily involves actions not only by farmers, but also by all the various actors in the degradation process.

MEASUREMENT AND ANALYSIS OF PEOPLE'S BELIEFS AND ATTITUDES TOWARDS THE ENVIRONMENT

Natural resources are unevenly distributed in any geographical space. They are unevenly perceived or known, unevenly available and exploited by local people. Therefore, local opinions, general beliefs and attitudes about the environment and the role of government in desertification control were assessed on an attitude scale based on a fixed-format response framework. The attitude scale consisted essentially of thirteen statement depicting varying degrees of favourable and unfavourable attitude to the environment from "strongly agree" to "strongly disagree".

In order to tap direction and intensity, these responses were broken down into five categories: "strongly agree", "agree", "undecided", "disagree" and "strongly disagree". The statements were given equal interval scale based on Likert's summated rating technique (Likert 1932) with 5 points response

Table 5.4. Beliefs and attitudes towards the environment, agriculture and adaptive mechanisms to environmental sustainability

Attitude statement by factor cause	Response[a] categories in %				
	Strongly agree	Agree	Undecided	Disagree	Strongly disagree
1. The decline in rainfall is a continuous phenomenon and is likely to continue	640 (38.9)	560 (42.6)	0 (0.0)	96 (14.6)	13 (4.0)
2. The land is degrading because the critical capacity has been exceeded. A solution lies in population control.	305 (19.0)	352 (27.0)	12 (1.2)	248 (38.0)	52 (16.0)
3. Land degradation and desertification can be reversed through local effort	105 (6.4)	336 (26.0)	0 (0.0)	172 (26.0)	38 (42.0)
4. Agro-forestry contributes to the rehabilitation of degraded land and would be generally preferred by farmers	440 (27.0)	536 (41.0)	36 (3.6)	150 (22.8)	20 (6.1)
5. Most farmers take adequate measures to protect the soil on their farms	440 (27.0)	448 (34.0)	0 (0.0)	194 (29.5)	32 (9.7)
6. Farmers must invest profits in soil and resource conservation	120 (7.3)	180 (13.7)	0 (0.0)	280 (42.6)	120 (36.6)
7. The government has already provided adequately for resource conservation and environmental protection in the region	0 (0.0)	0 (0.0)	0 (0.0)	240 (36.5)	209 (63.5)
8. Environmental laws are required to regulate and control land use	710 (43.1)	424 (32.2)	6 (0.6)	134 (20.3)	12 (3.6)
9. Drought and desertification can be reduced by small-scale irrigation	710 (43.1)	424 (32.2)	0 (0.0)	0 (0.0)	0 (0.0)
10. Desertification is accelerating because people misuse the land and local resources	405 (24.6)	352 (26.7)	0 (0.0)	164 (24.9)	78 (23.7)
11. If encouraged, people will support tree planting to avert fuelwood shortages in villages with a circular zone of denuded woodland	935 (56.5)	480 (36.5)	6 (0.6)	36 (5.5)	2 (0.6)
12. Bush burning will continue despite new legislative controls	495 (30.5)	432 (32.8)	15 (1.5)	168 (25.5)	33 (10.0)
13. The impact of land degradation is less dramatic and so the environment must be treated just like other sectors	65 (3.96)	88 (6.7)	18 (1.8)	189 (30.0)	378 (57.4)

Total sample size = 329. Only farmers were interviewed.
Total score (maximum) = 1645.
The numbers in parentheses are percentages.
[a]'Strongly agree' = 5; 'Agree' = 4; 'Undecided' = 3; 'Disagree' = 2; 'Strongly disagree' = 1.

continuum. These 5-point responses were given the weights of 5, 4, 3, 2 and 1 respectively for the favourable statements and 1, 2, 3, 4 and 5 for the unfavourable statements. If all respondents answered in the two extremes (i.e., "strongly agree" and "strongly disagree") to a specific question, then the theoretical maximum would be 1645 and the minimum 329. Of the thirteen statement categories in Table 5.4, the statements numbered 2, 3, 4, 5, 6, 7, 8, 9 and 11 are indicators of favourable attitudes, and 1, 10, 12 and 13 are indicators of unfavourable attitudes.

A summary of the profile of perception, beliefs, and attitudes of local people towards the environment show that local people, far from being ignorant of what goes on in the environment, are conscious and knowledgeable about the changes occurring on the landscape. About 81.5% (268) of the farmers are well aware of the changes in weather, especially declining rainfall, which is supported by available climatological data.

The majority of respondents were not satisfied with the record of government involvement in environmental protection and they unanimously believed that the government was not doing enough for them. Local people argued that more is needed from the government, because the resources allocated to the forestry sector in the region were below the optimum. The high score on this dimension shows that the government has not provided adequately for the environment.

LOCAL PEOPLE'S OPENNESS TO CHANGE AND ATTITUDES TO TREE PLANTING AS A DESERTIFICATION CONTROL MEASURE

The literature on production practices and the adoption of agricultural innovation, generally, assume that farmers will adopt new technologies because they are economically profitable. It also assumes that economically favoured farmers will tend to adopt new practices such as tree planting more readily than others.

Farmers of higher socio-economic status are usually better educated, which might make them more aware of the advantages of new technologies and conservation. Thus farmers who have higher incomes are able to acquire a new technology.

Since the success of desertification abatement projects, such as tree planting, depend on the motivation and willingness of rural people, the interview sought to elicit information on the level of interest in tree planting among the rural population, as well as what respondents thought they and others could do to control degradation and reverse the trend towards increasing desertification in the fragile ecosystem.

Experience with social forestry programmes (village or communal and farm forestry) in Pakistan, India, Burkina Faso and several other countries reveals significant differences in people's attitudes towards trees and tree planting, their use and management.

The importance people attach to growing scarcities and the motivation to plant trees depend on the relative weight of the benefits they derive from them. In many fuelwood-deficit countries, people have reacted to growing scarcities by planting trees or adopting agro-forestry farming systems to increase the supply base (e.g., Korea). Some have spread the scarcity through increased exploitation of the already dwindling supplies, which subsequently has led to an increase in the amount of time, proportion of household income and distances travelled to obtain fuelwood supply.

Many others substitute crop residues—roots, cow dung or agricultural waste—thereby increasing the soil's instability and depriving the soil of fertility restoration material needed to maintain crop production levels on infertile, fragile soils.

The implications of these differences in attitudes to tree planting projects, and local people's reaction to growing scarcities, are important for design of tree planting, agro-forestry, and environmental abatement programmes.

A question was asked to assess whether the assumptions outlined above fit practices designed to conserve natural resources (e.g., soil) or control desertification. Although local people have a thorough knowledge and understanding of their needs and environmental problems facing them (Brokensha et al., 1983), farmers had not adopted new technology and ways to cope with soil erosion and environmental degradation. When respondents were asked to suggest possible development interventions which may be necessary to solve the problems facing them, tree planting was the solution that was mentioned most often.

The cumulative profile of attitudes in the villages, in so far as these were accurately revealed by the survey, manifest a thorough knowledge of the benefits of trees to local people and the environment, but nowhere have local people embraced tree planting programmes or modern techniques to conserve the soil.

The general lack of interest in tree planting in the region was reflected in the absence of private plantations or community woodlots in the villages covered by the survey. The illegal encroachment and destruction of forest reserves by local people also demonstrate a lack of interest in protecting trees.

While tree planting has long been neglected, local people showed a willingness to plant trees if encouraged to do so. Two-thirds of the farmers who were interviewed indicated that they might consider planting an area on their farm with trees if given financial incentives and seedlings.

The responses confirm that certain socio-economic characteristics influence attitudes to tree planting. There appeared to be differences between the traditional small-scale farmer (one hectare or less) and the medium/large-scale operators. The more modern (that is, younger, better-educated) and more innovative of the farmers, with large farmholdings, appeared more interested and showed more favourable attitudes to tree planting whereas the older, less well-educated and less innovative farmers showed a lack of interest.

The total area that farmers were prepared to devote to tree planting varied between small and large farmers, with the more successful farmers willing to devote larger areas (more than 5%) of their farm holdings, while the small farmers indicated less than 5%. The smaller farmers had good reasons to show unfavourable attitudes. The initial investment required for tree planting schemes are simply beyond the economic means of the poor farmers. Unless they possess a certain minimum of economic resources to invest, tree planting cannot be embraced by farmers.

Respondents were unanimous in their answers that only degraded areas of their holdings would be used to plant trees while the more productive sections would be devoted to crop production. Areas along streets and compound houses were popularly suggested sites which respondents indicated could be considered in tree planting programmes. When respondents were asked if a village woodlot was required to counter the current fuelwood shortages in their localities, the majority of respondents from the densely settled areas unanimously agreed that their villages were fast running out of fuelwood and therefore village woodlots were necessary.

Questions related to the kind of trees that farmers would like to plant, or include in an agro-forestry farming system, showed significant differences between the species suggested by the Forestry Department and those farmers were willing to plant. While farmers frequently mentioned trees such as the shea butter tree (*Butyrospermum paradoxum*), the West African locust bean or "*dawadawa*" (*Parkia clappertoniana*), mango, akee apple and pawpaw, forestry officials were interested in economic trees as well as those that provide poles and protect the land from erosion. The species that were mentioned by the Forestry Department include: *Tectora grandis*, *Anogessus leocarpus*, *Kaya senegalensis* and *Leucaena leucocephala*.

SOCIO-ECONOMIC CONSTRAINTS ON NATURAL RESOURCE CONSERVATION

Since beneficiary participation is essential in strategies to control desertification, a question was asked concerning the constraints which stifled local initiative and prevented local people from becoming interested in resource conservation, particularly tree planting.

The main reservations expressed by respondents related to lack of finance for long-term investment and the economics of tree planting, which is explained in terms of the time lag between planting and harvesting. They also indicated that while they lacked inputs and extension advice, the financial return was too low compared to the initial investment cost.

This attitude may be explained, in part, by traditional cosmology in which trees or fuelwood (the main source of household fuel) is not tradeable, abundant everywhere and collected freely from the communal land.

It was observed in the survey villages that local people had not accepted tree planting because there is no monetary incentive to do so. Economically, for a land-user to have the interest to invest scarce resources in tree planting or soil conservation, the net return (NR) to the investor from tree planting, that is the total return (TR) on investment, minus the total costs (TC) on investment, must be positive (+) when all costs and benefits are appropriately discounted, to reflect the time when they occur and when perceived risks associated with the investment are assessed.

If the NR is negative, then the land-user has no financial incentive to invest. Only if the NR is positive is the investor interested and willing to invest. Although local people are aware of the benefits of trees to them and to the local environment, the low financial return on trees is a discouraging factor for those interested in tree growing.

There are environmental, technical and institutional constraints which make the adoption of tree planting programmes unattractive. These include labour constraints during the planting season, shortage of water in the long *harmattan* period, and inadequate supply and distribution of seedlings.

The damage to young plants due to animals, especially goats, whose destructive influence is most intense around compound houses and watering points, make tree planting a costly and a risky investment. Local opinion is supported by Obeid and Seif el Din (1970) who observed that goats are the animals most destructive of vegetation, especially seedlings.

Apart from widespread rural poverty, trees take a long time to reach maturity. The probability that trees would not reach maturity before the death of the investor is a strong factor in the lack of interest in tree planting, and the consequent absence of tree plantations in the survey villages. Other barriers to tree planting include:

(a) The "commons" syndrome. The lack of economic security gives the farmer an unfavourable psychological make-up for taking risks involving long-term investments such as tree planting, to which other members of the community may have access or lay claim by means of their usufructuary rights.
(b) Local leaders often appear reluctant, and not powerful enough, to enforce bye-laws and legislative restrictions on the use of trees.
(c) The long production cycle of trees weakens the confidence of those interested in planting trees today that they would mature in future.

The survey responses also show clearly that tree planting is highly and positively correlated with economic status. The wealthy farmers show greater
commitment to tree planting and soil conservation than poor farmers.
Among the poor farmers, their weak financial position prohibits them from
actively adopting tree planting, even if the motivation to do so exists. The
lack of interest is aggravated by the fact that poor farmers in the rural areas
were never reached by extension agents.

Those who lacked interest in tree planting were also sceptical about the
effectiveness of community woodlots, because responsibilities are not well
defined. Those who were more favourably disposed towards tree planting
believed that a tree planting strategy is necessary to restore degraded areas.

To summarize, so far this chapter has identified the variety of knowledge
and local attitudes to the environment in the Upper West Region. Second, it
has provided an understanding of the factors of degradation in the Upper
West Region which offers an important route to control land degradation.
Third, it has shown the variability of change by category and location of the
factors of degradation, the positive relationships and linkages between
human activity and desertification, and the necessity for an integrated and
interdisciplinary approach to control degradation. Three main conclusions
which have been noted here are:

(a) Local people often have a thorough knowledge and understanding of the
    environment and their needs. The reason why the environment is de-
    graded is not that farmers are ignorant, but that poor farmers who are
    risk-averse are more concerned with their immediate survival needs than
    in obtaining fuelwood in five or more years time.
(b) Substantial indigenous technical knowledge exists which planners and
    development experts cannot afford to ignore in the design and imple-
    mentation of environmental programmes.
(c) Local people have a positive commitment to tree planting and resource
    conservation. As the only labour force that can plant trees on the mag-
    nitude required, they must be supported with inputs in agro-forestry
    programmes.

These findings are significant indicators of the extent to which tree planting
and soil conservation are likely to be supported or opposed by local people.
It is also important in selecting target groups to which extension services and
planting programmes should be directed. The study has also revealed that
poverty is not a fertile ground for sowing the seed of conservation. Tree
planting and conservation projects are unlikely to be accepted by local
people unless they carry with them financial and input supply schemes.
These considerations have formed the framework for policy, strategy, and
alternative development interventions suggested for implementation in the

Upper West Region. In the final sections of this chapter we will consider the implications of local attitudes and behaviour, examining the strategies which might help stem environmental degradation in North West Ghana.

LOCAL STRATEGIES TO COPE WITH ENVIRONMENTAL DEGRADATION

The impact of environmental degradation and desertification on the local population include crop failure and famine, shortage of water, soil erosion, shortage of pasture for livestock and prolonged drought. Sustained drought not only leads to the loss of natural vegetation, it prevents farmers and pastoralists from re-establishing the necessary protective cover. Although the impact of desertification is a much more complex issue, its overall effect is observed in the inability of the ecosystem to provide the basic survival needs—food, water, clothing and shelter.

The view that desertification of farm and rangelands are entirely due to poor farming practices and over-grazing was at its peak during the Sahelian drought when farmers and pastoralists were frequently accused of over-stocking (Brown 1971); of cutting wood for construction and settlement; of cutting fodder for animals (Glantz 1976, UNCOD 1977); of over-exploiting the woody vegetation for fuelwood and charcoal; and of provoking ecological destruction through unsustainable farming practices.

Clayton's summary, cited by Blaikie and Brookfield (1987) aptly described what were seen as the misconceptions of the peasant farmer:

> The poor farming methods and soil depleting practices prevalent among [African] peasant cultivators stem from ignorance, custom and lethargy . . . the main obstacle to overcome is the native's lack of understanding of the need for the prevention of soil erosion. (Clayton 1964, p. 12)

Recently, ecologists and social scientists have become increasingly critical of this view. A recurrent theme in the literature on agro-pastoral systems in the last decade, is the recognition that agro-pastoralism, far from being ignorant or ecologically destructive, is perfectly rational in using scarce resources (Dyson-Hudson 1980). Several studies point to a plethora of adaptive mechanisms which reveal that farmers and herders' changing environmental pressures (e.g., bush fallowing), schemes of grazing, ways of life and technique afford considerable protection against soil erosion and soil fertility loss and contribute to conservation of nature in fragile ecosystems (Toupet 1975). Subsistence farmers and pastoralists are, therefore, expert practitioners of their respective modes of livelihood, and are particularly sensitive to the stability of the ecological systems of which they are a part (Hjort 1985, Raikes 1981, Richards 1985).

Although government relief efforts to victims of environmental degradation are often publicized and documented, no systematic attempts are made to investigate the suitability and effectiveness of local people's survival strategies and adaptive mechanisms for the benefit of environmental decision-making, planning and development.

The importance of ensuring an adequate understanding of the local adaptive mechanisms as a first step towards evolving an effective development programme was echoed by Feachem (1977) when he noted that environmental problems are caused by rural land-users and a knowledge of how rural people respond to the problems is necessary for the economic development of Africa. Moreover, since rural people "cause" degradation, it is they who can contribute to its solution.

What follows is a summary indication of the local adaptive strategies which vulnerable local groups in the Upper West Region have used to cope with environmental degradation and desertification. While some of these mechanisms have been capable of maintaining agriculture and ensured the survival of victims of degradation, some of the negative impacts have increased ecological disequilibrium and have robbed the region of all-season labour to sustain local development.

Local strategies and options

Environmental degradation and desertification, in their most devastating and subtle forms, provoke a variety of responses and adaptations by local people, some of which can be sustainable. In the arid and semi-arid regions of Africa, people have been engaged in a continuing process of adjusting to the environment and coping with environmental degradation, drought and desertification. In some cases they have accepted the environment as given and adjusted their activities accordingly.

When they have been able to predict changes in weather, adjustment has generally been effective, and to a large extent they have been successful in using available technology and local expertise to maximize the benefits of soil and weather, especially rainfall. However, where changes have been sudden and unpredictable, they have played a subservient role and have been very much at the mercy of soil and weather elements.

When local adaptive mechanisms have been inadequate and external assistance unavailable to victims of degradation, the most obvious and general adjustment has been the decision to bear the ordeal in resigned suffering (Benneh 1985). For example, the suffering which occurred during the Sahelian drought in 1968–72 and again in 1983–84 was reflected physically on the faces of poor people which changed in shape, size and form.

According to Williams (1979) local adaptive strategies range from indifference, fatalism, and inertia to active interest and firm commitment to soil conservation and environmental protection (Cunningham and Jenkins 1982, Chamaia 1985, Chamala and Rickson 1985, Barr 1985).

Some of the common adaptive mechanisms adopted to cope with environmental degradation are as follows.

Agricultural adjustment strategies

Rural people have, for centuries, evolved a complex, low-cost agriculture and forestry culture or elements of farming systems in which tree crops or seasonal crops are combined with livestock which is called social forestry by foresters today (Gregersen 1984).

In the Upper West Region's agriculture, the ecological effects of traditional farming practices such as crop rotation, bush fallowing and multiple cropping were positive adjustments to the climatic and physical conditions, especially infertile soils and variable rainfall, compared to the potentially damaging impact of modern mechanized systems.

Religious responses

In many African societies, the weather was assumed to be under the control of supernatural beings—thinking which exists today, especially in the rural areas. During periods of adverse weather conditions or disasters, traditional rulers make sacrifices to their gods, while Christians and Moslems offer prayers to God and Allah respectively.

Substitute or "famine" foods

The dire shortage of food, or crop failure as a result of environmental degradation, forces people to eat traditional substitute foods collected from the bush. Plants, wild foods including roots, barks and fruits which normally are not part of household diet, become palatable. Certain social norms and taboos regarding the consumption of certain types of meat and food are temporarily broken.

Schudder's (1971) succinct and thorough monograph about gathering among the Gwembe Tonga of Zambia, for example, is one of the most detailed studies in this area. Women and their children are usually responsible for gathering these wild products, while adult males hunt and trap game to meet the meat requirements of the household (Schudder 1971). Quite naturally, when conditions return to normal, the poor continue to consume these substitute foods while the rich often abandon them.

Socio-cultural responses

Communal sharing has remained an important means of coping with land degradation and environmental hazards in the region. In times of hardships such as crop failure, the food available to a household is not limited to those of the household alone but is shared with others in neighbouring compounds. However, when drought becomes pronounced and famine intensifies, the principle of communal sharing breaks down and people refuse to recognize the principle of communalism.

During difficult times, *rites de passage* are relegated to the background, and marriages and funerals become less frequent. Family visits are drastically reduced. However, remittances from migrants become an important source of supplementary income for victims of degradation. Remittances from migrants come in the form of cash, clothes and food.

Mixed cropping and the cultivation of drought-resistant crops

The possibilities for farmers to take preventive measures to manage drought lie in the choice of crops adapted to the environment and mixed cropping practices. The cultivation of drought-resistant crops (e.g., maize, millet and improved early-maturing crop varieties) which are capable of utilizing moisture and plant nutrient more efficiently, have been used by farmers. The cultivation of leguminous or nitrogen-fixing crops such as beans, and the use of manure, have been used as chemical fertilizer substitutes to increase productivity.

In addition to the choice of adapted crops, most applied risk-aversion strategies aim at the creation of multiplicity of cropping situations by diversification of time and space. The practice of mixed cropping has gained particular importance in local risk-aversion strategies because it increases crop yields. Experiments at ICRISAT have confirmed the effectiveness and greater yield stability of intercropping compared to sole crops. According to ICRISAT "At any given disaster level, intercropping showed a much lower probability of failure than either sole crops—sole pigeonpea would fail approximately one year in five, sole sorghum one year in eight—but intercropping only one year in thirty-six" (Rao and Willey 1980).

While the principal advantage of intercropping lies in the different susceptibilities of crops to drought, pest and diseases, local people use it as an insurance scheme against crop failure as well as to maximize labour input to benefit a number of crops simultaneously.

Other techniques exist. Although frequent biomass burning is ecologically damaging, rural people have used burning as a strategy to flush out game for meat, precipitate the growth of new grass for livestock and to return potash to the soil as a fertilizing agent. Similarly, in potentially flooded areas, mounds have been used to raise crops above the rooting zone. Yam mounds are often covered with grass to prevent erosion and the destruction of seedlings through excessive heating.

Sale of livestock

In more serious drought years local people depend on available stocks held in traditional barns. People also depend on savings to purchase food but poor households may resort to borrowing. When stocks of grain are exhausted and pasture is not available in the dry season, farmers sell livestock to reduce pressure on pasture and water resources. Firstly, the agro-pastoralist sells poultry, followed by goats, sheep and finally cattle. This is an adaptation practised by 90% of agro-pastoralists in the Upper West Region. It is an important strategy to raise money to supplement household income when food prices are highest.

In the following year after drought, farmers make efforts to compensate for the loss they incurred by expanding the area under crops. In surplus land areas, farmers bring more fallow land under crops, but in areas where land is scarce farmers cultivate their farmland more intensively.

The keeping of animals on free-range allows the animals to graze away from the compound. This practice allows damage to be spread over the whole landscape. The disadvantage of the free-range option is that animals are exposed to thieves and the occurrence of animal theft increases. Agro-pastoralists do not gain access to animal manure since the grazing practice denies the farmer access to the use of animal manure.

Trees are sometimes lopped to provide feed for livestock. Although this practice is capable of providing temporary nutritional needs for animals, without tree planting schemes or afforestation programmes they have long-term damaging ecological consequences on vegetation and plant growth. Frequent cutting of wood and burning often leads to increased water and wind erosion in areas of reduced vegetation cover.

Out-migration

Seasonal migration to take up paid employment in the south, particularly in the mines at Obuasi and on the farms in Ashanti and Brong Ahafo has been an important local adjustment strategy. It is very difficult to obtain precise figures of the seasonal induced inter- and intra-regional migratory movements of people because such movements are not administratively recorded. However, it was revealed by the survey that every compound had lost between two and three of its young people through such movements in the previous year. This is supported by a number of studies including Church (1980), who observed that about 35% of married women who were interviewed reported that either their husbands or their children had moved south for seasonal or permanent employment.

Similarly, Warren (1981), noted that out of a sample of 4262 respondents (representing 35%) of a total population of 12068 in Techiman, an agriculturally important town in the "middle belt", about 15% of the population were of northern origin. The majority of these were from the Wa district in the Upper West Region (Kasanga and Avis 1988).

Although seasonal labour migration is one mode of adaptation to famine and a source of supplementary income to households, it poses developmental problems because voluntary labour for community projects is scarce and only the aged and women are left to undertake community development.

Off-farm employment

Many local people take off-farm employment, doing odd jobs such as mending the compound house, hunting, fishing or trading. Local crafts such as weaving, pottery-making and carving become important activities during periods of drought when environmental conditions become unfavourable for crop production.

Fuelwood substitutes

A significant impact of desertification is the dwindling supplies and scarcity of fuelwood. Whereas in the past, rural households had access to wood as a free commodity, wood has acquired a monetary value as its scarcity and marketing potential has increased. Rural people's response to increasing fuelwood scarcity is that it is now used more sparingly, and greater quantities of alternative fuels are consumed.

Foods which require more energy to prepare are substituted for those which require smaller amounts of energy. For many poor rural households, crop residues such as millet and corn stalks, and cow dung, serve as the primary alternative fuels because of limited access to more technologically sophisticated fuels. While lower household incomes restrict access, the cost, non-availability and erratic supply of petroleum products make the consumption of fuelwood and agricultural residues the only viable alternatives. At the same time increasing use of fuelwood results in deforestation and accelerates desertification, the use of agricultural residues robs the soil of its soil fertility replenishing material.

The scarcity of trees in the environment means that collection of fuelwood is a time-consuming task for women and their children, who walk long distances and spend productive hours in its procurement. The use of children's labour in fuelwood procurement is done at the expense of their education and, therefore, constitutes an inadequate local strategy to cope with fuel-wood scarcity.

Local people's preferred strategies

It has been clearly shown that in Sahelian and sub-Sahelian countries, where the environment is being degraded, several adaptive mechanisms are employed by rural people to cope with the effects of drought, land degradation and desertification. While those keeping livestock on lands too dry for plough farming are accustomed to adjusting their composition of herds between sheep, goats, cattle and poultry, others move seasonally to distant grazing lands where adequate pasture is available. In many other areas, migration has been the best option for young people.

While some of these mechanisms have led to resource conservation, some have achieved limited success. An Overseas Development Institute paper *Coping with African Drought* (Briefing Paper, July 1987) cites the example among the Wodaabe Fulani of Niger where sociologists found that many poor households were unsuccessful in employing traditional adaptive mechanisms to rehabilitate the effects of the 1968–74 drought.

Since the impact of environmental degradation is critical on activities which depend on land and weather conditions, an attempt was made to understand the strategies that have been widely employed by land-users to cope with environmental degradation. A sub-sample of 329 farmers were asked to list the groups of strategies which they have followed in the past or prefer to adopt either concurrently or in some time sequence to cope with degradation. The responses are shown in Table 5.5.

It is clear that the most important local response to environmental degradation has been to purchase food from the local market after stored grain

Table 5.5. Local people's preference for coping with environmental degradation

STRATEGY	responses 1st option	(in percentages) 2nd option
Sale of livestock	50	50
Eat food substitutes	80	20
Sell household property	10	90
Take a loan from friends/bank	25	75
Outmigration	30	70
Depend on government relief	10	90
Purchase food from the south	90	10
Move cattle to new pastures	85	15
Change occupation (e.g., hunting)	60	40

Source: Survey data (Nsiah-Gyabaah 1991)

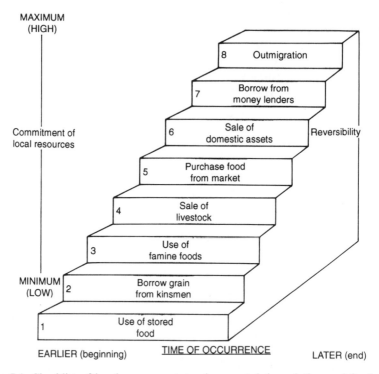

Figure 5.1. Checklist of local responses to environmental degradation and food short-age in the Upper West Region. (Note: As in the case of sale of assets, recourse to migration (permanent or seasonal) occurs generally under conditions of severe envir-onmental degradation, famine, drought and deprivation.) Source: Modified from Watts (1988)

reserves have been used up by the household. The consumption of substitute foods has widespread acceptability among 80% of farmers who were inter-viewed.

An important response as far as animals are concerned is to move them to watering points and grazing fields. While in 60% of the cases local people have changed occupations or would be prepared to do so, in 50% of the cases the livestock to supplement household income and to purchase food become significant. The movement of people to the urban centres, and to the towns of the south for paid jobs, was acceptable to 30% of respondents. Since the farmers own property such as livestock, they are often constrained by the nature of their economic activity and age from migrating. This explains the low response to the question about migration, which has been an important mechanism to cope with degradation in many arid and semi-arid areas.

Although the coping strategies and farmer adjustment mechanisms are many and generally vary from one area to another, evidence from most parts of Africa has documented common patterns that can be identified. A step-by-step checklist of the common responses that most households in the Upper West Region employ when faced with food shortage or famine has been modified from Watts (1988) and is illustrated diagrammatically in Figure 3.1.

According to the model, as land degradation accelerates and drought persists, resulting in food shortage, more precious domestic resources and assets are sold to raise money to purchase food. Those who command "entitlements" or wealthier families are not as vulnerable to food shortages as poor farm households (Sen 1981) because they are able to buy food from outside the region and can more extensively diversify their responses. At the final stage when there is a failure to cope with degradation and food crisis, land is abandoned by vulnerable groups and out-migration becomes the final outcome.

CONCLUSIONS

To summarize, most of the local adaptive strategies for coping with the drought, environmental degradation and desertification are low-cost innovations which are relatively simple to adopt and do not depend on imported technology or inputs. These strategies appeal to farmers and pastoralists because they address the short-term problems of rural agricultural production.

Although the benefits of these strategies are being eroded by widespread poverty and increasing human and livestock populations, most of these strategies continue to be the only viable alternatives capable of sustaining agriculture and maintaining ecological balance without external assistance.

The promotion and integration of local adaptive strategies into bureaucratically initiated and controlled projects, would make them acceptable to rural farmers and contribute to finding effective and lasting solutions to environmental degradation and accelerated desertification.

The central point of emphasis in this chapter is that planners and natural resource managers should look first at what rural people do, examine their existing practices and perceptions, and see how these can be improved, before recommending development interventions or innovative technologies. Through trial and error, local people have developed a complex, and sometimes very specific, knowledge of their local environment, which can be incorporated into innovations designed by outside agencies.

Although not all local beliefs are valid, and not all practices are sustainable, there are many of the more simple practices which can be improved and incorporated into rural development programmes. Simply introducing radical new institutions and technologies, or replacing local resource management systems with large-scale projects that do not meet local priorities, are bound to lead to rejection by local people, and are doomed to failure. In conclusion, development agencies which wish to help rural people to help themselves must carefully examine indigenous knowledge and beliefs, build upon existing knowledge and incorporate new ideas and innovation into indigenous systems.

This chapter suggests that people in rural areas of Northern Ghana show considerable awareness of the fragility of their environment, and the adverse effects of some agricultural practices. Villagers were frequently forced to choose between the demand for new pasture, or the need for fuelwood and the sustainable management of their resource base. Legislative controls frequently ignored local customs and practices, and were subsequently ignored themselves.

We have seen, in the Philippine case, how the lack of political will, and external indebtedness have hindered the adoption of more sustainable development. In Northern Ghana, where endogenous pressures of population and increased food production press on the available natural resources, local people demonstrate a high level of environmental consciousness. However, as we have seen, most people were not satisfied that government involvement in environmental protection was at all adequate, and distrusted government policy. Although tree planting in Northern Ghana has been neglected, local people showed considerable willingness to plant trees if encouraged to do so. There were environmental, technical and other constraints which made tree planting programmes unattractive.

In the next chapter we turn our attention to Mexico. The discussion of the Ghanaian case has established that local support for more sustainable practices in rural areas needs to be won, before government policy can be effective. In the central highland areas of Mexico there is similar suspicion of the state. Government involvement in Mexican rural development is frequently confined to political deals over land, and the provision of agricultural credit to those who place their land under the effective management of the state. Rarely, if ever, is the *campesino* producer encouraged to assume more responsibility, with official support, for sustainable management practices.

The next chapter focuses attention on the livelihood strategies which form the basis of the small farmer's calculations, and through which they tend to avoid risks and natural hazards. This takes us into the domestic economy of small agricultural producers and the gender divisions which underlie work roles and the political authority of the male household "head". As we shall see, when there is insufficient labour within the domestic economy it is the environment which suffers. The mixture of elements which compose livelihood systems need to be understood if policy interventions are to work, and sustainable development is to be translated into reality within the lives of ordinary people. The Mexican case demonstrates that when outside development assistance reaches the rural poor it is as likely to undermine the sustainability of the household economy as it is to support it.

REFERENCES

Ampadu-Agyei, O. (1986) "Bushfires and management policies in Ghana". *The Environmentalist*, **8**, (3), 221–228.
Barr, N.F. (1985) *Farmer Perception of Soil Salting*. Department of Psychology, University of Melbourne.
Benneh, G. (1971) "Land tenure and land use system in the forest–savanna contact zone in Ghana: a case study". *Factors of Agricultural Growth in West Africa*, Proceedings of International Conference held at Legon, April 1971 p. 107.
Benneh, G. (1985) "Socio-economic responses to climatic changes". *Workshop on Combating the Effects of Drought and Desertification*, EPC, 24–25 January, 1985, pp. 49–57.
Biswas, A.K. and Odero-Ogwell L.A. (1986) *Land Use*, **3**, special issue, No. 4.
Blaikie, P. (1985) *The Political Economy of Land Degradation*. Macmillan, London.
Blaikie, P. and Brookfield, H. (1987) *Land Degradation and Society*. Routledge, London.
Boudet, G. (1972) "Desertification de l'Afrique Tropicale Seche". *Adansonia*, Ser. 2 (12), 505–524.
Brokensha, D. and Riley, B.W. (1988) *The Mberere in Kenya, Vol. 1: Changing Rural Ecology*. Institute for Development Anthropology, IDA University Press.
Brokensha, D. Riley, B.W. and Cartro, A.P. (1983) *Fuelwood Use in Rural Kenya: Impacts of Deforestation*. Institute for Development Anthropology, Binghampton, NY, 54 pp.
Brown, L.H. (1971) "The biology of pastoralism as a factor in conservation". *Biological Conservation*, **3**, 93–100.
Bruk, S. (1985) *Methods of Computing Sedimentation in Lakes and Reservoirs*. Unesco, Paris, 224 pp.
Chamala, S. (1985) "Need for extension of sociological research in successfully transferring soil conservation technology". *Erosion Research Newlsetter*, **11**, 2–3.
Chamala, S. and Rickson, R.E. (1985) *Farmer's Perception and Knowledge of Soil Erosion and Conservation Practices in Australia: An Overview*. Department of Agriculture, University of Queensland, Brisbane.
Church, R.J.E. (1980) *West Africa*, 8th edn. Longman, Harlow, p. 372.
Clayton, E.S. (1964) *Agrarian Development in Peasant Economies*. London.
Cunningham, O.R. and Jenkins, Q.A.L. (1982) "Natural Disasters and farmers: a neglected area of research by rural sociologists". *The Rural Sociologist*, **2**, (5), 325–330.
Dregne, H.E. (1983) *Evaluation of the Implementation of the Plan of Action to Combat Desertification*. UNEP, Narobi.
Dyksterhuis, E.J. (1949) "Condition and management of rangeland based on quantitative ecology". *Journal of Range Management*, **2**, 104–115.
Dyson-Hudson, N. (1972) "The study of nomads". In *Perspective on Nomadism* (W. Irons ed.). E.J. Brill, Leyden, pp. 2–30.
Earle, T.R., Brownlea, A.A. and Rose, C.W. (1981) "Beliefs of a community with respect to environmental management: a case study of soil conservation beliefs on the Darling Downs". *J Environ Mgmt*, 12, 197–219.

Edroma, E.L. (1981) "Some effects of grazing on the productivity of grasslands in Rwenzori National Park, Uganda". *African Journal of Ecology*, **19**, 313–326.

Ellis, W.S. (1987) *National Geography*, **172**, 140.

FAO (1971) *Agricultural Commodity Projections 1970–1980*, Vol 1. FAO, Rome.

FAO (1979) *A Provisional Methodology for Soil Degradation Assessment.* FAO, Rome.

FAO (1983) *Provisional Methodology for the Assessment and Mapping of Desertification.* FAO, Rome, and Unesco, Paris.

FAO (1984) *World Food Reports.* FAO, Rome.

Feachem, R.G.A. (1977), "The human ecologist as Superman". In *Subsistence and Survival: Rural Ecology in the Pacific* T.P. Bayliss-Smith and R.G.A. Feachem eds.), Academic Press, New York, pp 3–10.

Foggie, A. and Piasecki, B. (1962) "Timber, fuel and minor forest products". In *Agriculture and Land Use in Ghana* (J.B. Wills ed.), Oxford University Press, Oxford, p. 236.

Forestry Department (1989) *ODA Forestry Inventory Data.* Forestry Department, Accra.

Glantz, M.H. (1976) *The Politics of Natural Disaster: The Case of the Sahel Drought.* Praeger, New York.

Grainger, A. (1990) *The Threatening Desert: Controlling Desertification.* Earthscan, London.

Gregersen, H.M. (1984) "Strategies and designs for afforestation, reforestation and tree planting". In *Proceedings of International Symposium* K.F. Wiersun (ed.). Agricultural University, Wageningen, Netherlands, 19–23 September, 432 pp.

Hardin, G. (1968) "The tragedy of the commons". *Science*, **162**, 1243–1248.

Harrison, P. (1987) *Inside the Third World.* Penguin Books, Harmondsworth.

Heberlein, T.A. (1972) "The land ethic realised: some social psychological explanations for changing environmental attitudes". *J Soc Issues*, **28**, 79–82

Hjort, A. (1985) *Land Management and Survival.* Scandinavian Institute for African Studies, Stockholm, pp. 48–108.

Ibrahim, F.N. (1979) *Desertification: A World-Wide Problem.* Hageman, Item no. 17 16 60, 1–30.

ICASLAS (1988) *Erosion, Productivity and Sustainable Agriculture.* Report of a Workshop held at Texas Tech University, 25–26 July 1980. International Centre for Arid and Semi-arid Land Studies.

IDI (1987) *"Coping with African drought"*, Briefing Paper. IDI, London, 4 pp.

Innes, R. (1972) "Fire in West African vegetation". *Proceding Annual Tall Timbers Fire Ecology Conference*, 11, 147–173.

Kasanga, K.R. and Avis M.R. (1988) "Internal migration and urbanization in developing countries: findings from a study of Ghana". Research Papers in Land Economy.

Kassaa, M. (1970a) In *Arid Lands in Transition* American Association for the Advancement of Science H.E. Dregne (ed.). Washington DC, pp. 123–142.

Kassaa, M. (1970b) "Desertification versus potential for recovery in circum-Saharan territories". *Arid Lands in Transition*, American Association for the Advancement of Science, Washington DC, p. 90.

Klaus, D. (1981) "Klimatologische und Klimatologische Aspekte der Durre im Sahel Erdwiss", Forsch, 16, Wiesbaden.

Lal, R. (ed.) (1988) *Soil Erosion Research Methods.* Soil and Water Conservation Society, Ankeny, Iowa, 244 pp.

Lamprey, H.F. (1975) "Report on the desert encroachment reconnaissance in Northern Sudan", 21 October–10 November. Unesco/UNEP mimeo, 16 pp.

Likert, R. (1932) "A technique for the measurement of attitudes". *Archives of Psychology*, No. 140.

Mainguet, M. and Cossus, L. (1980) "Le Sahel Bordure Meridionale du Sahara: etude de geographie". *Historiens et Geographes*, June–July, 813–830.

Mann, R. (1989) *Africa: The Urgent Need*. Methodist Church Overseas, London, p. 15

Manshard, (1986) "The West African middle belt: land use patterns and development problems". *Land Use Policy*, 3, (4), 307.

Marsh, G.P. (1864) *Man and Nature*. Scribners, New York.

McNamara, R.S. (1985) *"The challenges of sub-Saharan Africa"*. Sir John Crawford Memorial Lecture for Consultative Group on International Agricultural Research, published by the World Bank.

Mensching, H.G. (1980) "The Sahelian zone and the problems of desertification: climatic and anthropogenic causes of desert encroachment". *Palaeoecology of Africa and the Surrounding Islands*, Vol. 12, Balkema, pp. 257–266.

Milner, C. and Douglas, M.G. (1989) *Problems of Land Degradation in Commonwealth Africa. A Study on the Scope for Commonwealth Action*. Commonwealth Secretariat, London, 121 pp.

Norman, D.W., Quedraogo, L. and Newman, M. (1979) "Farm-level studies in the semi-arid tropics of West Africa". In *Socio-economic Constraints to Development of Semi-arid Tropical Agriculture*, Hyderabad, India, p.241.

Nowak, P.J. (1983) "Adoption and diffusion of soil and water conservation practices". *Rural Sociology*, 3 83–92.

Nsiah-Gyabaah K. (1991) "Environmental degradation and the threat of desertification in the Upper West Region of Ghana". PhD thesis, Wye College, University of London.

Nye, P.H. and Greenland, P.J. (1960) *The soil under Shifting Cultivation*. Commonwealth Agricultural Bureau.

Obeid, M. and Seif el Din, A. (1970) "Ecological studies of vegetation of Sudan". *Journal of Applied Ecology*, 7, 507–518.

ODA (1989) *National Seminar on Forest Inventory*, 15–16 March 1989. UST, Kumasi.

Omaboe, E.W. and Neustadt, I. (1962) *A Study of Contemporary Ghana*, Vol. 1 (Vol. 2 (1966).) George Allen & Unwin, London, 233 pp.

Pearce, D.W. (1988) "The sustainable use of natural resources in developing countries". In *Sustainable Environmental Management* R.K. Turner (ed.). Belhaven Press, London, and Westview Press, Boulder, CO.

Pearson, L.C. (1965) "Primary production in grazed and ungrazed desert communities of eastern idaho". *Ecology*, 46, 278–286.

Prospero, J. and Nees, R. (1977) "Dust concentration in the atmosphere of the Equatorial North Atlantic: possible relationship to Sahelian drought". *Science*, 196, 1196–1198.

Raikes, P. (1981) *Livestock and Policy in East Africa, Uppsala*. Scandinavian Institute for African Studies, Stockholm.

Rao, M.R. and Willey, R.W. (1980) "Evaluation of yield stability in Intercropping": studies on sorghum/pigeon pea. In *Experimental Agriculture*, 16, (2), 105–116.

Redclift, M.R. (1987) *Sustainable Development: Exploring the Contradictions*. Methuen, London.

Richards, P. (1985) *Indigenous Agricultural Revolution*. Hutchinson, London.

Schudder, T. (1971) *Gathering among African Woodland Savanna Cultivators. A Case Study: Gwembe Tonga*. Manchester University Press, Manchester, for the Institute of African Studies, University of Zambia (Zambian Papers, No. 5).

Sen, A.K. (1981) *Poverty and Famine: An Essay on Entitlement and Deprivation.* Clarendon Press, Oxford.

Stocking, M.A. (1987) "Measuring land degradation". In *Land Degradation and Society* P. Blaikie and H. Brookfield (eds). Methuen, London, pp. 49–63.

Thompson, J.T.A., Waldstein, G.S. and Miner, J. (1988) *Options for Promoting. User-based Governance of Sahelian Renewable Natural Resources.* USAID Contract No DHR-5446-Z-00-7033-00. Associates in Rural Development, Burlington, VT.

Tolba, M. (1985) "Desertification: moving beyond the laboratory". Paper presented to the Conference *Arid Lands: Today and Tomorrow"*, Tucson, Arizona, 20–25 October 1985.

Toupet, C. (1975), "La sedentarisation des nomads en Mauritanie Centrale sahe'liene". Thesis, University of Paris VII, Paris Librairie Honore Champion.

Tucker, C.J. (1985) "Africa land-cover classification Using satellite data". *Science,* **227**, (4685), 369–375.

UNCOD A/CONF 74/36 (1977) *Plan of Action to Combat Desertification.* Report of the UN Conference on Desertification in Nairobi.

Van Liere, K.D. and Dunlap, R.E. (1980) "The social basis of environmental concern: a review of hypothesis, explanation and empirical evidence. *Publ Opin Q,* **44**, 181–197.

Warren, A. and Maizels, J.K. (1977) "Ecological change and desertification". In *Desertification: Its Causes and Consequences,* Pergamon Press, Oxford, pp. 169–260; also UN conference on Desertification, Paper No A/CONF 74/7, United Nations, New York, pp. 35–63.

Warren, D.M. (1981) "Ethnic heterogeneity and the growth of market unions and ethnic associations in Techiman, Ghana". Papers on Anthropology, no. 5, Iowa State University.

Watske, G.E. Dana, J.M. and Rubenstein F.D. (1972) "An experimental study of individual and group interests". *Acta Sociologia,* **15**, 366–370.

Watts, M.J. (1988) *In Coping with Uncertainty in Food Supply* De Garime and G.A. Harrison (eds). Oxford University Press, Oxford.

Williams, M. (1979) "The perception of the hazard of soil degradation in South Australia: a review". In *Natural Hazards in Australia* R.L. Heathcote and B.G. Tom (eds). Australian Academy of Science, Canberra, pp. 275–289.

6 Local Environmental Knowledge. Agricultural Development and Livelihood Sustainability in Mexico

GRAHAM WOODGATE
Wye College, University of London, UK

INTRODUCTION

In this chapter we examine the relationship between rural livelihoods, local environmental knowledge, state promotion of agricultural "development" and the environment. The chapter draws on information gathered during a fifteenth-month field-work period spent in the central highland municipality of San Felipe del Progreso in the State of Mexico, Mexico.

The dynamics of socio-cultural and environmental change will be viewed from a coevolutionary perspective in order to elucidate the interactive character of processes of change. In his latest book Richard Norgaard has developed the concept of coevolution to show how Western science, resources and the environment have developed as a mutually interactive, coevolving system (Norgaard, 1993). In an earlier exposition on the notion of agricultural coevolution, Norgaard emphasized how people's "agricultural activities modify the ecosystem and how the ecosystem's responses provide cause for subsequent individual action and social organisation" (Norgaard 1984, p. 525).

In this chapter I shall outline the nature of small-scale agricultural production. State initiatives for its development and the way in which both are transformed in the pursuance of rural livelihoods at the margins of the formal economy. Finally, I shall consider the implications for the socio-cultural and ecological sustainability of the local livelihood systems.

Strategies for Sustainable Development: Local Agendas for the Southern Hemisphere
Edited by Michael Redclift and Colin Sage. © 1994 John Wiley & Sons Ltd

134

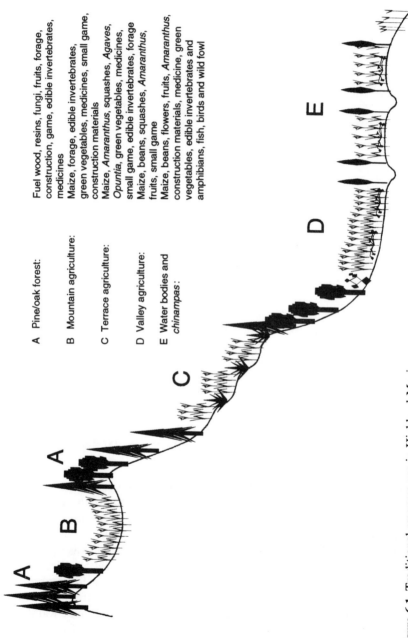

A Pine/oak forest:

B Mountain agriculture:

C Terrace agriculture:

D Valley agriculture:

E Water bodies and
   chinampas:

Fuel wood, resins, fungi, fruits, forage,
construction, game, edible invertebrates,
medicines

Maize, forage, edible invertebrates,
green vegetables, medicines, small game,
construction materials

Maize, Amaranthus, squashes, Agaves,
Opuntia, green vegetables, medicines,
small game, edible invertebrates, forage

Maize, beans, squashes, Amaranthus,
fruits, small game

Maize, beans, flowers, fruits, Amaranthus,
construction materials, medicine, green
vegetables, edible invertebrates and
amphibians, fish, birds and wild fowl

Figure 6.1. Traditional resource use in Highland Mexico
Source: Woodgate (1991, p. 161). Reproduced by permission of Manchester University Press

COEVOLUTION IN THE CENTRAL HIGHLANDS OF MEXICO

The coevolutionary history of Central Mexico, suggests that pre-Hispanic society was predicated on an indigenous agriculture which displayed an ability to manage a wide variety of crops in an equally diverse set of ecosystems (see Figure 6.1), using locally developed agroecological knowledge.

Following the conquest of the region between 1519 and 1525, however, much of this knowledge, vital to the sustainable utilization of local ecosystems, was devalued and destroyed by a variety of processes including: the transformation of indigenous society and production systems as a result of demographic collapse due largely to mass slaughter and the introduction of disease; the destruction of means of encoding, regulating and transmitting agricultural practices as a result of conversion to Catholicism; restriction of access to the full range of local ecosystems through the resettlement of indigenous peoples in "Indian towns" and; the rise of positivist science which dismissed other forms of knowledge as superstition (Woodgate 1992, Ch. 4).

Despite the declared objectives of the revolution in the early twentieth century and the commitment to agrarian reform displayed by the Cardenas administration (1934–40), the adoption of an import substitution industrialization strategy in the post-war period, without fostering the necessary conditions for the parallel modernization of the reform sector, meant that the State's alliance with peasantry could only be maintained through the preservation of peasant agriculture as a social sector. Although the reform has resulted in almost 50% of the national land area being transferred into the hands of the peasantry, peasant access to resources has remained limited in terms of both quantity and quality so that increasing numbers of small-scale producers now face the prospect of having to look outside agriculture for the means of their subsistence.

SMALL-SCALE AGRICULTURAL PRODUCTION IN SAN FELIPE DEL PROGRESO

San Felipe del Progreso comprises a region running westward from the northwestern corner of the Valley of Toluca bounded to the east by the River Lerma, over the mountains of the Sierra Madre, towards the border between the States of Mexico and Michoacan (Figure 6.2).

The area within San Felipe del Progreso where field-work was carried out, extends some 20 000 ha about the point 19°58′ North; 99°58′ West. At its highest point the land rises to over 3000 m, a.m.s.l., falling to around 2500 m, in the valley bottom. Mean annual temperatures range from 8 to 14°C, with average annual precipitation of between 800 and 1200 mm. Rainfall is concentrated between the months of April and September and frosts may be expected from October through to February.

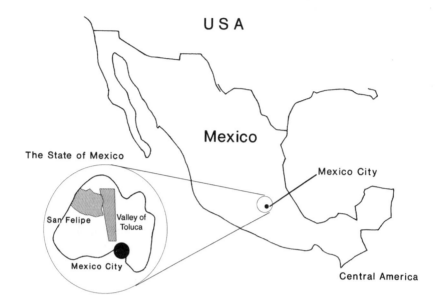

Figure 6.2. Location of the Valley of Toluca

The soils of San Felipe del Progreso range from lithosols on the sides of the steeply sloping volcanic peaks, through deep andosols in the small, intermontane valleys, to rich luvisols on the floor of the main Toluca Valley. The natural vegetation of the area, now greatly reduced in extent and composition, ranges from pine, through pine/oak and oak forest, to marshy, wetland willow (*Salix* spp) and alder (*Alnus* spp) forest in the valley bottom, an area originally endowed with a large number of shallow lagoons and their associated aquatic and semi-aquatic ecosystems.

FARMING SYSTEMS

Following the classification of Fresco and Westphal (1988) four distinct cropping systems are to be found in San Felipe. These are:

(1) Permanent upland cultivation, characterized by the permanent division of the holding with clearly demarcated fields in which predominantly annual crops are grown.
(2) Supplementary irrigation arable farming. The "*punta de riego*" system provides for between one and three irrigations at the beginning of the agricultural cycle to allow for crop establishment prior to the onset of the regular summer rains in order extend the growing season.

(3) Perennial crop cultivation, characterized by the permanent use of land for the same crop.
(4) Gardening or compound cultivation. This cropping system is characterized by the permanent use of small plots of land around the house with a variable number of annual, biennial and perennial inter-crops giving rise to a multistorey physiognomy.

Following the same classification scheme, the livestock systems of San Felipe del Progreso can be categorized as follows:

(1) Partial nomadism, characterized by the communal use of grazing land by herds, the sedentary nature of human communities and the dominance of arable agriculture.
(2) Small-scale stationary animal husbandry. These are intensive livestock systems distinguished by a diversity of animals, raised in small numbers on or near the house, often on the by-products of the farm, primarily with a subsistence perspective.
(3) Stationary animal husbandry systems, involving the intensive production and controlled feeding regimes were introduced into San Felipe del Progreso during the Echeverria administration (1970–76). However, the inappropriate nature of these systems resulted in a more or less generalized failure throughout the municipality.

In terms of cropping and livestock systems and biophysical factors then, the land-use system of San Felipe del Progreso falls rather neatly into Fresco and Westphal's (1988) "highland, sub-humid monsoon" category. Detailing the specific characteristics of local production systems would require more space than is available here. The following descriptions outline their basic features, however, and also makes reference to the local environmental knowledge which helps to sustain them.

Local environmental knowledge and resource use

Peasant producers, especially the older members of communities, typically possess a great deal of indigenous knowledge of their productive environments. Such knowledge relates to elements such as weather, soils, food and curative plants, the behavioural ecology of prey animals and crop and livestock pests, and the interaction between animals, plants and soils.

To take soils as just one example, field-work data show that the local producers recognize at least seven major categories of soil which are further subdivided by modifiers such as depth, texture, structure and the incidence of stones. Each soil is recognized by its physical characteristics, its agri-

138

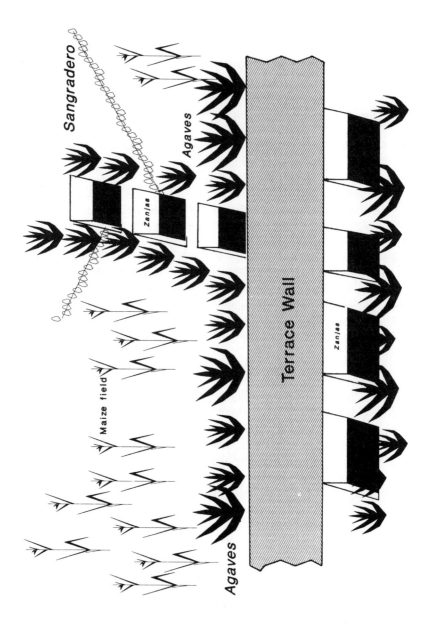

Figure 6.3. *Zanjas* or lock-and-spill drains
Source: Woodgate (1991, p. 172). Reproduced by permission of Manchester University Press

cultural, productive potential and its properties as a construction (e.g., adobe) or craftwork material.

The producers are clearly aware of the benefit of soil organic matter. When there were more extensive forests in the area it used to be common practice to gather leaf litter, compost it and then add it to the soil to improve moisture and nutrient retention, although as the forest area has diminished, this practice has become less common. Recognition of the benefits of organic matter is still widespread, however. Over 80% of households covered by a 105-household survey stated that they used whatever farmyard manure they had at their disposal to apply to their fields. Indeed production of manure was a frequently stated reason for keeping livestock.

Where households have insufficient manure to treat the entire holding, fields are fertilized with farmyard manure on a rotational basis and it was claimed that the benefits of organic fertilizer persisted for four or five years, whereas inorganic applications were required annually.

Of the variety of land management techniques employed by the local producers the lock-and-spill drains (*zanjas*), which are central to erosion prevention on steeply sloping land, are perhaps one of the most impressive examples (see Figure 6.3). The system relies on the annual construction of *sangraderos* or "bleed lines" which channel surface runoff from the fields to the adjacent *zanjas* which are aligned both parallel and perpendicular to the slope. The *zanjas* are regularly divided by locks, forming a series of small ponds approximately one metre wide by two metres long and up to one metre in depth.

The work of Mountjoy and Gliessman (1988) in the nearby State of Tlaxcala, comments on the high, innate sustainability of the *zanja* system, which functions by reducing the downslope force of run-off water, permitting the settling out of the sediment load at the bottom of each small pond. The sediment thus collected is excavated as many as four times each year and thrown up onto the maize fields, returning mineral and organic matter and nutrients to the soil and reducing the sediment load in the streams and rivers which feed the local reservoir. The drains also hold back water after the rain, allowing it to permeate into the subsoil, and providing an alternative, albeit transient, source of water for livestock.

Cropping and livestock systems

Permanent upland cultivation is by far the most common cropping system in the area, accounting for more than half of the total surface area, more than 90% of which is dedicated to maize production.

A plethora of different varieties or cultivars of maize is sown in the communities. Only 15.2% of households stated that they purchased maize seed, while 75.2% said that cobs selected from their own crops were their exclusive source of seed for the following year. In this way maize seed is locally selected and adapted to micro-environmental conditions. Traditionally, when a son leaves his parent's home and starts sowing his own maize fields, he is given seed by his parents, so that genetic material is passed on from generation to generation.

Different varieties of maize have different characteristics: the blue variety, for example, yields very little and is grown almost exclusively because it is said to make the most tasty *tortillas*. Pink maize is said to be a very strong plant with a short growing season, while the white and yellow varieties are high-yielding but require a longer growing season. Thus, by sowing a number of different varieties producers can spread risk, off setting maximum possible yield against the certainty of obtaining at least some yield if early autumn frosts cause the slower-developing but higher-yielding varieties to fail.

In terms of other crops, the *haba* or broad bean (*Faba* spp) is the second most commonly planted species under permanent upland systems of cultivation. It is rarely cultivated as a monocrop, but is frequently seen in conjunction with maize, especially in fields situated close to the houses. Besides its nutritional value, providing essential amino acids which are absent in maize, broad beans also fix nitrogen into the soil, off setting the demands of the nutrient-hungry maize.

Various species of squash (*Cucurbita* spp) are the other common ingredient of these systems. They are never sown as a monoculture, however; and when sown in mixture with the maize are usually limited to land close to the house. It is the three species mixture of maize beans and squash which, since the Conquest, has formed the basis of local polycultural systems.

The typical agricultural cycle for the maize/beans/squash crop system (see Figure 6.4) begins immediately after the completion of the previous harvest, usually in November, when the land is prepared by ploughing at right-angles to the old furrows. Cultivations are carried out using a pair of draught animals (oxen, horses or mules, rarely donkeys) which farmers either own, rent or borrow from a neighbour or relative.

The winter frosts then act on the soil to break down the clods and form a hard crust, so that the farmers must wait until the first gentle rains in March or April of the following year before they carry out the second cultivation or *barbecho*. Once the furrows have been demolished by the *barbechos* the field is ploughed again, this time perpendicular to the *barbecho* (*doblado*) to loosen and aerate the soil. Before the final levelling (*rastreo*), the *zanjas* are cleared out and the slit thrown up onto the maize field.

Sowing is carried out at the same time as the furrows are ploughed, once the light early rains have begun. Timing is critical. Farmers induced to sow by good early rainfall may lose part or even all of a crop owing to a late frost or drought when the main summer rains fail to materialize on time. On the other hand, if farmers were to wait for the onset of the heavier summer

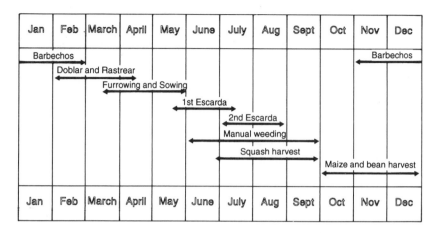

Figure 6.4. The agricultural calendar for maize/beans/squash crop system

rains before sowing, they would risk losing the crop to early frosts at the end of the season.

Furrowing involves two steps, *rayar* and *cruzar*, two passes of the plough, one perpendicular to the other, with furrows 50 to 80 cm apart. Sowing usually entails the participation of all able-bodied members of the household. There are numerous variations of sowing practices; exactly what is entailed may vary from household to household, field to field and year to year, depending on climatic conditions, soil consistency, current financial situation, other obligations and the availability of family members.

Once the fields are sown, the next task does not arise until three to six weeks after planting, in late May or early June, when the maize plants have emerged and reached a height of 30–60 cm. Then it is time for the *primera escarda* or first ridging-up. The purpose of the ridging-up operations is to weed the crop, conserve soil moisture, reduce the risk of lodging and, if fertilizer has been applied, to incorporate it into the soil.

As the plough passes between the rows of maize, the family follows behind, firming the plants and gathering any edible weeds, which are either eaten by the family or fed to the livestock. It is not uncommon for households to buy in hen or turkey chicks around planting time when they are too small to damage the emerging and developing maize plants. By the time the chicks are larger however, the maize is too tall to be damaged and hens, and especially turkeys, will often be herded into the field where the *escardas* are being carried out, so that they can eat crop pests such as wire-worms. The hens are later sold or eaten before the harvest, so that they will not steal the crop.

About one month after the first ridging-up, the operation is carried out again (*la segunda escarda*), when the largest of the plants have reached a height of 1–1.5 m. This is the last major task until the harvest; the family now has to wait and hope that the rains will continue and the crop will ripen before the on set of the first frosts. Between the *escardas* and following the *segunda* members of the household are occupied in the task of weeding the fields. This not only reduces competition with the crop plants, but also provides additional vegetables such as wild beans, potatoes and brassicas which provide extra nutrition in the diet.

Squashes may be ready for eating from July onwards and, once the maize crop has produced sufficiently large ears (early September), tender cobs may be harvested. It is not before October, however, that the crop will have ripened and it will be nearer the end of the month before the corn will be dry enough to harvest. Where beans have been sown in mixture, they are usually harvested prior to the maize to minimize losses caused by walking through the crop when the pods are ripe and splitting.

Harvesting is always carried out manually, with households working together in large groups or hiring casual labour to ensure that the harvest is gathered in as quickly as possible. Each harvester is responsible for a furrow and works with a *pizcador* (a small, sharply pointed metal implement similar to a large nail, possibly with a rough wooden handle). The *pizcador* is used to open the leaves which cover the cob, and help break it from the stem.

The remaining straw may either be havested immediately and stored in *mogotes* (stooks) in the fields or larger stacks at the house or left in the field to be cut as required. On completion of the harvest, the cobs are carefully examined and cleaned and the best examples (largest cobs and most even grain size) set aside for next year's seed. The remainder of the corn is stored either in *cincolotes* (wooden corncribs) or, in older houses, in the roof void, following a further period of outdoor exposure for more thorough drying. Once dry, the corn is shelled as and when necessary.

The next most common cropping system in terms of area covered, but not of number of households by which it is practised, is supplementary irrigation arable farming. The major effect of the *punta de riego* system to provide a good deal more certainty about the time of sowing as the second *barbecho* can be undertaken as soon as the first irrigation has been completed. From late February through March, those with access to irrigation water take turns to flood-irrigate their land.

Land with access to irrigation water is still most commonly sown to maize, although it appears to be less common to sow polycultures on irrigated land, probably because the presence of irrigation improves the performance of modern technological packages of fertilizers and pesticides, the herbicide component of which proscribes the sowing of broadleaved species such as beans and squash.

In terms of the number of households which practise the different cropping systems, the second most common is gardening or compound cultivation, which is practised by 77% of all households interviewed. However, the compound cultivation practised in San Felipe is not generally comparable with the highly complex systems of a similar *genre* practised in other parts of Latin America or Southeast Asia. Rather than a clearly demarcated plot of land, the home-gardens found in San Felipe del Progreso tend to consist of a few fruit trees and species of cacti planted close to the house, with haphazard scatterings of squashes, decorative flowers and herbs.

Perennial crop cultivation is represented locally by small *maqueyeras* which can still be found in a number of communities. These *maguey* plantations are probably vestigial systems left behind by the last of the *haciendas*; land is now far too scarce to plant to *magueyes*, especially since so many of the products they produce have been superseded by industrially manufactured goods. *Magueyes* are now most commonly found demarcating field and terrace boundaries, playing an important part in erosion control on sloping land. Today, the most common productive use of the *magueyes* is *pulque* production (*pulque* is the fermented sap of the *maguey*). *Pulque* is consumed at different levels of fermentation and thus alcohol concentration. It is a major source refreshment in San Felipe, with resultant high levels of alcohol-related illnesses such as liver disorders. Ironically, however, *pulque* is relatively high in proteins, vitamins and minerals, and is an important source of nutrition for those by whom it is drunk.

Livestock production makes a growing contribution to livelihoods in San Felipe. Livestock systems are predominantly partial nomadism and small-scale, stationary animal husbandry. In terms of animal numbers, systems are dominated by sheep and poultry. The number of animals owned by individual households is rarely more than a handful, however, which are usually kept in small corrals immediately adjacent to the house.

While animals are slaughtered and eaten on special occasions such as *fiestas*, it remains uncommon for the average family to eat the animals they rear; meat does not form a significant element of *campesino* diets. The most common reason given for producing and rearing livestock, from chickens to cattle, is as a form of saving. The mean value of the livestock owned by households was calculated in Mexican pesos as 6,044m or, at 1989 exchange rates, about £1500. When the need arises, an animal can be sold for cash, either to itinerant middlemen or at local and regional markets. In the months of November and December, and April and May, local markets fill to capacity with the animals of producers needing money to pay for labour, inputs and/or credit for the harvest and sowing respectively.

Another common reason cited for keeping animals is that of manure production. The benefits of animal manure are well recognized by the people of San Felipe, many producers were keen to demonstrate the difference between fields where they had been able to fertilize the soil using manure and those which had received only inorganic preparations. It was also frequently expressed, however, that the keeping of animals on the present scale is a recent development of the last 20 years or so. The reason appears to be related to the lack of cultivable land and the need to extract as much value as possible from the environment; this idea will be explored further later.

During the rainy summer months, older and younger members of the household herd the larger animals out to graze on the few remaining hectares of communal pasture or to browse along field boundaries, roadsides and, where the practice is still permitted, in the few enduring fragments of woodland. Such is the demand for grazing that towards the end of the dry season some farmers illegally set fire to the forest understorey to retard the growth of perennial species and provide an early bite at the onset of the rains. While semi-natural vegetation still exists it is possible to extract value from it by converting it into animal products.

It is also common for fodder to be cut and carried back to the household; maize field weed species form a significant element of livestock feeding regimes in the wet summer months. Although no hard data were gathered in this respect, it was apparent that fewer animals are kept during the dry season when fodder is scarce. Those which are kept are fed on maize straw, ground cobs or, occasionally, bought-in fodder. Pigs are an exception to this generalized rule, often being bought at the end of the wet season to be fed on maize which spoils in storage.

Having reviewed the various techniques and technologies which describe the different natural resource-using sub-systems then, it is now time to move on to look at the role of the Mexican State in the promotion of agricultural development.

THE STATE AND AGRICULTURAL MODERNIZATION

Modernization Strategies

Two basic strategies have been used to promote agricultural modernization in the State of México. The first and longest standing is the promotion of research activities by the State. Policies oriented toward the development of technological packages were initiated towards the end of the 1950s with the objective of producing high yielding seed varieties, mainly wheat, for use in the irrigated areas in the north of the country. It was not until the mid-1960s that attention was turned to high yielding maize.

In the State of México, from 1970 onwards the "Plan Maíz" was put into operation by DAGEM (the Directorate of Agriculture and Livestock of the State of México). The "Plan Maíz" consisted of two main strategies:

(a) The recruitment of the most efficient producers (technical leaders and natural promoters) to promote modernization. The *Jefes*, as they were known, were required to promote the formation of groups of producers well disposed to the incorporation of new technology and the creation of necessary infrastructure.
(b) The design and implementation of suitable credit programmes for producer groups which could not meet the credit requirements of normal banking institutions. To achieve this, the state government established an agreement with BANRURAL (the National Rural Credit Bank) whereby the State received and underwrote the credit which was necessary for the modernization programme. Nevertheless, BANRURAL made the provision of such credit conditional on the purchase of agricultural insurance from ANAGSA, the national agricultural insurance agency.

Secondly, coinciding with this state-level strategy, CEDEMEX (Central de Servicios para el Desarrollo, affiliated to the Mexican Foundation for Rural Development (la Fundación Mexicana para el Desarrollo Rural)) was also working in the region with a similar strategy aimed at organizing groups of small-scale producers to receive credit from the then private banks with the assistance of state employees, who were, at the same time, often members of the administrative boards of the same banks. In this way the state bureaucratic apparatus was accommodated within the development drive.

Owing to the State's eagerness to participate in the organization of the modernization process, and the dynamics of large-scale credit provision, from 1975 the sphere of cover of these services was expanded in an attempt to close the basic credit cycle—that is until its repayment. For this purpose CODAGEM (la Comisión Coordinadora para el Desarrollo Agrícola y Ganadero del Estado de México) was established, through which UADMs (Municipal Agricultural Development Units) were established in the majority of the of municipalities in the region. By 1980 there were two in San Felipe del Progreso.

It can be seen then, that from the State's point of view, rural development was to be achieved principally through the adoption of methods of production and forms of organization and behaviour, which were appropriate to capitalist cycles of production and reproduction of capital The following extract demonstrates the point.

> The agricultural problem of the State of Mexico claims and has the priority attention of the state authorities, as the production of foods is of the utmost importance . . . The agricultural sector is of great social importance, accounting for at least 1.7 million people. This sector is of key importance to elevating the lives of the population, due to the great potential which it has for opening new alternatives for employment and production in almost all the state.

In these circumstances the objective of the current agricultural development programme is clear: to consolidate agricultural activities and pursue greater productive efficiency in conjunction with greater equality in the distribution of its benefits without which sustained rural development cannot be achieved. . . . The efforts made by the State are directed toward problems of the first order: lack of improved seeds; lack of inputs and their high cost; limited access to credit; and, as if that were not enough, limited and controlled markets.

One of the most important factors for agricultural development rests on the organization of producers. There has been a constant struggle which has already achieved the formation of Ejido Unions, Rural Production Societies, Credit Unions and Specialized Cropping and Livestock Unions. . . . [E]xtreme atomization explains the necessity of grouping the producers together in order to allow economic improvement by making production and marketing more efficient, expedite the supply of fertilizers, agrochemicals and other indispensable inputs, through a better utilization of the supports and services provided by federal, state and municipal governments. The introduction of Unions of Ejidos, Rural Production Societies, Credit Unions and Specialized Cropping and Livestock Unions contemplates attractive alternatives which previously did not exist. (CODAGEM 1988, p. 105–109)

One of the fundamental conditions for the success of the credit system in the field was the restructuring of the entire system of agricultural support in function of the principal objectives of the technological package. However, it is clear that the necessary unification of purpose and strategy was not achieved between the various credit institutions, so that there was a duplication of functions, allowing maize producers to duplicate credit for the same crop. Thus some producers either received credit simultaneously from both CODAGEM and BANRURAL or, asked for credit from one that was destined to pay off the other. Fraudulent activities are not restricted to the producers, however, as the following article from the local newspaper *Sol de Toluca* reports:

All of the credits that, from [the start of] the 1988–89 [agricultural] cycle, are to be dispersed in the countryside will be scrupulously controlled, by activities coordinated with the SARH, BANRURAL and ANAGSA, both to impede duplication [of credit] and to put an end to the corrupt activities of [state] functionaries towards this [the agricultural] sector. (*Sol de Toluca*, No. 14 715, 10 July 1989, p. 1-A).

During both formal and informal interviews with producers, a number of accusations were made against credit and insurance agencies' staff. The credit agency staff were accused of promoting the idea of claiming for more than the actual area cultivated and then claiming a share of the additional payments and likewise, ANAGSA staff were accused of assessing crop losses much greater than the actual losses incurred, and then claiming part of the payment.

Production credits and technological packages

Technical advice and infrastructural support is provided by the SARH (Secretariat of Agriculture and Water Resources), although with fewer than ten technicians to cover the entire municipality, the service is very limited. The experience of the producers is that, rather than receiving help towards solving their existing problems, advice is usually centred around the implementation of technological packages.

The two main credit agencies are the CODAGEM and BANRURAL. The former is the major supplier of credit to the households which cultivate communally owned land, while the latter deals mainly with private landowners. Both are in the business of extending credit facilities for crop production using predetermined packages of chemical inputs: fertilizers, herbicides and other pesticides. The vast majority of the credit received by producers in the 29 communities is directed towards maize production.

Those communities which have access to irrigation water from the local reservoir were also reliant upon the SARH for ensuring that they receive their water quotas at the correct time. Annual timetables are drawn up with minimal recourse to user–supplier communication. Added to the fact that the SARH has prohibited the growing of commercially valuable crops such as alfalfa and forage oats (owing to their high demand for water), it is clear that the production process on irrigated land is strictly controlled by the State.

As CODAGEM is the major supplier of credit to producers in the study area, this section reviews the technological packages it has on offer for maize production. It should be noted that despite the wide variety of soils and topographic conditions in the study area, only two different packages are available. During formal and informal interviews with both individual producers and community leaders, a common request from the FSR project with which the author was involved was for the team to carry out detailed soil analyses and make specific recommendations for future fertilizer applications.

The first of the two packages, "Programa 2.3 de Temporal', as the name indicates, is for rain-fed land which, under the following package of inputs, is expected to yield 2.3 tonnes of maize per hectare:

		N	P	K
Fertilizer regime:		120	60	0
made up of either:				
(a)		N	P	K
	200 kg 46% urea	92	0	0
	+ 150 kg 18:46:00	27	69	0
		= 119	69	0

or:

	N	P	K
(b)			
600 kg 20.05% ammonium sulphate	120.3	0	0
+ 300 kg 20.05% calcium superphosphate	0	60.15	0
	= 120.3	60.15	0

The recommended regime is to apply all of the phosphate and one-third of the nitrogen at sowing, followed by another third of the nitrogen at the first *escarda*, with the final dose of nitrogen when the maize is flowering. However, the most commonly followed practice is to apply all of the phosphate and two-thirds of the nitrogen at the time of sowing and make the final application of nitrogen at the first or second *escarda*.

The second package is "Programa 3.2, Punta de Riego" which is expected to yield 3.2 tonnes of maize per hectare on irrigated land.

	N	P	K
Fertilizer regime:	150	60	30

made up of:

	N	P	K
300 kg 46% urea	138	0	0
+ 150 kg 18:46:00	27	69	0
+ 50 kg (50%) KCL	0	0	25
	= 165	69	25

The recommended regime is to apply 100 kg of urea and all of the phosphate and potash at the time of sowing with a second dose of 100 kg of urea at the first *escarda* and the final 100 kg of nitrogen being applied at the time of flowering. Again, the usual practice is different, half of the nitrogen together with all the phosphate and potash is applied at sowing and the remaining 150 kg of urea at the first or second *escarda*.

Both packages follow the same pesticide regime. Granular or powder insecticides are applied to the soil at sowing to control the following pests: gusano de alambre (*Agriotes* spp.), four common species of *Diabrotica*, *Gallina ciega* (*Phyllophaga* spp). and gusano trosador (*Feltia* spp). The most commonly used insecticide is "Volatón", applied at a rate of 25 kg ha^{-1}. The active ingredient of "Volatón" is aldrin (5%) which has been banned in many industrial nations for some years now. In Britain it was associated with the deaths of large numbers of birds of prey. Because aldrin cannot be metabolized, it accumulates in fatty tissues, becoming more and more concentrated at progressive trophic levels in the food chain.

Both pre- and post-emergent herbicides are used to control the maize field weeds. Pre-emergent applications of "Azinotox" and "Gesaprim 50" (active ingredient 2% atrazine, a wide-spectrum broadleaf herbicide) are used in order to attain weed-free fields for the first 60 days, in order to give a good start to the maize plants. Post-emergent applications consist of either "Hierbamina" or "Hierbipal". Both have the wide-spectrum broadleaf herbicide 2,4-D as active ingredient and are applied to weeds of 10–15 cm. in height, at the first or second *escarda*.

Although the CODAGEM *técnicos* claimed that neither herbicide is persistent, in Britain both atrazine and 2,4-D are strictly controlled, specifically because of their long-term residual effects. Atrazine is currently under review in Britain with the possibility that its use may soon be prohibited, while 2,4-D has already been banned in the USA. The residual effect of atrazine was clear from field inspections. Plots treated with the chemical in the previous year remained virtually weed-free until well into the following season.

While visiting a household in the village of Fresno Nichi, a farmer produced an empty packet of "Azinotox", and asked if I could obtain any more for him. Noticing that his fields were virtually weed-free, I asked him why he wanted more? He replied that it was an extremely good fertilizer. Although I tried hard to convince him that atrazine was a herbicide, he was adamant that it was not. "Look! Just look how well the plants are growing, just one dose of the fertilizer at the beginning of last season, nothing more!"

The man was eventually persuaded that the "fertilizer effect" of the herbicide was due to the reduction of weed species competition for nutrients, but the facts remain that firstly, illiteracy and lack of "modern scientific knowledge" had allowed him to perceive the herbicide as a fertilizer and secondly, if the misinterpretation of empirical evidence could be made by one person, it could be made by others. Atrazine can have a residual effect for up to three years, so annual applications may result in a build-up of the chemical in the soil, making it impossible to plant anything but monocotyledonous crops.

The minimum land area which an individual must bring into the CODAGEM credit schemes is one hectare; the maximum for producers who cultivate communally owned land is 10 ha, and 20 ha for owners of private land. CODAGEM prefer to deal with rural credit societies composed of five to thirty members. Credit is paid in kind and includes an insurance premium paid to ANAGSA. A common problem with receiving credit in the form of fertilizers and pesticides is that transportation difficulties mean that inputs often arrive late, delaying sowing and thus increasing the risk of frost damage at the end of the season when the crop is ripening.

In 1989 the average, total per hectare cost of CODAGEM credit packages was 366 000 pesos while the insurance payment for total crop loss was 919 500 pesos per hectare. From this sum the credit plus interest at 46% per annum over ten months, a total of 406K pesos, is deducted to leave 513 500 ha^{-1}. This figure is supposed to cover the cost of cultivation and labour. If a conservative estimate of the average cost of ground preparation and intermediate cultivations is taken to be 250K pesos ha^{-1}, then the farmer is left with 263.5K pesos ha^{-1}. These figures do not take into account additional family labour or the opportunity cost of leaving wage labour to carry out other necessary tasks associated with agriculture. Indeed, the CODAGEM *técnicos* estimated that the cost of producing one hectare of maize on a commercial, mechanized farm could be as high as 1.8 m pesos.

The guarantee price for maize during 1989 was 375K pesos per tonne. Thus, it can be seen that the whole system of credits and insurance appears to be completely inadequate. If the maize harvest is good, depending on the weather, land quality, technological package and seed variety, 1–3 tonnes of maize will be produced per hectare, yielding a market value 350K to 1.2 m pesos. This is often bearly sufficient to pay off the credit, let alone cover the cost of cultivation and other labours.

As a result, many people in San Felipe have become heavily indebted to either CODAGEM or BANRURAL and have no means of repayment. Furthermore, once a debt has gone unpaid, no further credit can now be obtained. Little wonder then that many of the producers of San Felipe del Progreso talk about becoming "*endrogado*" (drugged, or perhaps addicted) by the credit.

A further problem associated with the acceptance of credit and insurance, is the need to delay the harvest until ANAGSA staff have visited and assessed the loss. During the months of November and December one of the most common queries posed by producers who have taken up production credits concerns the progress of the insurance assessors, and the likely date of their visit to the community. It would seem then, that maize credit rarely fulfils either its production objectives or any useful social support role. Furthermore, there seem to be some potentially serious environmental and health-related externalities.

In conclusion, it becomes clear that, as a result of the institutional programmes for promoting modernization, the producers in the region have modified their production systems and rely more and more on the decisions of institutional employees for the initiation of each new production cycle, becoming captive purchasers of agricultural inputs.

Examples of modifications thus induced in the maize production systems of the region include:

(1) The elimination of mixed cropping such as maize with beans and squash.
(2) The necessity of managing financial resources far greater than any they have previously had to deal with, which supposes a new productive rationality.
(3) Producers find themselves dependent on a bureaucracy which tells them what, when and how to sow.

(4) They become tied into a cycle of debt from which it becomes increasing difficult to escape.
(5) A great deal of time and money has to be spent on bureaucratic negotiations.

Having reviewed some of the organizational and institutional aspects of agricultural production, it is now time to move on to the idea of livelihood systems.

IDENTIFYING LIVELIHOOD SYSTEMS

Rivera's (1989) concept of household strategies can be equated with the combination of activities which Conway (1990) associates with the livelihood system. Rivera identifies three major strategies, based on how households distribute their labour resources among various spheres of activity. Here, in order to avoid confusion with the survival strategies which individuals follow, Conway's concept of livelihood systems is preferred to Rivera's notion of household strategies. Every individual has a survival strategy; the livelihood system represents the more or less coordinated sum of the survival strategies of its individual members.

Following Rivera's (1989) outline, agricultural subsistence systems refer to households which opt to deploy their land, labour and capital resources in agricultural production of both use and exchange values in order to achieve their reproduction and reduce risks to a minimum. Accumulation systems consist of expanding the capacity for agricultural production or, alternatively, insertion into other sectors of the economy in order to generate profit so that two types of producer can be seen to develop from accumulation systems, namely capitalized family farmers and rural entrepreneurs.

The third type of system is the basic survival system, representing those households which do not have sufficient land to secure their reproduction and are forced to employ their labour in whatever spheres of activity afford them the possibility of survival.

The 105 households covered by the livelihood systems survey were categorized into six different groups using cluster analysis. In order to add more depth to the analysis, cluster membership was cross-tabulated against a variety of other variables. Rather than present this information in tabular form, the data will be used in conjunction with field-work notes to provide case study-like descriptions of the different systems. However, as the majority of households fall into the basic survival systems categories, the aggregated data relating to the other systems are based on very small samples, implying that they should be treated with caution.

Basic survival systems

Given the average size of holdings in the study area (c. 2 ha), it is not surprising that classification on the basis of labour allocation identified the vast majority (78.1%) of households as basic survival units. Two sub-groups were identified however, which are differentiated on the basis of the relative emphasis given to on-farm and off-farm labour.

Those households which emphasize on-farm activities have access to marginally more land than those which emphasize off-farm wage labour (just over two hectares as opposed to just under two), although the difference is not significant. The more important difference lies in the ratio of on-farm workers to land area, with those households emphasizing on-farm work employing 2.63 times the quantity of labour per hectare, suggesting a well-defined strategy to concentrate labour resources on the holding. There is also a difference in the number of domestic and craft workers per hectare, with on-farm basic survival households having, on average, 47% more domestic and craft workers available per hectare of land farmed. The most significant point here is that the off-farm wage labour sub-group appeared to be substituting mainly female domestic and craft workers for male on-farm workers as they concentrate their economic efforts on obtaining cash income from the labour market.

In terms of location, as might be expected, both of the basic survival system groups are located in resource-poor communities (88% of those emphasizing wage labour and 74% of those concentrating labour on-farm). Moreover, households in the cluster which stresses wage labour are concentrated (62%) in communities with access to good roads and transport systems, while those emphasizing on-farm labour are concentrated (62%) in isolated settlements, suggesting one plausible explanation of why labour allocation differs between the two.

With regard to agricultural production, the difference between the two sub-groups is highlighted by the greater diversity of crop species and maize varieties cultivated by those households which devote more labour to the land. On average 21% more crops and 23% more maize varieties are utilized by these households. On-farm basic survival systems also tend to employ more agricultural capital and use credit more frequently than those which opt for wage-labour survival, although both sub-groups have similar livestock value to land area ratios of 2.4 m pesos per hectare of land.

All of the households which were identified as basic survival units tend to make significant use of communal "free goods", using a variety of wild medicinal and edible plant species and, together with subsistence agriculturalists, being the only groups which undertake hunting and fishing activities.

The most significant characteristic of basic survival households, however, is the extent to which they employ labour resources in all spheres of economic activity considered by this study. Not only do they undertake on-farm labour, domestic and craft work, wage labour and, to a lesser extent, commercial activities, they also participate in a greater number of minor activities than any other group.

Agricultural subsistence systems

This cluster of households, although the third largest, only accounts for 11 out of the total of 105 households. They are distinguished by the fact that all of their economically active members work on the holding and/or at domestic and craft activities in the home. Subsistence agriculture households seem to be distributed fairly equally between resource-poor and resource-rich communities but tend to be concentrated (nine out of eleven) in communities with access to good roads.

The average size of holding is three hectares (including 1.3 ha of privately owned land) which must provide for an average of six people. This group tends, however, to have better access to the more productive, irrigated land than any group save the agricultural accumulation cluster. The greater productivity and stability of irrigated cropping systems, means that this group appears to be relatively resource-rich.

Besides cultivating a wide variety of crop plants and maize varieties, as was anticipated, subsistence agriculture households tend to make use of the full range of natural resources at their disposal. What is interesting, however, is the fact that the livestock value to land area ratio among this group is lower than any other, which may suggest a greater awareness of the problems associated with high stocking rates.

Field-work notes indicate that this group of households also tend to achieve high standards of infrastructural maintenance; their *zanjas* are regularly excavated, *Agaves* are replanted and maize fields tend to be hand rather than chemically weeded. It was among this group that there seemed to be the greatest awareness of the problems associated with the adoption of external inputs and devoting high proportions of available labour to off-farm wage earning activities. However, rather than identifying problems intrinsic to the technology, a more personal analysis was highlighted, which attributed the environmental problems associated with using agrochemicals to the user group being "lazy" and "not wanting to get their hands dirty".

As suggested by Rivera (1989), subsistence agriculture households tend to produce and sell a varied range of products. In San Felipe del Progreso subsistence agriculture households tend to be very active in the production and sale of craftwork such as weaving and embroidery and the local *Agave* beer, *pulque*.

Accumulation systems

Together, agricultural and diversification accumulation systems account for just 8.6% of the households studied. As for the subsistence agriculture cluster, there seems to be no particular pattern to the location of their holdings. While it may have been anticipated that they were likely to be concentrated in resource-rich areas, or areas with access to all-weather roads, there is no evidence to substantiate this. This may be partly understood by looking at the nature of their land resources and activities.

Both groups have access to private land. Those units which emphasize agriculture have an average total land holding of just over five hectares (1.4 ha of which are irrigated) including two hectares of private land, whilst those which stress diversification have an average of 2.75 ha total land area, none of which is irrigated although half of it (1.4 ha) is privately owned.

Agriculture is a prominent feature in the livelihood systems of both sub-groups, the main difference being in land area and livestock value. Both groups tend to plant a variety of crops including more commercial species such as potatoes, but make relatively little use of wild plants and animals. The two sub-groups are clearly distinguished by livestock numbers, however, with those favouring agricultural intensification owning animals to an average total value of 25.34 m pesos, compared to only 7 m pesos for those by whom diversification is favoured.

Of the five agricultural accumulation households identified by the analysis, three owned flocks of 20 or more sheep, one was producing chickens and eggs in a relatively intensive system and the other was fattening 50 head of beef cattle using concentrated feeds on a small ranch which included ten hectares of cultivated land. The overall intensity of livestock production within this small sub-group is demonstrated by the fact that, at 5.05 m pesos/ha, the ratio of livestock value to land area is more than double that of any other group.

Both groups are involved in commercial activities such as having a small store at the house from where they sell basic foodstuffs. Those which put more emphasis on commercial activities tend also to stock goods such as clothing, hardware and perhaps agricultural inputs. They may also be involved in buying crops, livestock and craftwork from the surrounding area and either selling-on to wholesale businesses or making the round of local markets such as Ixtlahuaca, San Felipe, Atlacomulco, San Bernabé and even Toluca.

Left agriculture

This group contains just three families, in all of which the male head of household has permanent employment as a wage labourer. Two work in factories in the nearby town of Atlacomulco and one is an electrician in San Felipe del Progreso. They are classified as having left agriculture rather than as not participating in agriculture because, without exception, all come from farming families and own houses built on *ejido*[1] land.

Not only do these families not participate in agriculture, neither were they recorded as utilizing any of the available natural resources such as edible and medicinal plants. Although all of the adult males were born and raised in *ejido* households and have houses built on *ejido* land, they are no longer producers.

THE DYNAMICS OF LIVELIHOOD SYSTEMS

The preceding sections of this chapter have identified livelihood systems and added some flesh to the bones by way of aggregate statistics. The images which have been developed are, however, rather static, with only an occasional allusion to the dynamic nature of livelihood systems. In order to facilitate an appreciation of change and the factors which precipitate it, four short life-histories will now be detailed before going on to discuss some of the implications of particular systems for the socio-cultural and biophysical environment. The names used in the following life-histories have been changed in order to preserve the anonymity of the individuals and families involved.

María and Francisco Reyes: surviving at the margins

Francisco (Pancho) Reyes was born in 1956, the second son of a family of three boys and four girls. His grandfather had been one of the original recipients of land when the local hacienda was dissolved and the *ejido* was founded in 1939. His father inherited two hectares of rain-fed land in 1954 which, supplemented by income from occasional agricultural labouring, sustained the young family.

When he reached the age of six, Pancho enrolled at the local primary school. He only stayed for one year, however, after which he began work tending the family's flock of 20 *criollo* sheep. Although both his mother and father are able to speak and understand the local Mazahua language, Pancho understands very little and is also unable to read and write other than the most simple of Spanish sentences.

As the family grew, so the need to supplement the family income increased. "There was very little to eat in those days and no money for luxuries, so I decided to take myself to the city to see what could be had

---

[1]The *ejido* is a community land holding granted to groups of peasants who enjoy usufruct rights to cultivate individual parcels.

there." Pancho first went to Mexico City in 1971. In 1976 he met María and they were married the following year. María had come from the State of Morelos originally, moving to the city in the early 1970s to work in domestic service. She can both read and write and also speaks Náhuatl.

Together they managed to start saving some money with the intention of moving back to San Felipe and building their own house on a small plot of land which had been promised to Pancho by his father. Towards the end of 1977 María gave birth to their first child, Victoria. Unfortunately early in the next year the construction company which Pancho had been working for went bankrupt and he lost his job. After several months of odd jobs and unemployment, Pancho found himself on one of the city's large rubbish heaps, looking for work among the rubbish-pickers.

> When I looked at that place and saw the little kids picking through all the stinking rubbish and all the bloody rats running around them I thought to myself, Pancho you may be poor but you're not this bloody desperate. So I decided that we should go home to San Felipe and that I could find work there.

When they first moved back to the municipality there was not much work to be had. María stayed with Pancho's parents while he split his time between the family holding, days labouring on other fields and occasional periods in the city. In 1981 María gave birth to their second child and a chance encounter with a distant relative in Mexico City found Pancho employment on a building site, where he continued to work more or less permanently until 1986, coming home only at weekends and for the sowing and harvest of the family's fields.

In 1984 Pancho asked the *ejido* authorities and the Agrarian Reform Committee to grant him a small patch of land in the community. He was registered and received his ¼ hectare plot the following year. Although the land was sloping and of rather poor quality (sticky and difficult to cultivate) Pancho cleared the larger stones and planted his first crop in the same year. In 1986 he set about building himself and his family a house.

First, the land had to be levelled using a pick and shovel. Then he used some of the large stones from the field for the first metre of the walls, taking it up to two metres with adobe which he made from clay and pine needles at the edge of a small lagoon, and then carried three kilometres up the hill to the site. The roof is of corrugated tar paper resting on poles cut and dragged from a small patch of community forest on the top of a nearby hill.

In total, Pancho reckons that it took him two full months of work to build his house. When the house was finished and María and the children had moved in, Pancho's father gave him ⅜ ha of his 2 ha plot of land, giving Pancho and María a total of ⅝ ha. The land his father had given him was of better quality than the newly cultivated land that he had obtained from the *ejido*. After four years of cultivation and the addition of organic manure, however, the new plot has improved in texture and structure.

The slope makes the land liable to erosion but Pancho has spent time constructing and maintaining *zanjas*, and by constructing a stone wall at the downslope boundary ,of the plot has initiated the gradual process of terrace formation. On the upslope boundary he has constructed another *zanja* to channel water away from the back of the house, and a small dam to store it, offering a transient source of water for the donkeys, chickens and turkeys that María tends.

In 1988 the couple decided to experiment with keeping bees, intending to sell the honey to raise a little extra cash. The bees were purchased and seemed to be making a successful start until June when the hive was killed, according to Pancho and María, by insecticides being sprayed on a neighbouring plot of land.

On their own land the couple plant mainly maize. On the *ejido* plot this is usually mixed with broad beans. If the maize fails to germinate the spaces are filled with barley and oats which are used as fodder for the donkey and its foal. At the beginning of the wet season hen and turkey chicks are purchased and, once the crop plants are out of reach, allowed to scratch around in the field for weeds and insects. The couple also bought a young pig during the 1988–89 dry season which they fed on household waste and maize which had spoiled in storage. The pig was sold in June 1989 to buy a little extra fertilizer for the maize crop.

Pancho applied herbicide for the first time in 1989 because he said, "I didn't have time to weed by hand". He does not have sufficient land to apply for credit from official government sources, however, and when asked about credit replied, "No, it is better to buy the inputs, the maize doesn't pay enough to cover the credit".

When the crop is ready for harvest Pancho finishes his work in the city and returns home. The outlying land is tackled first and the crop gathered in as quickly as possible. The maize in the house plot is harvested with less haste and straw left standing to be cut a little at a time which, says Pancho, helps the soil to retain its humidity. Once the harvest is completed Pancho and María may take the opportunity to glean over the fields of some of the larger producers in the region. In this way they obtained 2 *costales* (C 120 kg) in onc afternoon in November 1989.

The house has no water or electricity. Water is collected from a spring approximately 2 km from the house and carried home on the donkey. The donkey is also used for bringing back firewood from the small patch of community forest. Pancho complains of people from other communities coming to steal wood from the local forest. The *ejido* has organized tree planting schemes and a forest guard rota to try and combat this problem.

During the 1988–89 dry season Pancho spent his weekends working with other members of the *ejido* to install water pipes from the bottom of the valley to the upper reaches of the hill where they built a 10 000-litre storage tank. The *ejido* group which carried out the work are now waiting for a pump which is needed to transfer water from the well to the tank. By the end of 1991 Pancho hoped to have piped water at the house. Talking about community projects in general, however, Pancho said that they were often not very successful "the people are divided now and at times they don't want to work."

With the best of growing seasons Pancho and María reckon that their ⅝ ha could provide their family (since March 1989 they have had another girl and there is now another baby on the way) with sufficient maize to last the year. Really good years are few and far between these days, however: like many of the people of San Felipe del Progreso, the Reyes believe that the weather has been deteriorating for ten or twenty years now.

To be self-sufficient from agriculture they say that they would need 1 ha for maize production and another two from which to earn sufficient money to buy "the shopping" (*las compras*). However, Pancho says that he would not want to work full-time as a farmer.

In the country (*el campo*) it is clean and safe and the tortillas don't cost anything. In the city you can earn money but everything is so expensive. What we really need are permanent sources of work here in the community. That way I could earn money and look after the family and fields at the same time.

Federico and Amparo Hernández: disenchanted with the State

Federico and Amparo live in an *ejido* community on the fertile plain of the Toluca Ixtlahuaca Valley. They live together with their five children (four sons and a daughter aged between 15 and two years) and Federico's mother and sister, after inheriting the land and house when his father died in 1984. Prior to his father's death, Federico had worked in Mexico City on the construction sites since the age of 14, having reached the fifth grade in primary school.

The house was originally a two-roomed adobe structure but Federico has put his construction skills to use and built another two rooms of breeze-block and reinforced concrete. The house has electricity and piped water, and is on the sewer system. The family farm consists of two hectares of irrigated land which is situated two kilometres from the house which always causes problems "whether they be related to getting the fertilizers onto the land or getting the harvest out."

Everybody lends a hand in the fields when necessary and the women and children look after a variety of around thirty hens, turkeys and ducks which are sold, when needs be, in San Felipe market on a Sunday. Nobody works away from the house on a permanent basis, although all of them undertake

occasional waged labour in the area and Federico may take a few weeks
work in the city if extra money is needed. All of the family's land is
dedicated to maize production, until recently under a CODAGEM credit
scheme. With the specified package of inputs the land will yield up to 2.5
tonnes of maize per hectare, even though Federico sows exclusively his own
pink maize seed. Irrigation water from the local reservoir is a highly prized
resource, although not without its problems: "most of the people have their
land close to the irrigation canals and really benefit from the water but I
have my parcels at a distance of 1.5 km from the canal and, whereas they
get water twice a year, there is only enough for me to irrigate once".

Apart from a wheelbarrow and the usual machetes, shovels and rakes,
Federico rents all of the capital equipment he needs to cultivate his plot. He
rents a tractor and driver for the main preparatory cultivations at a cost of
200 000 pesos per hectare and a close friend lends him mules and a plough
for the *escardas* at a cost of 50 000 pesos/ha. At harvest time Federico also
hires a few workers whom he pays in kind with maize and refreshments.

Federico no longer gets credit from CODAGEM as he got into debt
which he is still trying to repay. He is very bitter about the way he has been
treated by both CODAGEM and the insurance agency, ANAGSA, and
about the cropping restrictions placed on irrigated land by the SARH.

> We have never had any benefit from government programmes around here,
> nothing has improved because the government is nothing more than promises,
> it never fulfils its word. They never support anything but maize production and
> maize is the product that pays the least. They charge the highest rates of inter-
> est and give us no time to pay. The insurance is useless, they never pay up,
> that's why I don't work with insurance any more, it's pure stories. I wouldn't
> sell my harvest to CONASUPO either, the standards are too high and they
> never pay on time. No, I sell to the middlemen, they pay well and they pay
> before they take the maize.
>
> What we need here are more places to work in the community, because us
> producers are the poorest, most fucked-up bunch of people. We could organize
> ourselves within a Union of Ejidos or a collective and form a group to start an
> industry of some sort. Maize production is no use to us. SARH, INI and
> BANRURAL are all the same, they never fulfil their promises. The SARH has
> *técnicos* but they don't help us. The INI has machinery, but they don't help us
> either. Pure promises, nothing else. Well it might offend but I believe that it
> would be better if we producers were the *técnicos* because many of the agrono-
> mists (graduates) don't know anything about our little plots of land.

When I asked Federico what he would like to see by way of help from the
government he said:

> They should sell us improved seed at a lower price, that would help. If the
> SARH *técnicos* were more efficient that would help too. I would like to see the
> credit arriving on time so that people could sow their fields on time. The gov-

ernment should employ more capable people in CODAGEM, not the mediocre ones. Why don't the INI help the real, authentic indigenous people like us poor whores. The government should not accept corruption amongst their officials. There are various government agencies which are supposedly there to help producers, but it's all lies, it is always those who have money that benefit.

Emiliano and Eugenia Martínez: living from the land

Emiliano Martínez was born in 1948, the youngest son of a relatively well-off peasant family. Although his father had worked as a foreman on the local *hacienda*, he had been instrumental in the formation of the *ejido*, resulting in him being nominated secretary to the first ejidal commissary and becoming commissary himself in the 1950s.

Emiliano's father received four hectares of land when the *ejido* was first formed, including two hectares with access to irrigation plus an additional two hectares when the community was granted further land in 1962. Although Emiliano has always worked on the family holding, his eldest brother used to go to Mexico City to work on the construction sites during the 1970s. Towards the end of the 1970s his brother was granted two hectares of *ejido* land and was part-way through building himself a house there when he was killed in a road traffic accident. The house-building was abandoned and his brother's widow and son remained living in the family house.

Emiliano and Eugenia were married in 1980 when Emiliano was 32, two years before the death of his father. When their father died, the eight hectares of land were split equally between Emiliano and his surviving brother Carmelo, who completed the work on the temporarily abandoned house before moving in with his wife and two children. Since then Carmelo and his wife have set up a small bakery where they produce bread rolls which are sold locally in the community.

Emiliano and Eugenia now live in the original family house with Emiliano's mother, sister-in-law and nephew who is now 16 years old. Emiliano and his wife have not had any children of their own. Their land is devoted mainly to maize which is inter-cropped with broad beans and squash around the house. Pink, blue and yellow maize varieties are sown separately and in rotation on the rain-fed land. The pink because of its rapid maturation, the blue for its flavoursome *tortillas* and the yellow for its potential yield.

The hectare of irrigated land is sown with a hybrid maize monocrop to which Emiliano applies the recommended doses of nitrogen and phosphate fertilizers, mixed with manure from the families flock of sheep; Emiliano considers regular applications of organic manure to be essential for the "health" of the soil. "The fertilizers are not worth anything without the manure. Without good manure the land just gets poorer every year."

Although herbicides are used on the irrigated land, they are not part of a credit package; rather they are used because the land is situated some 3 km from the house and Emiliano does not consider it to be worthwhile cutting the weeds and carrying the fodder back to the house. Half a hectare of land is usually sown to forage oats which are cut whole and dried before feeding to the livestock. In recent years, they have also sown a few furrows of potatoes for domestic consumption.

The flock of sheep is kept at a minimum of about 10 animals but may rise to 20 if the family are planning to make a large purchase. When Emiliano's mother was in need of hospital treatment three years ago, five sheep were sold to cover the expenses. During 1989 the family had one ox, two cows and two calves. For the main preparatory cultivations Emiliano and Carmelo work jointly, bringing their oxen together to form the team. The *escardas* are carried out using a single horse, Emiliano has two and a foal, which he hopes to sell for 2 m pesos in a couple of years' time.

As well as the usual assortment of pigs and poultry, the family also keep as many as a dozen rabbits in hutches at the side of the house. The rabbits are slaughtered for home consumption or occasionally sold to neighbours. The livestock are mostly cared for by the women, although Emiliano usually has something to say or ask about the animals when he arrives at the house after a day in the fields.

The women also make use of the sheep's wool which they spin and weave into *gabanes*, *capas* and *fajas*, all items of traditional clothing. All of the women in the family wear traditional clothing although Emiliano and his nephew dress in Western-style slacks and shirts. Eugenia and the other women also take on orders from around the community which they make up either with wool from their own flock or wool provided by those submitting orders.

Emiliano collects *agua miel* from which he makes *pulque*. Besides his own plants, he rents others at 5000 pesos per plant. Also, after he has finished with them and the plants have died, he is obliged to replace any which failed to reproduce vegetatively. The *pulque* takes up to two weeks to ferment after which it is sold locally at 800 pesos per litre.

The total production of maize is usually between five and seven tonnes per year. Up to two tonnes may be sold to the middlemen soon after harvest and then smaller quantities are sold to local shops as and when money is needed. If larger amounts of cash are needed animals to the required amount are sold either to itinerant middlemen, or occasionally to the butcher in Santa Ana Nichi.

Juan Coyote: a well-travelled entrepreneur

Juan Coyote is married to Angélica; together they have nine children; the eldest is 25 years old, married, with two young children of his own and living in a newly constructed breeze-block and concrete house, built on land given to him by Juan when the couple were married. The youngest of Angél-ost two others in childbirth and one from pneumonia at the age of three.

Juan was born in 1936 and worked at home on his father's 5 ha holding until he was 30, when he went to find work in Toluca. Angélica stayed at home with the children, Juan returning at weekends to help out with agricultural work. "I was always looking for a way to make more money in those days, so when they offered to guide me, I went wetback up to the United States." Juan worked in the USA for two years in which time he managed to save up enough money to buy himself his first pick-up truck. Since then he has not looked back.

Today, through a variety of well-taken opportunities and gambles, Juan has become a politically important actor on the local scene. On his return from the United States he bought ten hectares of land from a local rancher and built himself a small house there. More recently he has built a new house in the centre of the local village which is served by running water, electricity and a sewer system.

Juan's land is all rain-fed. Six hectares are sown to maize and worked with the aid of credit from BANRURAL. In 1988 Juan planted several rows of potatoes, he was pleased with the yield but was not able to obtain credit to expand production in 1989. One or two hectares are usually planted to forage oats on a rotational basis in order to rest the land after maize production.

Juan is well-versed in the history of the development of the local community and *ejido* and was a prime mover in the establishment of the local agricultural technical college, the health centre and the new classrooms at the primary school. In 1984 he helped to obtain a State grant for the founding of a communal dairy unit. The information which Juan gave should probably be treated with some caution, but it appears that the community were not prepared to give land for the construction of the unit and so Juan allowed it to be built on his own land, adjoining the technical college:

> They [the state government] offered us 20 m pesos of credit for an intensive milking system and the *ejidatarios* put it to the vote, but they weren't interested in a collective dairy unit. Then we reduced the agreement to 6 m pesos for a sheep unit to be put in the same place but they didn't want that either, the *ejidatarios* and the authorities said that they didn't want it on communal land and that they didn't want all the bother of managing the unit, they didn't want to receive anything.
>
> Then I, as a private landowner, donated half a hectare of land for the building of the stables; and there it is waiting for the day . . . Well they [the government] gave us the opportunity to improve ourselves. They gave us credit with which we bought five rams and 200 sheep which were imported from the USA.

The whole lot went into the stables and we worked there for two years with the
ejidatarios and in those days we hoped that we would still be operating there
today. But we don't have any sheep any more; we had problems due to a lack
of management.

The problem to which Juan was referring was a liver fluke infestation. The
stables had been installed without a reliable source of drinking water for the
sheep. When the supply failed, the pedigree Suffolk flock was herded down
to a stream where they were left to pasture. Once the supply was re-estab-
lished the flock was returned to the stables only to start dying from the liver
fluke infestation which they had picked up from the wet land around the
stream. Vets from the local agricultural college pointed out that because the
local *criollo* sheep seem to have an endemic level of liver fluke infestation
which is rarely sufficient to kill them, the problem was not perceived in
advance.

Don Juan continued to relate his story thus:

Right now we have a chicken-fattening project which is giving us good results
but we have the idea to rehabilitate the stables with more sheep and continue
giving the opportunity to the *ejidatarios* who truly want to work and improve
themselves and, well, change their lives.

Going onto another subject then, we are now seeing the restlessness caused
by our failure to obtain the right credits, the *ejidatarios* want credits from
BANRURAL but we are only sowing maize and that isn't very productive,
maize doesn't produce good [economic] results. What we need to do now is
change crops, we want to get some potato projects going, they would give good
results. Well, we would be earning no more than a million pesos if we could
produce two or three tonnes of maize per hectare, when with a good yield of
potatoes we could be getting 20 m pesos. With all costs included, planting a
hectare of potatoes would cost us 10 m pesos and it would yield 20 to 25 million . . . what I'm trying to say here is that we are only utilizing 30% to 40%
of our potential.

I believe that that [producing potatoes] is what we ought to do, but we have
to put more effort into it, because if we don't get one or two *ejidatarios* sowing
a few hectares of potatoes so that the others can see that the potato is an
effective crop, we are not going to develop. In this community we already have
an effective trajectory whereby if one person doesn't get ahead nobody follows
them. They don't go ahead with projects on their own because they don't know
how to and they believe they will lose a quantity [of money] which they don't
have. So I believe it would be most effective for us to start a project in order
that the others would follow us, but with a good credit. With the support of a
good credit we could achieve progress and if . . . I'm not saying that the people
here are useless, that they don't know how to do anything . . . if it's a good
idea they just need to see a project producing good results and they will follow,
that is the only way. Chicken, pig and beef fattening and rearing projects,
potato production projects they would all work, the people here are working
people, the only thing they need to see first is an effective project giving good
results and then they would all join in and work.

Q. So, it seems that one problem is that credit is only available for maize production?

Yes yes, the problem right now is that credit is only available for maize and even that is hardly sufficient, but we are still doing it, for no other reason than custom (*pero pués lo estamos haciendo y nada más como costumbre*). But I am restless now and have already sent a letter to the President of the Republic complaining that that [credit for maize production] is not effective and, moreover, it is because of the bad management by bank administrators that we are unable to derive any benefit with this small credit that they give to the *ejidatarios* for maize.

For [this community] we need more frequent credit of some 10 m pesos to each *ejidatario* for potato production and some livestock projects with good credit too, and one or two good tractors for the community in order to be able to carry out the necessary work and ox teams because some poor peasants don't even have ox teams and every *ejidatario* should at least have a pair of draught animals. And that is the work we want to undertake, with good credit we can recuperate other resources. It is not to have luxuries, the greatest need in this community is to be able to feed, dress and educate our children. . . . We have no other objectives, we don't want money to buy luxury cars, no no, what we need here are good houses, and a little production in order to be able to cover the costs of educating our children. I want to see a future when we will not be able to say that we are isolated here in the mountains, overlooked and forgotten by the government; no, we have good land and we are only an hour's journey from the state capital [Toluca]. We already have schools and teachers, what preoccupies us most now is economic remuneration so that we can afford to clothe and educate our children properly.

Angélica runs a small business producing and buying and selling woven and embroidered craftwork. In their house in the centre of the community, Angélica and Juan have set aside a room where they have installed looms and, more recently, sewing machines. They provide work for five or six women in the house and also make the rounds of the community buying woven and embroidered goods from private houses. Angélica takes up the story:

We as women, as artisans, know that when Jiménez Cantú was State Governor (1975–81) it was a time when we could move [sell] our products. Because we could talk to him, we told him of all the problems we used to have, that we couldn't sell our goods. I'm not just talking of three or five women but of the whole community; well girls just twelve years of age have already started to grasp the craft of embroidery, what we lack are markets. But Cantú ordered that CASART[2] should buy our produce and yes, they bought all we could produce.

---

[2]CASART is a State-run chain of stores which sells indigenous Mexican art and crafts to the public.

When Cantú's term was over we wanted to continue in the same way, but Alfredo del Mazo (1981–87) [the new governor] wouldn't talk to us and since that time we haven't sold a single item to CASART. Well we have already spoken with Ramón Beteta [governor 1987–89] well he was the same [as Cantú] he ordered CASART to purchase our products, but up until this moment they still haven't purchased a thing.

Our situation is very sad since for us, the women, it is the only way we can work to feed, clothe and educate our children. So, yes, we demand that they buy our work from us, because if we can't do artisan work and sell it in order to give our children a good education, having a well-developed education complex [school buildings and facilities] is worth nothing to us. We need money to buy them all their (*útiles*) [texts, exercise books, pens, pencils etc]. Right now the men are having to go to Mexico [City] to work but that is nothing compared to the traumas (*friega*) a mother has to put up with in the home all day with her children . . .

I need a pencil! I need a book! I need a contribution for this or that!

. . . and who is it who has to respond? Well it's always the mum.

I think that the little that their dads are earning isn't even enough to give them something to eat and so, if we thought there was an opportunity, and that there really was no market for our craftwork but that the government could give us some industry so that both men and women could work, I think that we could get ahead. Why? Because we would not be financial prisoners (*atenidas*) until Saturdays when the men arrive home, waiting to see if they have brought us any money. But I think that a mum's worst trauma is that every day the children come with . . .

Give me 100 pesos! I'm going to school now and I don't have any money! Well haven't you even got anything for me to eat?

The truth is that the government has not heard us. We even tried to start exporting our products ourselves. We had all the paper work sorted out, all we needed to do was take the documents to the Home Office (*gobernación*) for them to counter-sign and we would have had an export permit. And I don't know what happened there but they didn't accept them and the documents were detained there and never submitted. I don't know who held up those papers but we never got our export licence. If the government had helped us I believe we would have been better off by now.

Summary

There are many factors conditioning livelihood systems then, from demographic and geographic to political and ecological. The type of social relation and the actors and institutions with which the producers interact, all play their part in conditioning the path that any one household will follow in the pursuance of its overall reproduction. What has been shown here, though, is that human agency (the intentional acts of ordinary men and women) also plays a very important part in the equation. Given a range of options, under a variety of socio-economic conditions, different people are likely to tackle the same problems in different ways.

Livelihood systems are conjuncturally specific, not just based on the demographic cycle, but on the prevailing natural, economic and policy environments. If members of a household can make the right socio-political connections they may hope to benefit more from available help. Power is very transient, however, and what may be an advantageous association today may become a millstone tomorrow.

It is clear that size of holding, size of family, and the age and gender structure of the household in combination are extremely important factors: without land there is no agriculture, while a lack of labour means that activities in other economic spheres cannot be entered into without resulting in a certain degree of neglect or abuse of the natural economy. That is, the processes which govern the regeneration of the natural productive potential and stability of the agroecosystem.

The general characteristics and dynamics of livelihood systems seem to suggest that the domestic economy is the sphere within which all of the other activities that household members enter into are articulated. The domestic economy is largely the preserve of women and children and it seems to be they that have to adapt most to change.

If increasing family size means that male members must migrate to earn more money, it is the domestic economy which provides the labour to maintain agricultural activities. If a decision is taken to use herbicides to reduce the time needed for manual weeding operations, it is the women and children left at home who suffer most. Their diets are impoverished and they must spend more time searching for fodder with which to feed the animals.

Thus, when available labour in the domestic economy becomes stretched to its limits, it is the environment which suffers. It is the socio-cultural and environmental implications of different livelihood systems which are the focus of the final section of this chapter.

LIVELIHOOD SYSTEMS: SOME SOCIO-CULTURAL AND ENVIRONMENTAL IMPLICATIONS

Socio-cultural implications

Economic activity and cultural identity are closely bound together. Passing time in the community, participating in communal projects, developing local social networks and practising traditional production techniques provide a framework within which traditional knowledge has value and group identity or culture can develop along autochthonous lines.

When a local economy can, for whatever reasons, no longer sustain the local population or when the economic system of an invasive culture penetrates into the local arena, people are drawn into a wider environment. Whether new conditions actually penetrate the local milieu (as in the case of State promotion of off-farm energy-intensive production systems) or the people migrate to participate in the market economy, frames of reference indigenous to the local milieu are devalued. In order to associate, communicate and enter into productive processes in the wider economy, people must learn new frames of reference, new ways of perceiving the world which are often contradictory to those which serve as the matrix that guides coevolutionary processes in the local arena.

Peasants who leave their communities to work in the city are often ridiculed there when they speak in their native tongue. They are introduced into a society in which individual endeavour is praised and communal action often absent. When they return to their home communities the contradictions between the two cultures are internalized. While it may be quite evident to them that new technologies form an uneasy alliance with their own indigenous epistemology, their exposure to the supposed merits of the "industrial" culture and the market economy may encourage them to adopt patterns of market behaviour simply in order to refute an acquired perception of indigenous "backwardness". They resist the notion by complying with the model even when they do not possess sufficient knowledge of how the model actually works.

The consequences of such contradictory behaviour are expressed in the loss of social cohesion which may translate into environmental degradation as each household struggles in its own way to understand and comply with the model with which it is presented.

Environmental implications

As the average size of producers' plots has decreased, more and more people have had to look to waged employment in distant urban centres, as a means of ensuring their families' survival. Although it is often women who make the day-to-day decisions concerning agricultural production, it is still the men who decide upon the overall strategy. To many of them, the use of agrochemicals represents a reduction in the time required for manual weeding, allowing them to spend more time earning cash on the construction sites in Mexico City. The fact that the women and children who remain at home have one less source of "free" food and animal fodder, appears to be given less consideration.

Under the BANRURAL and CODAGEM credit programmes the application of wide spectrum herbicides such as Atrazine is obligatory. Hence, in place of the traditional inter-cropping of maize, beans and squash, the acceptance of credit dictates the cultivation of a maize monocrop. The use of herbicides kills the numerous "weed" species associated with indigenous production systems, which have traditionally been used as green vegetables for human consumption and/or fodder for their domestic animals. Reduced availability of green vegetables from the household plot also increases pressure on communal resources which themselves, are quite evidently diminishing

The "weeds" also have great utility in erosion control as the interlocking root mass, which they form together with the crop plants, has the effect of binding the soil together and so protecting it from the torrential summer rains. Denuded of the weed cover, any small holes in the soil allow water to enter and so the formation of small rills begins. If left unrepaired the rills soon become gullies which, in turn, may go on to form badlands, completely devoid of any productive value.

In the upland areas the eroded soil is carried further downslope in the many small streams and rivers, its ultimate destination, the local reservoir which is slowly silting up. Thus, neglect of traditional slope and water management practices or the replacement of hand by chemical weeding in the upland region of the study area, not only affects the small plots of the producers who live there, but also leads to sedimentation of the reservoir so that those who live and work on the irrigated land in valley have experienced a slow but certain reduction in the amount of water available for irrigation (SARH, 1981).

Also, as plot size has decreased, the number of livestock has tended to increase. Field-work notes suggest that the relative importance of the livestock sub-system has grown significantly in recent years, especially amongst the basic survival system households. Animal products do not figure highly in the diet of the majority of the population, however. It seems that the main reasons for livestock ownership are: as a source of draught power, manure production, and investment. Investment is in terms of the buying in or breeding of livestock, rearing them, and then selling when cash is required—either for an emergency such as the need for medical treatment, for the repayment of credit debts, for the hiring of seasonal labour and/or equipment for agricultural activities, or for a planned expenditure such as is incurred by taking on the responsibility of organizing part of a fiesta, or the marriage of one's children.

It appears then that the "livestock option", represents the chance to extract the maximum possible utility, not just from one's personal resource endowment, but more especially from whatever browsing is available in whatever location. The result is the failure of the forests to regenerate, a general deterioration in the communal resource base, and another important contribution to the process of soil erosion.

CONCLUSIONS

The current work has shown that peasant society which, from the outside at least, appears to be more or less homogeneous in terms of the resources (both natural and socio-economic) at their disposal, may manage overall livelihood systems which are quite distinct. The mixture of elements which compose livelihood systems must be understood if development interventions are to assist small-scale producers in maintaining the productive potential of local agroecosystems.

With regard to the majority of basic survival households identified by the current work, it is clear that any movement in this direction requires either the consolidation of production units into larger "farms", in order to free labour for employment in the cities, or the development of alternative, local employment opportunities. Both of these strategies would facilitate more responsive resource management.

Similar livelihood choices carry different implications for different households, depending on the type of livelihood systems they manage and the quality and quantity of resources at their disposal. While an accumulation system based on agriculture and devoting a significant proportion of available labour to agricultural activities may well be able successfully to integrate chemical inputs into their production systems, the same does not necessarily apply to a basic survival unit.

The relatively resource-rich accumulation systems are better placed to recognize, accommodate and respond to the externalities which may result from the incorporation of agrochemicals. They are likely to be better educated and thus better able to communicate with the suppliers of agrochemicals (whether they be State officials or commercial firms). They are also less dependent on the complementary products which are forgone when wide-spectrum herbicides restrict mixed cropping practices and eradicate associated weed species.

On the other hand, owing to the lesser innate stability of high external input agroecosystems, agricultural accumulation systems are not so well placed if the need should arise to devote labour time to off-farm income-earning activities. In low input systems, a few weeks' absence may have little or no effect on production owing to the preservation of maintenance feedback functions as an integral component of the natural capital of the ecosystem. If, on the other hand, chemical-reliant systems, which depend on industrial capital, are not continually monitored by the farmer, a pest or disease outbreak may devastate the entire crop.

In a similar vein, if an accumulation through diversification household experiments with a new crop, the risks are likely to be less than those experienced by an agricultural subsistence unit, whose livelihood is entirely reliant on what can be produced from the land and animals.

It is also clear that the fate of the peasantry is intimately linked to its cultural existence, sustainability is threatened because cultural integrity has been undermined by "development". Much of the locally developed agroecosystems knowledge is ignored or even responded to with derision by many of the State-employed extension technicians. Rather than aid the producers in the search for solutions to existing problems, State help revolves exclusively around the provision of credit, often in the form of technological packages, which pay little, if any, regard either to the nature of local soils, topographic conditions and production systems or to role of agriculture within overall livelihood systems.

Be this as it may, State agencies such as CODAGEM and BANRURAL represent the only source of external "help" to which the producers have recourse and, despite a certain feeling of betrayal, producers consider State tutelage to be an import factor conditioning livelihood possibilities. It is perhaps not surprising then that, on the receiving end of a one-way flow of information which lauds "modern", scientific technological packages as a panacea to boost productivity and modernize "outdated" agroecosystems, the producers themselves begin to devalue and ignore the lessons which their ancestors accumulated over generations of productive experience.

REFERENCES

CODAGEM (Comite para el Desarrollo Agropecuario del Estado de Mexico) (1988) "Produccion agropecuaria en marcha". *Dos Valles: Revissta del Estado de Mexico*, **1**, (3), 105–109.

Conway, G.R. (1990) In *Systems Theory Applied to Agriculture and the Food Chain* J.G.W. Jones and P.R. Street eds.). Elsevier Applied Science, Barking, Essex, pp. xvi, 365.

Fresco, L.O. and Westphal, E. (1988) "A hierarchical classification of farm systems". *Experimental Agriculture*, **24** 399–419.

Mountjoy, D.C. and Gliessman, S.R. (1988) "Traditional management of a hillside agroecosystem in Tlaxacala, Mexico: an ecologically based maintenance system". *American Journal of Alternative Agriculture*, **3**, (1), 3–10.

Norgaard, R.B. (1984) "Coevolutionary agricultural development". *Economic Development and Cultural Change*, **32**, (3), 525–546.

Rivera, A.R. (1989) "Campesinado: el enfoque de las estrategias del hogar". *Estudios Rurales Latinoamericanos*, **12**, (3), 326–362.

SARH (Secretaria de Agricultura y Recursos Hidraulicos) (1981) "Evaluacion Tecnica, Social y Economica del Proyecto Tepetitlan". SARH unpublished internal document.

Sol de Toluca, No 14 715, 10 July 1989, p. 1 – A

Woodgate, G.R. (1991) "Agreocological possibilities and organisational limits some initial impressions from a Mexican case study". In *Environment and Development in Latin America: the politics of sustainability* Goodman and Redclift (eds.) Manchester University Press, Manchester, pp. 155–183

Woodgate, G.R. (1992) "Sustainability and the fate of the peasantry: the political ecology of livelihood systems in an upland agroecosystem in the central highlands of Mexico. PhD thesis, University of London.

7 Coca, Development and Environment in Bolivia

COLIN SAGE
Wye College, University of London, UK

INTRODUCTION

The international drugs connection linking producers in the South to consumers in the North has a long history but since the early 1980s has become one of the most intractable development problems confronting many Latin American and Caribbean countries. The cultivation, processing and refining of coca leaf, and the international distribution of a powerful derivative to consumers in industrialized countries has been labelled "Latin America's most successful multinational". Yet below the pinnacle of the international cocaine industry, represented by the competing Colombian cartels and lesser national "drug barons", are the hundreds of thousands of peasants and urban poor who have sought a livelihood from the cultivation and processing of coca leaf amidst a prolonged and severe economic recession. Thus, the drugs trade has generated employment, raised rural incomes and stimulated aggregate demand with the consequential benefits for legitimate economic activities. Indeed,

> the coca industry does almost all that the "current view" on rural and agricultural development in lesser-developed countries calls for: it is labour-intensive, decentralized, growth-pole oriented, cottage-industry promoting, and foreign exchange earning. If the coca industry were completely licit and high returns to growers held, it could be the final answer to rural development in economically stagnating areas. (Tullis 1987, p. 257).

Yet while cocaine production appears to increase incomes, the demand for goods and services and overall national production (Franco and Godoy 1992), the United States has sought to impose supply-side controls involving the eradication of coca at source. This has increased pressure on the governments of Bolivia, Peru and Colombia to play a full and active part in the

Strategies for Sustainable Development: Local Agendas for the Southern Hemisphere
Edited by Michael Redclift and Colin Sage. © 1994 John Wiley & Sons Ltd

"war on drugs", with the US offering military and logistical support and tying its disbursement of aid to the achievement of crop-substitution targets. These measures have been accompanied by a discourse that has attempted to create a common language and shared experience between producer and consumer countries. The objective has been to establish a convergence of international sentiment in which drugs are represented as a common plague that undermine and irredeemably transform shared "traditional" values. A useful tool in this respect has been the application of the term "narcotic" to cocaine, which is a stimulant and not an opiate to which "narcotic" correctly applies. This has provided a universal, utilitarian and discreditable prefix, "narco-" that works equally well in Spanish and English (del Olmo 1989). So while coca production and processing fundamentally represents a problem of development (more accurately, distorted development or underdevelopment), it is instead treated as a security issue with a military solution. In this case the globalization of a doctrine of national security (Queiser Morales 1989) has become a very effective mechanism to formulate responses to the challenge of uncertainty, disorder and threats to international social equilibrium.

In the absence of the spectre of "communist aggression", drug diplomacy has become the cornerstone of US foreign policy in much of Andean America in which aid is allocated on the basis of performance in eradication. Yet this is a region-specific tool which has never been used against the Mujhadeen or Pakistan (Lee 1989). On the other hand, a "war on drugs" can trigger responses by traditional enemies and create that heady cocktail, "the narco-guerrilla conspiracy". In Peru, for example, coca eradication programmes involving the aerial spraying of chemical defoliants and biocides probably led to increased Sendero activity (Morales 1989) and has resulted in the convergence of drug control and counter-insurgency into a permanent state of low-intensity conflict.

In 1992 President Fujimori of Peru announced the suspension of eradication efforts involving biological and chemical agents to be replaced by a programme of "alternative development". In Bolivia, this highly ambiguous slogan has been in place for some time, along with the equally transparent "coca por desarrollo". Broadly, this is a policy of agricultural conversion in which farmers are being encouraged to replace coca with high-value agro-export crops. As we shall see, the underlying dynamic of the policy has little to do with "alternatives" but plenty to do with a process of agricultural modernization, in which the objective appears to be to stimulate the emergence of a class of capitalist family farms at the expense of the peasant economy. Intriguingly, while the campaign of opposition to the Bolivian government's programme of alternative development has stimulated an active internal debate about the cultural value of coca, the organizational slogan in 1990 of "militarizacion no, desarrollo si" was equally enigmatic and ambiguous. It is certain that there is a desperate need to give some intellectual content to the notion of "development", especially in the context of a diminishing public sector and retreating state. It is also time to bring to bear some of the concepts developed in the debate around sustainable development to the specific problem of coca and cocaine in Bolivia.

THE DISCOURSE ON SUSTAINABLE DEVELOPMENT

Earlier chapters of this volume have elaborated upon the origin and meaning of sustainable development and so it will not be discussed in detail here. However, it is important to note that some critics have dismissed the term altogether, arguing either that it is merely a rhetorical device with so many different definitions as to be devoid of substance, or alternatively that it serves as a new weapon of conditionality wielded by the North against the poor of the South. As we have seen, there are difficulties in attempting to create universally agreed definitions, but vagueness is not always a problem and multiple meanings should make us beware of the dangers in singular truths. Sustainable development has the ability to convey important underlying principles: productivity, stability, equity, diversity and resilience across the biological, economic and social systems. The objective of sustainable development, then, is to maximize goal achievement across these three systems through an adaptive process of trade-offs, a process that ensures that these are place- and time-specific (Holmberg and Sandbrook 1992). Consequently, sustainable development is not to be seen as a blueprint but as a set of guiding principles in an unfolding, negotiated process in which there are conflicts and dilemmas.

At the grassroots or community level, a strategy for achieving sustainable development is represented by the notion of primary environmental care (PEC) (Pretty and Guijt 1992). This has three essential elements: meeting basic needs and livelihood security; ensuring the optimal use of environmental resources; and the empowerment of groups and communities. While the satisfaction of basic needs has long been a goal of rural development, the key to PEC is the indispensable participation and active involvement of local people in achieving this aim. By building upon local knowledge, indigenous management systems, and an understanding of the existing diversity and complexity of resources in order to strengthen livelihoods, there is a role for outside agencies to facilitate and contribute to sustainable development. But the notion of state institutions or other agencies delivering services and promoting alternative production packages to grateful beneficiaries represents thinking from a different era. The evident failure of this approach to reach sufficient numbers of people, as well as the considerable constraints on public spending and development aid that mark the current era, mean that alternative models of rural development that enable people to meet their own needs are long overdue.

In practice the pusuit of sustainable development has to start where people are in terms of place and their socio-economic and cultural environment. Yet too often development strategies have been dominated by a mindset of top-down thinking, the concentration of power and the centralization of institutions which are often seized-up by bureaucratic practices and narrow sectoralism. Not only is decentralization an indispensable prerequisite for sustainable development, but successful regional development requires building appropriate institutions from the grassroots level upwards to ensure the exercise of democratic rights. Too often in Latin America political participation has been blocked or mediated by traditional elites, so that representation without accountability predominates, encouraging corruption and alienation.

The crisis of the 1980s has come to represent the collapse of the old clientalist state with its models of economic development based on the role of government intervention and strategic investment. The imposition of fiscal authority originating in Washington, in which deregulation, privatization and liberalization have been the required criteria, has served to undermine the notion of the strong state, especially given the failure of concerted action to confront the debt issue (O'Brien 1991). The apparent success of the US in leading the restructuring of the Latin American state during a period of democratization raised popular expectations, but has failed to deliver the anticipated dividends of economic growth and full employment. This has led to a process of deep and increasingly bitter disillusionment with governments and politicians, and even the democratic process, as the demands of the poor have remained unfulfilled. Indeed, in certain quarters this has resulted in a challenge to the very legitimacy and sovereignty of the state. One can speak of the social and political decomposition of the state and a growing divergence between the state and civil society as different social groups find unorthodox, unregulated and sometimes illegal solutions to their livelihood needs.

This has created the conditions for a long overdue re-evaluation of pre-existing notions of development, especially regarding the role of the state. Gradually, new initiatives are emerging which advocate more self-reliant, egalitarian development based upon cultural pluralism, increased autonomy and political empowerment. Combining these highly normative political goals with ecological principles provides a powerful basis for defining strategies for sustainable development. The aim is to build more self-reliant regional economies in which there is an improved functional integration of rural and urban areas, ensuring food security, better service provision, an enhancement of local production systems and a strengthening of livelihoods. These are the features which would characterize a throughgoing programme of "alternative development" in the true sense of the term.

THE ENVIRONMENTAL CONSEQUENCES OF COCA, COCAINE AND ERADICATION EFFORTS

Coca (*Erythroxylum* spp) forms part of the natural pharmacopoeia of the Andes and its use has been dated back into the third millennium BC (Plowman 1986). Coca leaves are widely used throughout the Andean region and Amazon Basin as a masticatory that serves as a mild stimulant and sustenance for work, and they possess a nutritional value providing essential vitamins and minerals. As the "sacred leaf of the Incas", coca performs an important sacramental role, and is a strong symbol of cultural identity amongst native Andean people (Allen 1986). It is vital, therefore, to distinguish the traditional role of coca from the use of more powerful derivatives such as "crack" and cocaine.

Today approximately 300 000 hectares are planted to coca, of which Peru accounts for some 60%, Bolivia 30%, Colombia around 10% with small amounts in Ecuador and Brazil (Smith 1992). This represents almost a doubling of the area under coca during the last eight years, and reflects the massive process of frontier expansion that has occurred, especially in the Chapare region of Bolivia and the Upper Huallaga Valley of Peru, the two main coca-growing areas. The dramatic increase in coca production during the 1980s can be attributed to two major factors. First, the high price of coca compared to alternative crops: for example, in Bolivia in the mid-1980s its price advantage was between 4 and 24 times the returns on traditional food and cash crops (Eastwood and Pollard 1986). Secondly, the scale of the crisis affecting highland agriculture in Peru and Bolivia, in which drought and economic recession severely hit an already structurally impoverished rural population, encouraging outmigration in search of improved livelihood prospects. That many rural migrants headed for the coca-growing frontier underlines the importance of this sector as the main, if not only, source of economic growth and employment within Bolivia and Peru during the 1980s.

Much of the casual labour that has sought work on the frontier has been employed in refining operations in which coca leaf is turned into paste. This relatively simple process, using principally lime, kerosene and sulphuric acid, has become widely practised amongst small producers for several reasons. It avoids the wild fluctuations in price of coca leaves, it allows producers to retain more value-added from their labour, and it reduces the bulk of 500 kg of leaves to a more manageable 2.5 kg of paste which is then sold to merchants. Most of this paste then passes through two further stages of refining: the first yields cocaine sulphate (base); the second cocaine hydrochloride, its purest form. These two operations are performed by more specialized laboratories, most of which have hitherto been located in Colombia.

However, setting to one side processing activities for the moment, let us first examine the environmental impact of coca as a perennial plant.

Amongst the array of arguments deployed by the prohibitionist lobby, perhaps one of the most disingenuous is that the cultivation of coca causes serious environmental damage. Coca, it is argued, is singularly responsible for encouraging spontaneous colonization and forest clearance. After a few years under coca, exhausted soils are then abandoned and colonists extend the frontier once more in search of new stocks of soil fertility: an endless cycle of destruction. It is not intended to refute in detail this argument which represents a selective reading of the facts to suit a perspective which seeks the elimination of coca entirely. Moreover, there is not the space to elaborate upon the fairly well documented details of farming systems in Chapare to assert that coca has traditionally formed part of a diversified cropping system in a transition to perennials. Coca has emerged as a preferred crop, not only because of its own price attractiveness but because the market prices of alternative crops have long been so low, and up to half of perishable crops can be lost for lack of market demand and transport. As for coca encouraging migration and frontier expansion then this has certainly been the impression during a period that has seen the collapse of many existing livelihood systems, whether in the towns, mines or highland villages. But economic crisis, drought and increasing land scarcity in the valleys and Altiplano are the principal driving forces of spatial mobility, not the temporary insecurity offered by coca.

The scale of deforestation in Bolivia has been estimated at between 120 000 and 200 000 hectares per year which, for a total forest area of 56m hectares, is well below the rates of depletion found in neighbouring countries (WRI 1990). While many official sources emphasize the destruction wrought by colonists, it is forestry concessions to logging companies that cause greater destruction. Indeed, it has been groups of forest indians and coca producers who have separately organized campaigns to reduce logging operations. During 1990 some 53 000 hectares in the Isiboro-Securé Park was finally granted as territory to native peoples. Yet this Park has been under increasing pressure as those sectors most closely allied to narco-capital have expanded the frontier of the Zona Roja along the flanks of the Serrania de Mosetennes, which offers soil and humidity conditions well-suited to coca cultivation. The lawlessness accompanying the expansion of the coca economy into the forest (the hunting of animals for live export and for skins; cocaine-processing laboratories), together with the institutional paralysis of the forest service, has made it difficult to exert control over developments in the Isiboro-Securé Park.

Although coca is a perennial bush and in many ways ecologically preferable to annual crops, it is nevertheless a poor substitute for the forest canopy. As leaves are stripped from the bush four times or more per year, and with the clean weeding of *cocales*, the soils are exposed to heavy rainfall, which in the Chapare exceeds 2 000 mm/year, and without careful management can result in erosion. However, the nutrient demands of coca are less clearly established. Lee observes that, "the coca plant robs the soil of essential vitamins and nutrients" (1989, p. 27). Most plants do, that is how they grow; the question is how quickly, and whether under appropriate management this represents an irreversible process. There is plenty of evidence to suggest this is not. Morales notes that coca thrives in areas with marginal soil conditions unsuitable for most other cash crops, and makes better use of available resources of water and nutrients while being less susceptible to diseases (Morales 1989). Reference to the Yungas, where coca has been grown on terraced hillsides for many generations, should emphasize the fact that under appropriate soil management practices coca is no more responsible for soil degradation than any other crop. Indeed, a recent study commissioned by USAID (the United States Agency for International Development) highlighted the capacity of coca to help control erosion and to contribute to the recovery of soil fertility compared to other subtropical crops (CEEDI-LIDEMA 1990). These findings may help to explain why the Report received so little circulation outside the Agency. Another USAID-commissioned study concluded that, "*as a crop* coca's effects on the environment seem average or even benign, especially with other crops grown in the (Chapare) region" (Tolisano *et al.*, 1989, F3). Nevertheless, there may be some evidence to suggest that good soil management practices are not always employed by farmers accustomed to farming under different agroecological conditions, or by those who spend much time travelling between their holdings in the Chapare and highland communities where they retain and cultivate land.

The most environmentally damaging aspect of the drug trade results, not from the cultivation of coca, but from the dumping of toxic substances derived as by-products from processing operations. The disposal of sulphuric acid, ethyl ether, acetone and other chemicals, together with kerosene, diesel and lime, all in substantial quantities, has enormous potential to create major pollution problems. For example, when petroleum products enter the river system they create a thin surface film which inhibits oxygenization of the water. In the slower moving lowland rivers there is insufficient turbulence to break this film resulting in the asphyxia of fish life. Meanwhile, on the sand banks of these rivers, which are important feeding grounds for birdlife that live from fishing, birds suffer direct intoxication from deposited oil products. Many of the tributaries that rise in the Isiboro-Securé Park, for example, are important sources of fish life which migrate downstream and grow in the larger confluences. If small fish are being eliminated in these headwaters this may dramatically reduce the quantity of fish life downstream which provides important protein sources for large riverside populations.

In Bolivia it is estimated that 38 000 tonnes of toxic waste are dumped this way each year, involving some 3 million gallons of kerosene and 6 500 tonnes of lavatory paper used in the drying process (Curi and Arze 1990). In Peru it was estimated that in 1986 in order to produce 6 400 tonnes of basic paste, the following quantities of precursor chemicals were used and discarded: 57 m litres of kerosene, 32 m litres of sulphuric acid, 16 000 tonnes of lime and the same quantity of toilet paper, and 13 m litres of acetone and toluene (reported in Garcia-Sayán (1989) and Alvarez (1992). This has posed a grave threat to the many species of fish, amphibians, reptiles and crustaceans that were once found in the rivers and streams where the maceration pits are located.

Yet serious ecological damage is also being caused by the efforts of the anti-drug forces and coca eradication schemes. First, with regard to the search and destroy missions led by the United States Drug Enforcement Agency (DEA), the discovery of coca processing operations results in the destruction of all materials and precursor chemicals *in situ* by use of fire. Dumps of many hundreds of litres of chemicals thus go up in flames, including large quantities of sulphuric acid. However, fire does not destroy the acid but sends the molecules into the atmosphere where they are dispersed, combine with water droplets and fall as acid rain. Soil micro-organisms, which are responsible for the fertility and productivity of tropical soils through the decomposition of organic matter, are extremely sensitive to even slight changes in pH, so that areas well removed from the site of the destroyed "kitchen" may be seriously affected.

Coca eradication programmes and policy proposals have also generated considerable ecological concern. Coca producers in Bolivia fought a long campaign to secure legal agreement for voluntary substitution, which was enshrined in Law 1008 of November 1988. While they have argued this commitment was jeopardized by Supreme Decree DS22373 introduced in August 1989, they have maintained a high level of vigilance to ensure forcible eradication does not proceed. Meanwhile the US has yet to relinquish its commitment to developing chemical and biological agents aimed at coca, and trials have brought forth a storm of protest from across the breadth of public opinion.

In 1982 in the Chapare, US officials used 2,4-D, a chemical defoliant, in highly publicized field trials—until public demonstrations brought this exercise to a halt. It was later alleged that the trials may actually have been using Agent Orange which, true or not, effectively served to eliminate further chemical testing in Bolivia. With the US Congress providing $1 m in 1986 for coca herbicide research, Eli Lilly emerged in 1988 with Tebuthurion ("Spike"), a product designed to kill woody plants. Aerial spraying in Peru's Huallaga Valley proved the product was effective, but the Environmental Protection Agency, while approving the product, warned that Spike was an extremely active herbicide which will kill trees, shrubs, and other desirable forms of vegetation, and should be kept out of ponds, lakes and streams.

In wetlands, the herbicide could quickly leach away and remain in rivers and farmlands for up to five years; food crops, small birds, and small animals in the area would be killed; residues would be left in the meat and milk of livestock. Because the Huallaga River is a tributary to the Amazon, both rivers could be contaminated. (Yet) some US researchers even doubted the effectiveness of Spike against coca bushes. (McClintock 1988, p. 134)

In May 1988 Eli Lilly announced that it would no longer supply Spike for fear of legal and possibly other reprisals against its interests (Gladwell 1988). While the Company described the product as capable of causing irreversible harm to flora and fauna, and pulmonary and heart damage in humans, the US Assistant Secretary for Narcotics Matters said that Spike was "less toxic than aspirin, nicotine and nitrate fertilizers" (quoted in Lee 1989, p. 206).

Apparently undaunted by the arguments of the environmental lobby, the US government has been supporting research into biological agents in its search for a "magic bullet" against coca (Kawell 1989). It has been experimenting in the Huallaga Valley with the larvae "Malumbia" (*Eloria Noyesi*), which is "seeded" from light aircraft over coca-growing areas. Peruvian and Bolivian peasants have long fought the voracious appetite of this larva on citrus crops, a potential commercial alternative to coca. Yet these examples of almost indiscriminate use of chemical and biological agents to eradicate coca exemplifies a style of intervention that not only has contributed to the high level of conflict in the region, but also demonstrates little real interest or concern in securing an environmentally sustainable, long-term alternative to coca cultivation.

CROP SUBSTITUTION AND "ALTERNATIVE" DEVELOPMENT

The main dynamic behind the apparent success of "voluntary eradication" in Bolivia is the existence of a repressive paramilitary apparatus creating a climate of fear and uncertainty that has done most to drive down the price of coca leaves. Contrary to the normal laws of economics, a reduction in coca supply caused by interdiction does not result in a price rise, but the reverse as demand melts away during local "search and destroy" operations. During the period 1985–89 the average price of a 100-lb *carga* of coca leaves was $70; by early 1990 the price was around $5 per *carga*, the lowest for more than 15 years. With estimated costs of production of $30 per *carga* many people without a significant stake in the Chapare have begun to move away: casual labour, *partidarios* (sharecroppers), even the occasional small colonist tired of the continuing insecurity and threat of violence. Some have also decided to take the route of agricultural reconversion, hoping to establish a more secure productive base with the package of incentives on offer under the Regional Programme for Alternative Development (PDAR).

The first step in this route is for the producer to approach DIRECO, the

Bolivian bureau in charge of eradication, and claim compensation for the loss of his coca. It has been widely publicized that producers receive an incentive of $2000 per hectare, but it is less well known that pro rata payments are also judged on the quality of the coca as well as the area. The DIRECO agents instruct the producers in the correct way of cutting the bushes and inspect the work once it has been performed before providing the certificate which enables producers to collect their compensation. With the fall in the price of coca in early 1990 the DIRECO office in Villa Tunari was open for just two days per month, which provided sufficient numbers of clients to occupy DIRECO staff for the remaining 28 days. It is not known, incidentally, how many producers secure compensation for eradicating their old and low productivity coca—then move on to the frontier to clear new land for coca which for some is clearly an option.

With the certificate from DIRECO in their hands, producers are then eligible to secure loans, acquire substitute crops and receive training from IBTA (the agricultural development and extension agency) once they have agreed a crop and livestock farming system. But there is little participation and negotiation by producers in this process, and the terms on which they take on substitute crops are very unattractive. First, with respect to loans, these are derived from the United States' PL480 (Food for Peace) credit programme, in which there is some irony given the impact that concessionary food aid has had on highland producers, and are agreed at extremely unfavourable rates. Discussions with producers in the Chimoré area of the Chapare and a review of their documentation showed that loans are agreed in US dollars but paid in Bolivian pesos; that the rate of interest is equal to 13% plus the rate of inflation; and that there is no grace period: the first instalment is due 6 months after receiving the loan and comprises capital repayment and interest. Those who had coca and removed it under the scheme are eligible to receive credit. Those who never had coca (for example because of unsuitable soils, or that they are members of a Protestant church), or removed it earlier are refused credit entirely. Consequently, the credit programme, which should be an indispensable, generous and inclusive service, appears arbitrary, unattractive and, frankly, corrupt.

A central plank of IBTA's crop substitution programme has been the introduction of new institutional structures to challenge and ultimately undermine the authority of the *sindicato*, the local farmers' union. Their attempts to foster producer associations around substitute crops, and the recruitment of local "promoters", young males chosen for their "progressive" attitudes, are devices clearly designed to splinter collective commitment to traditional, community-based institutions. The promoters are paid a salary of $30 per month to cover expenses, and they receive training and the opportunity for foreign travel. For example, by early 1990, 30 of them had visited Costa Rica or Ecuador to view projects. Yet many are under considerable pressure from the *sindicato*; while there were originally 90 volunteers to become promoters, 45 were forced to withdraw. But those that remain within the scheme are an indispensable link in the diffusion of substitute crops, as IBTA supports the promoters to establish profit-making nurseries for the multiplication and sale of plant stock.

The single most incongruous feature of the crop substitution programme, however, is the issue of scale. This, above all, reveals the ideological leanings implicit in official notions of "alternative development" in which the ultimate objective is to create a class of capitalist family farms in the Chapare at the expense of the peasant economy. For example, the model of a typically diversified 10-ha farm in the Chapare might comprise: 1–2 ha of coca; 2 ha of traditional perennials (citrus, banana); 1–2 ha of annual crops (rice, yuca, maize); and pasture on 4–5 ha. This system has generally proved well-suited to the agroecological possibilities of the Chapare, makes effective use of household labour resources and provides a significant level of self-provisioning. Thus, the system scores well in terms of sustainability and livelihood security. This cannot be said for the alternative models promoted by the agricultural conversion programme in which minimum and optimum scales of production exceed the resources and capabilities of all but a small group of producers in the Chapare.

Starting from the actual, specific conditions that prevail in the Chapare, rather than those that would ideally exist, is vital in formulating a strategy to encourage conversion from coca. This requires recognizing the fragmentation of holdings, increasing land scarcity and differentiation. The development of *minifundismo* in the Chapare means that many households can only survive by monocropping coca at a high market price. It is clearly intended under the PDAR that such households should be encouraged to return to the highlands, hence the High Valleys Project in which USAID is supporting the creation of new employment opportunities in a few highland communities. Yet for every beneficiary in Mizque-Aiquile or Tapacari there will be scores more without prospects of improvements in their home communities. Consequently, developing alternatives requires building upon the limited resources of small agricultural units not those of agro-industrial enterprises.

That the promotion of exotic crop species and improved livestock breeds is on a scale entirely incongruent with the land, labour and other resources available to the majority of producers in the Chapare can be easily illustrated. Macadamia seedlings are being imported from Costa Rica at a cost of $26 per plant and sold to producers at the subsidized price of $13 each. The recommended cropping system promoted by IBTA is for a macadamia and black pepper combination at a minimum scale of one hectare. This requires 100 macadamia and 360 pepper plants (sold at $1.45 each) which involves a total investment of $6000 per hectare including the cost of all inputs. While much of this sum can be borrowed under the PL480 credit scheme, it will be remembered that the producer is liable to begin repayment of capital and interest immediately. *Yet macadamia takes 7–10 years before producing its first harvest.*

The same large-scale thinking is in evidence with the promotion of improved livestock breeds. The Head of the Chipiriri Experimental Station emphasized that IBTA only supported those producers willing to sustain optimum numbers of stock which amounted to 500–1000 hens, 10–20 pigs and a minimum of five head of cattle. These are enormous numbers, given the resources and mode of operation of small household production, even on the idealized 10 hectares mentioned above, let alone those a fraction of this size; yet this was the scale proposed for a *mixed livestock–arable farm* also involved in the production of non-traditional crops.

While producers are being encouraged to move out of coca because of low prices, many of the substitute crops do not offer very much more remuneration or security. For example, in Senda B, a community in the Chimoré area, some households have planted tea and made their first delivery of leaf to CORDECO, the Regional Development Corporation, in February 1990. Five months later they were still awaiting payment (at 0.5 pesos/kg). At that time CORDECO had stockpiled 28 tonnes of tea without a market, and $300 000 in tea-processing equipment and storage facilities was looking a very poor investment. Similar problems beset other crops. In 1989, 60 tonnes of ginger was produced of which only 16 tonnes had been sold by May 1990, and that with the help of $36 000 in grants and loans authorized by USAID to foster small processing plants and export companies. By June 1990 some 600–700 tonnes of turmeric had been produced, for which not one tonne appeared to have a market. Again, USAID stepped in with at least $100 000 to ensure producers received some minimal remuneration.

Consequently, while producers are making the move from coca into other cash crops, there are desperate efforts being made to find markets outside Bolivia which can purchase these goods and to construct an entire infrastructure capable of processing and transporting them. The dream is to find market windows of counter-seasonal production in North America, but the costs of transport from Bolivia make this unlikely, given the competition from countries with much better infrastructure closer to these major centres of consumption. Identifying market niches in high-value, low-bulk goods probably represents a more likely option, which might create opportunities in the growth sector of essential oils, medicinal plants and natural care products, and, to a limited extent, in spices, condiments and colourings. However, this is to assume that building alternatives to coca begins from the identification of possible export markets, an assumption that has to be challenged if sustainable development and secure livelihoods is a desired outcome.

MOVING TOWARDS A SUSTAINABLE "ALTERNATIVE DEVELOPMENT"

The preceding discussion has illustrated the extent to which an imposed solution to the "problem" of coca production is entirely out of step with the prevailing reality. Indeed, in an age where one assumes that the rhetoric of sustainable development has penetrated most spheres of the development industry, it is surprising to appreciate the degree to which current eradication–substitution efforts have failed to address these universal concerns. A consultant's report, prepared following an evaluation of a sanitation project in the Chapare, notes that the perceived urgency of the international drugs problem is justification for a rapid response where caution and normal development criteria are discarded in the cause of being seen to act.

> The result is a process of shooting from the hip in which large poorly considered projects are thrown at complex situations. The approach of the agro-industrial projects, particularly, is evocative of 1960s development thinking where it was felt that we had all the answers and simply had to "transfer" them to the grateful peasantry. In short, the drug control imperative is being used to justify the worst features of naive top-down development. (Dudley 1991)

Top-down and short-term thinking dominates the entire institutional structure, from the policymakers in Washington to project personnel in the field. A highly bureaucratic structure exists, as Malamud-Goti (1992) has recently suggested, dedicated to the protection of its own interests rather than those of "client" groups. This is most apparent in IBTA: of the 106 staff working in the Chapare programme, only six are extension agents and another six are research technicians; the remainder are involved in management and administration, and in providing support services. Moreover, within the regional programme there are very evident conflicts, eg between IBTA and PL480, and between IBTA and the marketing side in which there is little coordination of activities. There is also an unhealthy overlap of professional interests with opportunities for personal gain, eg with regard to the importation and distribution of plants, the selection of recipients for credit, the opportunities for well-paid jobs for unskilled people in inflated bureaucracies and so on. Yet all of these extraordinary dynamics are being played out with hardly any regard for the target group: the coca producers.

It is clear that the rural economy is very much more complex than simply comprising the production and sale of agricultural commodities which are considered infinitely substitutable. Despite the efforts of the state and other agencies, there are limits to their ability to regulate the production and distribution of coca, which is the dynamic for an array of activities and relationships within and beyond the Chapare. Moreover, maintaining conditions

of insecurity—through repression, violence and fluctuations in price—undermines confidence in the integrity of any development intervention. Indeed,
efforts to weaken the authority of the *sindicatos* and their federations
demonstrates the utter failure to understand the conditions for a successful
transition from coca to a sustainable post-coca future.

The *sindicatos* themselves are an extremely varied collection of organizations demonstrating different degrees of militancy, alliances with narco-
capital and capacities to work for a better future (Healy 1988). Yet they
provide an important vehicle for contesting dominant notions of development which are growth-centred and into which communities of people fit
uneasily. But they also offer an institutional structure around which a strategy of sustainable development can be organized. What might be the principal elements of such a strategy?

It would surely need to begin with an identification of what the needs of
people in the Chapare actually are. Currently, the region is experiencing
significant investment in the fields of rural sanitation services, agro-proces-
sing, road construction and forest management. But there appears to be,
according to consultants reports, minimal community participation in the
projects with the danger that, once donor funding and management systems
withdraw, they are liable to collapse. Moreover, the "beneficiaries" are clear
that the rationale for the delivery of such services is as incentives to end
their association with coca. For what is the stake of recipients of top-down
aid in the maintenance of such services?

One of the problems that donors have in working in the Chapare is the
mobility of the population, and concentrating aid in one location will not
eliminate this. However, by identifying a strategy that meets the needs of
people and for which they are made ultimately responsible, the use of donor
funds might not begin with major capital investment in infrastructural
improvement. True, health indicators in the Chapare are extremely poor and
efforts do need to be made to improve them; but the first requirement in
effective primary health care is information and education on personal
hygiene and ways of reducing disease transmission. It is often the case that,
before clean water, rural people desire secure livelihoods, that is reliable and
assured sources of income, and it is for them to consider the trade-offs and
to make the choice between different options. The role of outside professionals should therefore be to support institutional strengthening and capacity building by furnishing information and drip-feeding resources, not by
imposing solutions and throwing money at perceived problems.

Strengthening rural livelihoods has to address conditions of production in
both the highlands and lowlands, for they are inseparably linked. However,
in order to revitalize production it is necessary to have a national food
policy that recognizes the role of the small farming sector, and to build upon
its strengths rather than to constantly promote large-scale, agro-industrial

models. Emphasizing, once again, the basic principle of sustainable development, which is to build upon what exists, means making use of site-specific agroecological knowledge and local organizations in order to develop low external-input farming systems. This approach would help to reduce dependence on the market for agrochemicals which are proving so damaging to human health in the country. It would also help to achieve better management of environmental resources on which the future well-being of local communities is based.

The structural dislocations of the Bolivian economy have historically been created and partially overcome by recourse to the plunder of the country's natural capital. What has passed for development during the last five hundred years has been based upon the exploitation of non-renewable resources, and increasingly upon the unsustainable utilization of renewable resources, principally forests and soils. Successive resource frontiers trigger inherently unstable conditions of growth and create little long-term development. New combinations of export commodities may appear (gold, lumber, minerals, cocaine, macadamia nuts), and may temporarily ease debt service burdens and provide some short-term stimulus to regional economies. But creating sustainable futures requires building secure livelihoods and empowering rural people to make optimal use of their local environment. Such a future will for many include a role for coca alongside a range of other perennial and annual crops. But the quantities of coca that are produced and what happens to the leaves (and to the rivers, the forests and the people), will depend upon demand for derivatives in the North and the prospects offered by alternative crops. What is certain is that a solution to the coca "problem" in Bolivia will only emerge once the existing repressive, top-down structures are replaced by participatory institutions engaged in dialogue with producers, and the principles of sustainability are fully grasped to create a truly authentic alternative development.

REFERENCES

Allen, C. (1986) "Coca and cultural identity in Andean communities". In *Coca and Cocaine: Effects on People and Policy in Latin America*. D. Pacini and C. Franquemont (eds). Cultural Survival Report, 23, Cultural Survival Inc., Cambridge MA.
Alvarez, E. (1992) "Coca production in Peru". In *Drug Policy in the Americas* P.H. Smith (ed.). Westview Press, Boulder, CO.
CEEDI-LIDEMA (1990) *Evaluacion Ecologica del Cultivo de la Coca en los Yungas de La Paz*. CEEDI, LIDEMA, USAID, La Paz, Bolivia.
Curi, C. and Arze, C. (1990) "Estudio del impacto de los precursores en la produccion de cocaina sobre el medio ambiente en Bolivia". USAID/IDEMA, La Paz, Bolivia.
Dudley, E. (1991) Report prepared for Overseas Development Administration, UK.
Eastwood, D. and Pollard, H. (1986) "Colonisation and coca in the Chapare, Bolivia:

a development paradox for colonisation theory". *Tijdschrift voor Economische en Social Geografie*, **77**, (4), 258–68.

Franco, M. de and Godoy, R. (1992) "The economic consequences of cocaine production in Bolivia: historical, local and macroeconomic perspectives". *Journal of Latin American Studies*, **24**, 2, 375–406.

Garcia-Sayán, D. (1989) "Narcotrafico y region andina: una vision general". In *Coca, Cocaina y Narcotrafico: Laberinto en los Andes* D. Garcia-Sayan (ed.). Comision Andina de Juristas, Lima, Peru.

Gladwell, M. (1988) "Coca war checked in pesticide debacle". *International Herald Tribune*, 2 June.

Healy, K. (1988) "Coca, the state and the peasantry in Bolivia 1982–1988". *"Journal of InterAmerican Studies and World Affairs*, **30**, 2/3, 105–126.

Holmberg, J. and Sandbrook, R. (1992) "Sustainable development: what is to be done?" In *Policies for a Small Planet* J. Holmberg (ed.). Earthscan, London.

Kawell, J.A. (1989) "Going to the source". *Report on the Americas*, **XXII**, 6, 13–21.

Lee, R. (1989) *The White Labyrinth: Cocaine and Political Power*. Transaction Publishers, New Brunswick.

McClintock, C. (1988) "The war on drugs: the Peruvian case". *Journal of Inter-American Studies and World Affairs*, **30**, 2/3, 127–142.

Malamud-Goti, J. (1992) *Smoke and Mirrors: The Paradox of the Drug Wars*. Westview Press, Boulder, CO.

Morales, E. (1989) *Cocaine: White Gold Rush in Peru*. University of Arizona Press, Tucson, AZ.

O"Brien, P. (1991) "Debt and sustainable development in Latin America". In *Environment and Development in Latin America: The Politics of Sustainability* D. Goodman and M. Redclift (eds). Manchester University Press, Manchester.

Olmo, R. del (1989) *Los Discursos sobre la Droga*. HISBOL, La Paz, Bolivia.

Plowman, T. (1986) "Coca chewing and the botanical origins of coca in South America". In *Coca and Cocaine: Effects on People and Policy in Latin America* D. Pacini and C. Franquemont (eds). Cultural Survival Report, 23, Cultural Survival Inc., Cambridge, MA.

Pretty, J. and Guijt, I. (1992) "Primary environmental care: an alternative paradigm for development assistance". *Environment and Urbanization*, **4**, 1, 22–35.

Queiser Morales, W. (1989) "The war on drugs: a new US national security doctrine?" *Third World Quarterly*, **11**, 147–169.

Smith, P.H. (1992) The political economy of drugs: conceptual issues and policy options. In *Drug Policy in the Americas* P.H. Smith (ed.). Westview Press, Boulder, CO.

Tolisano, J., Bossi, R., Henkel, R., Rivera, A., Seubert, C., Smith, D., Sutton, J. and Swagerty, J. (1990) "Environmental assessment of the Chapare Regional Development Project, Bolivia". Development Alternatives Inc, Washington DC.

Tullis, F.L. (1987) "Cocaine and food: likely effects of a burgeoning transnational industry on food production in Bolivia and Peru". In *Pursuing Food Security: Strategies and Obstacles in Africa, Asia, Latin America and the Middle East* W.L. Hollist and F.L. Tullis (eds). Lynne Rienner, Boulder, CO.

WRI (World Resources Institute) (1990) *World Resources 1990–91*. Oxford University Press, Oxford.

8 Conclusion: Ecological Imperatives and Global Nemesis

MICHAEL REDCLIFT AND COLIN SAGE
Wye College, University of London, UK

According to the World Bank our global natural capital has been depleted to the point where sustainable resource systems are increasingly difficult to achieve:

- Two hundred million people depend directly upon depleted forest resources.
- Eight hundred million people are affected by dryland degradation.
- One billion people rely upon increasingly fragile irrigation systems, which suffer from inadequate supply of water and salinization of soils.
- Five hundred million people occupy degraded watersheds.
- Four hundred million are vulnerable to the resulting downstream siltation.
- Over one billion people lack an adequate, safe, water supply.
- Nearly two billion people suffer from malnutrition or lack proper sanitation.
- Each year thirteen and a half million children (under five) die as a result: two million of malaria.
- Over one billion people live in cities where air pollution is below World Health Organization standards.
- Almost one billion people live in cities where sulphur dioxide standards exceed safe levels.
- *Each day* thirty-five thousand children die from environmentally related diseases, attributable to pollution and unsafe water. (World Bank, *World Development Report* 1992)

These are the cold, almost unintelligible statistics, which formed the backcloth to the meeting of the United Nations Conference on Environment and Development (UNCED) in Rio de Janeiro in 1992. They also form the backcloth to this book. Where do these global figures meet the day-to-day

Strategies for Sustainable Development: Local Agendas for the Southern Hemisphere
Edited by Michael Redclift and Colin Sage. © 1994 John Wiley & Sons Ltd

realities documented throughout this book? How do these experiences fit into the wider picture presented at UNCED?

In answering these questions it might be useful to return to two of the issues with which we began: How do people *value their environments?* How can *institutional changes* seek to help *empower local people to assume control of their own environments, and to manage them more sustainably?* In addition, a third issue needs to be addressed: How can we ensure that the global political economy is refashioned in ways that enhance increased sustainability at the local level? In fact, the UNCED process considered these questions at some length, and made a number of recommendations about future policy. It is these to which we now turn.

ENVIRONMENTAL VALUES AND THE VALUATION OF THE ENVIRONMENT

The importance of understanding the value which people place on their environments has emerged throughout this book. The discussion of deforestation in the Philippines suggests that natural resources have been used as a source of capital, and used to pay for an accumulated financial deficit. The adoption by the Philippine government of an export-led model of development, undermined endogenous attempts at conservation.

In the Ghanaian case endogenous pressures of population and increased food production have placed considerable pressure on natural resources in the drier north of the country. People in this region were fully aware of the value of the trees and water sources in their area, but the combined effect of policies was to make their conservation unattractive. There was considerable suspicion of the state, and little confidence in its ability to deliver on it promises. Similarly, in Mexico, the environmental knowledge which poor people possessed was devalued by technical "experts", while their exposure to development "opportunities", largely through capital inputs and new technologies, has served to undermine the viability of the peasant household.

At UNCED considerable attention was paid to the competing claims of local communities and international interests in the conservation or depletion of natural resources. It was acknowledged that preserving forests had a global environmental benefit which was not captured by the host country in the South. There was an acknowledged need to transfer, to internalize, the benefits for local people. At the same time the developing countries defended the sovereignty of their own resources, and argued that they would only sign away part of their sovereign control of their resources in exchange for effective compensation. Countries like Malaysia and India opposed the idea of a binding statement on forest principles.

Similarly, the value locked up in biodiversity, for which no adequate payment was made, exercised the feelings of representatives from the South at

UNCED. A number of options were put forward for accommodating both the interests of the North (in gaining access to biodiversity) and the South (in seeking to protect its stake in natural capital). These would involve establishing non-profit institutes which would contract for the use of wild genetic material. Alternatively, private companies could support national scientific institutes in the South, in return for exclusive rights to screen collections of genetic materials. Finally, host governments could exploit resources and foreign companies could be granted exploratory concessions. However, none of these suggestions meets the problem which the conservation of biological resources *in situ* poses for environmental management: How can host communities acquire rights which translate into incentives to conserve biodiversity?

The result of these deliberations has passed into history. After fifteen weeks of negotiation, spread over four years, the Biodiversity Treaty was presented to UNCED. The Treaty had already been diluted to produce what the head of UNEP, Mostafa Tolba, described as "the minimum on which the international community can agree". However, even this weakened Treaty did not satisfy the United States government. President Bush refused to ratify the Treaty, saying that "the American way of life is not up for negotiation".

INSTITUTIONAL CHANGE, HUMAN AGENCY AND LOCAL EMPOWERMENT

The case studies included in this volume have all paid attention to the difficulty of releasing the energies of local people from the straitjacket so often represented by government. At best the state was so removed from the kinds of choices local communities faced, that it proved ineffective in influencing their behaviour. At worst, and the Philippines is an obvious case, the state connived at resource depletion. It seldom sought to empower the poor.

Agenda 21, the document which preceded the Rio conference, was intended to be the instrument through which the Earth Charter would be implemented. It was "an agenda for action . . . listing priorities, targets, costings, modalities and the assignment of responsibilities to different parties". In fact several sections of the report lived up to this promise. The legal framework was given emphasis at many points, and it was suggested that domestic policy interventions should give legal title to local groups and households as a prerequisite for the sustainable management of resources. Similarly, rural people in the South are referred to at various stages as critical actors in agricultural and rural regeneration. It is suggested in *Agenda 21* that their participation must be sought, and planning, implementation and monitoring functions, should be devolved to groups of local people.

The intention of *Agenda 21* is that multilateral agencies, including the agencies of the United Nations system, should work through the national

institutions and plans of different countries. At the same time the performance of different governments in delivering *Agenda 21* was to be the concern
of Non-Governmental Organizations (NGOs), whose views would be channelled through the United Nations. The intention, at least, is that sustainable
development should be the responsibility of governments accountable to their
people, and the wider international community. However, no coordinating or
monitoring mechanism was established in Rio to carry out these guidelines.
To be effective *Agenda 21* would need to be translated into disaggregated,
operational plans, whose performance could be closely monitored.

There is little doubt that *Agenda 21* reflects a willingness to embark on
structural changes at the international and national levels. However, this has
not been translated into workable programmes to encourage more popular
participation in environmental management, nor into concrete changes in the
way international organizations work. As the International Institute for
Environment and Development (IIED) has suggested "a major weakness
exists in the indication of training requirements without stating the modalities of such training, namely that it must be interactive, participatory,
problem-solving and attitude-changing" (IIED (1992) "Rio: the lessons
leathed". *Perspectives*, No. 9, p. 15). In the cases we have discussed what
was clearly lacking, in the Philippines, Ghana and Mexico, was a willingness
to learn from local populations, and a commitment to more collaborative
environmental management.

GLOBAL POLITICAL ECONOMY AND LOCAL-LEVEL SOLUTIONS

Changes in global political economy depend on more than political goodwill
and a well-rehearsed agenda for action. They depend, ultimately, on the
power of different groups, governments and transnational organizations, in
the international arena. Changes in global political economy also depend on
adequate resources, and agreement about priorities.

The divisions between North and South, and to some extent within these
camps, became evident in the preparatory meetings of UNCED, and the discussions of the Working Groups which helped to prepare the business of the
Rio meeting. In reflecting on the global agenda, it is worth considering some
of these divisions.

The focus of the climate discussions in advance of the UNCED meeting
was the role of technology transfer in reducing the effects of rapid industrialization in the South on global warming. Several large countries, with
impressive supplies of fossil fuels, notably China, were impatient with any
restriction on their energy production which threatened their economic
growth. Other countries in the South emphasized the role of additional
funds in encouraging the adoption of cleaner technologies. Similarly, there
was considerable discussion surrounding mitigation costs in the South, and

procedures for evaluating them. Since the developed countries were largely responsible for the global warming that is anticipated, most (but not all) of the developing countries argued that a climate agreement should precede any agreement about tropical forests. They refused to accept that global warming could be averted by concentrating on "sink based" solutions, requiring them to conserve their forests.

Similar problems arose in advance of the Biodiversity Convention. The focus of the discussion was one of definition: Could a useful distinction be made between biodiversity in nature, and the development of genetic materials in laboratories and collections? As we have already noted the developing countries wanted control of biodiversity to protect their stake in natural capital; the North wanted guaranteed access to biodiversity to ensure corporate profitability. Most biodiversity is in the South; most biotechnology is in the North. Problems immediately arose over the idea of sovereignty, which meant control of their own resources to governments in the South, but to the North represented a barrier to what were perceived as "global" solutions.

The issue of greatest concern to the developed world, though scarcely mentioned at Rio, was that of population increase. As we have argued in this volume, general agreement on reducing tropical deforestation and population growth has characterized the recent discourse about environment and development in the North. However, there has been less convergence in the North about formulating effective policy responses to meet global climate change. As we saw in Chapter 3, above, the developing countries believe that a reduction in rates of population growth can only begin when economic growth has raised living standards in the South. Before UNCED was convened in Rio it was requested, by the developing world, that population be omitted from consideration of poverty/environment linkages. The North insisted that population be retained. There followed a heated discussion over the responsibility of North and South for global poverty, which was variously attributed to "demographic factors" (by the North) and "over-consumption" (by the South).

The second major area of global political economy which needed to be successfully addressed was that of adequate international financial provisions. Prior to Rio, the UNCED Secretariat had argued that the provisions of *Agenda 21* would require *an additional* $125 billion, almost twice what the World Bank had estimated. The Global Environmental Facility (GEF) had already been established in May 1991, with an interim life of three years. There were three main sources of funds available to the GEF: core funds ($800 million) committed by official donors; concessionary funds ($300 million); and funds released in the wake of the Montreal Protocol, which were intended to enable the South to phase-out CFCs ($200 million). The existing funding, of $1.3 billion, then, was far short of that which would be required to carry out the programme agreed at UNCED.

At Rio some of the developing countries argued for a "Green Fund", financed by the North on an agreed formula, and based on an international carbon tax. The North was hostile to this suggestion, and it was eventually dropped. But there were other, perhaps less predictable, objections to establishing such a fund. Many of the Non-Governmental Organizations based their suspicion of a new Green Fund on the problems surrounding existing international aid, which they saw as politically motivated, inefficient and counter-productive. The NGO community was, for the first time, an important actor in the UNCED deliberations and, through its own parallel summit, the Global Forum, was able to exert considerable influence on thinking in some areas.

In the event only $2.5 billion was pledged for the work of Agenda 21 at the summit, and these modest pledges have yet to be supported by hard cash. Although the powers of the GEF were enhanced, its budget remained modest, and little evidence exists that more funds will be forthcoming. Indeed, the prospect of continued economic recession in much of the North, and accelerated conflict over international trade and the GATT, does not bode well for the continued funding of the GEF on the scale required. The promotion of sustainable development, at least at a global level, waits on the adequate financing of international programmes, and a willingness to bury (or, negotiate about) differences over critical issues like responsibility for global warming and population increase.

Where do the difficulties surrounding UNCED leave the discussion of natural capital, and the role of local-level changes in its conservation? Clearly we are unlikely to see, in the immediate future, a reorientation of political will and resources towards addressing the kind of issues raised at Rio. There are likely to be piecemeal changes, and greater sensitivity to the environmental consequences of development policies. More resources are likely to be devoted to mitigating the worst effects of economic growth in the South, but little attention is likely to be paid to seriously revising our view of growth in the North. Action in some areas, such as carbon taxes, is probable, but it is unlikely to be linked to ways of facilitating the transfer of cleaner technologies to the South, or their indemnification against environmental damage.

The cases described in this book acquire importance in other ways, which in no sense detract from the urgency of "global" policy initiatives. First, measures taken to address the life-threatening issues raised at the beginning of this chapter, are a prerequisite for development, not a brake on it. Measures to reduce soil erosion or the salinization of irrigation systems would be given enormous assistance if they were supported by a global strategy, adequately resourced. However, they remain urgent even if this is not forthcoming.

Index